THE CASE METHOD OF TEACHING

Human Relations and Administration

THE CASE METHOD OF TEACHING

Human Relations

AND

Administration

AN INTERIM STATEMENT

EDITED BY

KENNETH R. ANDREWS

HARVARD UNIVERSITY PRESS

Cambridge, Massachusetts

1 9 6 0

TO

WALLACE BRETT DONHAM

Introductory Note

This book is a collection of papers by those who teach and do research in human relations at the Harvard Business School. It is addressed to the educators and administrators in schools, in governments, and in businesses who sense the need for better teaching and learning of executive skills. New courses in human relations taught by the case method have spread since the war into many schools and into industry. The men who staff these courses have more than once asked that we record our own experience in applying the case method of teaching to the new materials made available by research into human relations.

This is, then, a miscellany on teaching human relations and administration by the case method. It is offered hesitantly. The writers know that in five years they have not answered many of the questions encountered in the establishment of their new courses. They have often talked together, discussing in frequent group meetings the problems of teaching just as much as the interpretation of research data. They have explored in seminars every topic mentioned in every one of these essays. Even so, they are not ready to issue a credo. They have not formulated an all-embracing theory to explain and unify their work, partly from diffidence and partly from desire for more data from which theory is properly derived. They have asked the editor to say very clearly that this is an interim statement of teaching practices and an incomplete analysis of early experience in a new discipline.

Since 1945, the writers of these papers, working together, have collected cases for, established, and taught a group of courses now part of the various curricula of Harvard University. They have resumed, after a wartime interruption, a program of basic research and of training for research which began as early as the Hawthorne experiments. The courses include: (1) Social Sciences 112, a course in General Education offered to undergraduates in Harvard College and Radcliffe, (2) Administrative Practices I and II, required of all first-year graduate students at the Business School, (3) a shorter version of Administrative Practices required of the businessmen in the Advanced Management Program, and another in Radcliffe's Management Training Program, and (4) Human Relations, an advanced course offered to second-year graduate students at the Business School. The basic research, subordinated in the immediate postwar years to course-building, has consisted of doctoral theses and a few books listed in the bibliography. The experience accumulated in teaching and research has been shared systematically with visiting professors who have, in turn, introduced similar courses in their own universities.

A vitally important activity (expensive in time and thus a deduction from current visible accomplishment) has been the training of younger members of the group. The essays on research techniques and on teaching problems make clear the need for such training. Courses were staffed in large part with men who had not grown up in human relations but in older fields—history, economics, literature, marketing, sociology, personnel, and the like. New men were continually joining the staff. Training became a group, as well as an individual, activity. Under the leadership of George F. F. Lombard, for example, regular meetings have systematically provided opportunity to discuss common problems. Most of the writers of these papers attended these informal seminars and learned a good deal from each other. It was at these meetings that the need for a better formulation of the case method of instruction was expressed and explored. The result is in part this collection of papers.

These varied activities focus upon one goal: the training of people for the achievement of coöperation in organization—coöperation embracing the attainment of individual satisfactions and organization purposes. In the undergraduate courses the organization is often the family, fraternity, church, or club; in the graduate courses it is always a business or government organization. The method is always the same. Students study individual problems drawn with the greatest possible fidelity from actual events. They are asked to disentangle the relations evident in the description of the case situation, to become aware of the different points of view of the major participants, to decide what the situation requires by way of responsible action from the executive most concerned. Case by case the students proceed, thinking out for themselves the perplexities before them without benefit of verbal solution and abstract principle, and evolving a way of thinking which does not collapse before the demands of concrete experience.

Fritz J. Roethlisberger believes that the core discipline of human relations consists of (1) study of the growing body of data resulting from examination of "concrete situations of human beings at work in an organized human activity," (2) "the point of view and methods characteristic of such study," and (3) "the result obtained therefrom in terms of both more explicit skill and better theoretical formulation for adjusting to and administering change." The subject is concerned with "general problems of communication and understanding between individuals, between individuals and groups, and between groups under different conditions and varying relationships," and with "general problems of securing action and coöperation under different conditions and in varying formal organizations." The advanced course in Human Relations concentrates on face-to-face communication and (within this framework) on the skills by which individual and group understanding are achieved, coöperation encouraged, and conflict contained.

Administrative Practices is the first-year course, which, in close coördination with the other first-year courses (Marketing, Control, Finance, Production, and Business Responsibilities in the American Society), covers a wide gamut of interpersonal and intergroup relations as it surveys the human problems attending organized activity. The course is designed to increase the student's understanding and acceptance of the responsibilities of group membership. Its case-by-case progression usually leads him to at least an awareness of a need for the integration of the different points of view in organizations, and sometimes to some skill in achieving it.

All these courses (and consequently all these essays) are concerned with (1) a set of attitudes comprising awareness, acceptance of people as people, and a mature willingness to work with people, (2) a body of substantive knowledge accumulated through field studies and business experience, (3) a way of thinking which provides one means of usefully ordering observations and of bringing substantive knowledge to bear on concrete situations, and (4) a set of skills which constitutes adequate behavior in the face of unique situations requiring action. These points are extended, developed, and subjected to many emphases in the essays that follow.

Part One, Teaching and Learning, not only carries us further into the realm of definition, and makes much clearer what human relations is here conceived to be, but also describes in detail the classroom process. The order of essays is unimportant, but roughly it takes the reader from a panoramic view of the method, through techniques of instruction, student confusion and rebellion, remedial counseling, problems of examining for what has been learned—all this accompanied by implications for business practice as well as for educational theory.

First published in the *Harvard Alumni Bulletin* of October 19, 1940 (and reprinted here with permission of its editor), Professor Gragg's article has achieved considerable attention in the last ten years as an introduction to the case system of instruction and a description of the teacher's and student's roles therein. Professor Gragg has at various times taught Administrative Practices. His most important contribution to his colleagues in that course is perhaps his definition of the relations between instructor and student which in his judgment encourage learning. His concept of the nature of classroom "rapport" has been freely borrowed by other contributors to this volume.

John D. Glover and Ralph M. Hower published most of the cases used in Administrative Practices in 1949 under the title: *The Administrator: Cases on Human Relations in Business* (revised edition, 1952). A year later, for instructors using the book in various universities, they published *Some Notes on the Use of* The Administrator, from which, with the permission of Richard D. Irwin, the publisher, these excerpts are reprinted. Their subject is the instructor's behavior in the classroom, and their purpose is to help the instructor who is willing to try teaching administration by the case method. Their paper applies the point of view described in general terms by Professor Gragg to classroom problems.

David N. Ulrich's paper is a perceptive view of the case method as a whole, different from the two preceding articles in that two vantage points are especially emphasized—that of case writer and that of student. The sensitive description of what can happen to a student under the case method should be compared with later references to student casualties. The section on case material should be compared with Paul Lawrence's essay on case collection.

Sometimes students, temporarily halted by the impediments to learning described by Mr. Ulrich, rebel under the pressure imposed by the case method. In an afternoon class on October 27, 1948, the rebellion of one section of 100 students was sharp and loud enough to be readily summarized. Joseph Bailey's paper is a unique description of a classroom protest. It will reward the analyst interested in early student adjustment to case-teaching, and in skillful response by an instructor not easily taken aback.

Anyone reading the Ulrich and Bailey essays, noting therein the disturbance which the case method can set off in students, and then reading Dean Fox's statement that up to one-third of all students need individual help in adjusting to the system, could well conclude that the case method is a lethal instrument. It might be mentioned here, therefore, that these three writers are talking about the *early* stages of adjustment to a wholly new environment. The victims usually recover, particularly if the therapy, like the classroom instruction, is student-centered.

Miss Ronken's analysis of Allen Price's progress serves as a case history to document some of the statements made earlier about the impact of case instruction upon students.

The contribution of semantic studies to the interpretation of field data and to the study of communication in organization has been very great indeed. Persons newly interested in problems of communication will appreciate Professor Lee's summary of Korzybski's work for its own sake. The observations which general semantics has equipped Professor Lee to make about the educational processes he saw in motion here will interest newcomers and old hands equally.

Mrs. Fuller's illustrative lectures, delivered at the end of two different runs of the undergraduate course in Human Relations, may serve two purposes for the readers of this volume. First, they may correct a misapprehension that in a case course one must never lecture. Second, they will acquaint readers with the substance of Social Sciences 112, with the point of view from which cases are attacked, and with some notion of the accomplishments of the term, as Mrs. Fuller knew after listening to her classes what would be the proper dimensions of a summary.

Like Mrs. Fuller's summary lectures, the text of Ralph M. Hower's lecture provides insight into course substance, this time the version of Administrative Practices presented to the executives of the 14th session of the Advanced Management Program in 1948. Those who were not there can still follow the continuity and see in general how a series of case discussions can be the basis of significant general observation.

In the literature on the case method, there are few detailed descriptions of a case with student comments. Professor Learned enables us to sample the analyses of 100 students writing for one hour on a two-page case as part of their final examination. Since the same variety of interpretations would appear in a class discussion, the reader can get a vivid impression of the range and depth of interpretation an instructor must preside over and at examination time to evaluate. This article was first published by and is now reprinted by permission of the Harvard Business School *Alumni Bulletin*.

Professor Stephen H. Fuller takes us to the evaluation of the papers in which such responses appear. He considers the worst papers of a recent examination period and decides what it is he dislikes about them. This analysis of a set of unsatisfactory examinations indicates very vividly the misunderstanding and distortion to which Administrative Practices is subjected by the students for whom the classroom procedures are not adequate.

The dozen papers carrying the reader from Professor Gragg's opening article through Professor Fuller's final examinations may arouse curiosity about what a case discussion actually reads like. For technical reasons incident to large classes in rooms not designed for recording, accurate transcripts are almost nonexistent. Professor Glover provides enough of the discussion of a small group of second-year students to give analysts of the learning process an opportunity to decide for themselves whether anything interesting is going on.

Mr. Towl's paper is about problems of teaching inasmuch as it discusses the curricular difficulties arising from the separation of executive functions for course purposes. But even more crucially this essay concerns itself with the executive environment for which courses in Human Relations as well as in technical functions prepare a student. Its observation about "business" as opposed to "administrative" decisions throws light on the perennially confusing problem of how to classify executive activity and disentangle business knowledge and judgment from leadership in organizations. The section on the evolution of purpose in organizations is a contribution to administrative theory which has implications not only for classroom activity but for business practice.

Part Two of this volume, Training in Industry, is a brief reference to the inadequacy of conventional training programs in industry, and to the successful extension of the case method to fill the need there. This development, if the bottleneck in experienced instructors is ever successfully broken, should be an important extension of the case method beyond the school into offices and factories. The success of Advanced Management Programs in various business schools in bringing executives back to re-evaluate their executive experience, will facilitate the introduction of executive training inside industry.

Professor Roethlisberger's article, reprinted here by permission of the *Harvard Business Review*, arises from industry's growing interest in human-relations training. Read in association with A. Zaleznik's *Foreman Training in a Growing Enterprise*, a new book which documents some of the observations made here, it provides a compelling indictment of misdirected training effort.

Kenneth R. Andrews' article describes applications of the case method to the training objectives of two organizations. Other members of the teaching group have conducted case discussions in companies; their experience, as well as the writer's, is drawn upon. The case system of teaching, as well adapted to education in companies as in schools, will eventually be more widely used in industry.

Part Three, Research Problems in Human Relations, is concerned with the twofold direction of field investigation—case collection and primary research. The special problems of research in the social sciences as they pertain to the teaching of administration are discussed for those who wish to look into them. In a field so new as this, continuous research is essential. The case method makes peculiar demands for continuous application to real life to provide data for classroom interpretation and to make possible on-the-job training for the research workers. Primary research in human relations must be painstakingly clinical. The practical as well as the professional difficulties will concern all those interested in working in the area.

Paul Lawrence describes in simple terms the nature of case collecting in Human Relations and answers the questions which are usually raised by those beginning this activity. Even though the Business School makes its cases available to companies and to other schools, sooner or later most instructors want at least a few cases of their own to serve particular purposes.

Professor Lombard writes here of the clinical method of research and of the research case. The research case differs from the teaching case in that it contains (besides a definitive clinical description of a single situation) an interpretation. The diagnosis is designed to be of practical use to administrators as well as to social scientists.

Professor Lombard's second paper, reprinted here with permission, was first published in *Science*, September 15, 1950. Its subject is the relation of the observer to the data observed, and what is said here may be usefully compared to the Scott-Lynton essay which follows. Of interest principally to those conducting primary research (rather than to those newly interested in a case method), this article is a significant comment on the central limitation on human relations as a science.

The greater part of the paper by Jerome F. Scott and R. P. Lynton is taken from Chapter V of the authors' forthcoming book, *Community and Technology*, to be published by UNESCO. It is published here with permission of UNESCO and the Columbia University Press. Although neither author is currently a member of the Harvard Human Relations group, this paper is germane to the research method underlying the courses in Human Relations and Administrative Practices and to all knowledge in the area covered by these courses.

No lack of knowledge, no difficulties in teaching, and no defects in these essays can obscure the satisfaction which has accrued for the writers around the activities described here and their debt of gratitude to those who have made progress possible. Work in human relations is an integral part of the total mission of the Harvard Business School, and its administration has for a long time fully supported with limitless patience the explorations undertaken. In addition, the intense interest of informed American business which makes case research and primary research possible has been a continuous encouragement. The interest of men in other free countries, aware of the urgency in the Western world of learning to deal with conflict before conflict engulfs us all, has also been a constant stimulus. We have been grateful for such support and interest from those with whom we work. It is this interest which leads us to commit this volume to print.

KENNETH R. ANDREWS

July 1, 1952

Contents

CONTENTS

PART ONE

TEACHING AND LEARNING

Because Wisdom Can't Be Told

CHARLES I. GRAGG

*So he had grown rich at last, and thought to transmit to his only son
all the cut-and-dried experience which he himself had purchased at the
price of his lost illusions; a noble last illusion of age . . .* BALZAC

*The essential fact which makes the case system . . . an educational
method of the greatest power is that it arouses the interest of the student
by making him an active rather than a passive participant . . .*

Dean DONHAM

Students must be accepted as the important part of the academic picture. This article about the case system of instruction of the Harvard
Graduate School of Business Administration is concerned therefore with
the effects which the case system has upon students. The object is not to
describe the cases themselves, the methods of their collection, or even
the routine of their classroom use. For the benefit of those unfamiliar with
business-school cases, it is merely necessary to explain that, as now used,
a case typically is a record of a business issue which *actually* has been
faced by business executives, together with surrounding facts, opinions,
and prejudices upon which executive decisions had to depend. These real
and particularized cases are presented to students for considered analysis,
open discussion, and final decision as to the type of action which should
be taken. Day by day the number of atomic business situations thus
brought before the students grows and forms a backlog for observing
coherent patterns and drawing out general principles.

It can be said flatly that the mere act of listening to wise statements
and sound advice does little for anyone. In the process of learning, the
learner's dynamic coöperation is required. Such coöperation from students
does not arise automatically, however. It has to be provided for and continually encouraged.

Thus, the key to an understanding of the Business School case plan

of teaching is to be found in the fact that this plan dignifies and drama-
tizes student life by opening the way for students to make positive contributions to thought and, by so doing, to prepare themselves for action.
Indeed, independent, constructive thinking on the part of students is
essential to the sound operation of the plan. This result is achieved in two
ways.

In the first place, students are provided with materials which make it
possible for them to think purposefully. They are not given general theories or hypotheses to criticize. Rather, they are given the specific facts,
the raw materials, out of which decisions have to be reached in life and
from which they can realistically and usefully draw conclusions. This opportunity for students to make significant contributions is enhanced by
the very nature of business management. Business management is not a
technical but a human matter. It turns upon an understanding of how
people—producers, bankers, investors, sellers, consumers—will respond to
specific business actions, and the behavior of such groups always is changing, rapidly or slowly. Students consequently, being people, and also being
in the very stream of sociological trends, are in a particularly good position to anticipate and interpret popular reactions. A recent conspicuous
example is found in the area of labor relations.

In the second place, the desired result of student participation is
achieved by the opening of free channels of communication between students and students, and between students and teachers. The confidence
the student can be given under the case system that he can, and is expected to, make contributions to the understanding of the group is a
powerful encouragement to effort. The corollary fact that all members
of the group are in the same situation provides the student with exercise
in receiving as well as in giving out ideas. In short, true intercommu-
nication is established.

In these facts lie the unique values of the case system, and from these
facts also arise certain difficulties encountered in its use. It is not easy
for students to accept the challenge of responsible activity in the face of
realistic situations. Nor is it always easy for teachers to preserve the
needed open-mindedness toward their students' contribution. Nevertheless, the very existence of the assumption, implicit in the case system, that
students are in a position to and will exert themselves to think with a lively
independence toward a useful end in itself provides a real stimulus. By
the same token, the stage is so set as to simplify the teacher's task of encouraging students to participate actively in the process of learning. The
students are given the raw materials and are expected to use them. The
teacher, for his part, has every opportunity and reason to demonstrate
an encouraging receptivity as well as to inform and guide.

Thinking out original answers to new problems or giving new inter-pretations to old problems is assumed in much undergraduate instruc-tion to be an adult function and, as such, one properly denied to students. The task of the student commonly is taken to be one chiefly of familiariz-ing himself with accepted thoughts and accepted techniques, these to be actively used at some later time. The instruction period, in other words, often is regarded by both students and teachers as a time for absorption.

Thus many students entering graduate schools have become habitu-ated to the role of the receiver. The time inevitably arrives, however, when young people must engage in practical action on their own responsibility. Students at professional school have a little time, at the Harvard Graduate School of Business Administration two years, to achieve the transition from what may be described as a childlike dependence on parents and teachers to a state of what may be called dependable self-reliance.

If the hearts of the young men entering a graduate school of business administration could be clearly read, it is likely that many would be found to cherish a hope that upon graduation they would find positions of au-thority and power awaiting them. This is a carefully guarded hope, be-cause for some reason there is a general feeling that it is an unseemly one for young men to harbor. Yet, although the students who possess this hope may be said to be unrealistic under conditions as they exist, they cannot be said to be other than logical. For if a young man is to occupy more or less permanently a humble position in the business hierarchy, he can make better use of two years of his time than spending it at a school of business administration. The apprentice system is open to the young man who wishes to enter business in a fuller way than it is to the young man who seeks to work in the field of law or of medicine, for example. Except in a few instances, such as the plumbing and electrical trades, there are no restrictions similar to those imposed by bar or medical examinations as to who can start in business. And if a young man who is to spend his life as a salesman, floorwalker, clerk, or minor official has several years to de-vote to acquiring background, he is likely to find that study of sonnets, or operas, or fishing, or philosophy will be more sustaining to his soul than a broad knowledge of business operations.

The work of a graduate school of business consequently must be aimed at fitting students for administrative positions of importance. The quali-ties needed by businessmen in such positions are ability to see vividly the potential meanings and relationships of facts, both those facts having to do with persons and those having to do with things; capacity to make sound judgments on the basis of these perceptions; and skill in communi-cating their judgments to others so as to produce the desired results in the field of action. Business education, then, must be directed to developing in students these qualities of understanding, judgment, and communication leading to action.

Furthermore, since young men who contemplate entering a graduate business school customarily have an alternative opportunity to enter business immediately, the business school must be able to do more for its students than could be accomplished in a corresponding period of actual business experience. Formal professional education necessarily postpones the time of responsible action. Yet a principal object of professional education is to accelerate the student's ability to act in mature fashion under conditions of responsibility. A young man who completes a professional course is expected to demonstrate a more mature judgment, or to demonstrate mature judgment at an earlier period, than the young man who enters upon a career of action without benefit of formal training. The presumption in this situation obviously must be that it is possible to arrange programs of training in such a way as to do more than offset the effect of prolonging the student's period of ostensible immaturity.

It would be easy to accept the unanalyzed assumption that by passing on, by lectures and readings, to young men of intelligence the accumulated experience and wisdom of those who have made business their study, the desired results could be achieved. Surely if more or less carefully selected young men were to begin their business careers with the advantage of having been provided with information and general principles which it has taken others a lifetime to acquire and develop, they might be expected to have a decided head start over their less informed contemporaries.

This assumption, however, rests on another, decidedly questionable one, namely, that it is possible by a simple process of telling to pass on knowledge in a useful form. This is a stumbling block of the ages. If the learning process is to be effective, something dynamic must take place in the learner. The truth of this statement becomes more and more apparent as the learner approaches the inevitable time when he must go into action.

We are all familiar with the popular belief that it is possible to learn how to act wisely only by experience—in the school of hard knocks. But everyone knows that, from a practical point of view, strict adherence to the literal meaning of this belief would have a decidedly limiting effect upon the extent of our learning. Time is all against it. So we all try to tell others what we know or what we think we know. A great part of our educational system, perhaps necessarily, rests on this basis. It is the simple, obvious way of passing the torch of culture from hand to hand.

Entirely aside from the seemingly sound logic of this course, there exists a natural and strong tendency for people to tell others what is what

—how to think, or feel, or act. Often this tendency seems, to the one having it, like an urge to duty. A friend of ours, for example, may remark that he is worried because he doesn't seem to be getting anywhere with the president of the company. "He doesn't seem to know I'm around," our friend explains. Ah ha! We know the answer to that one and will tell our friend how to solve his problem. "Look here, old boy, the trouble with you is you are too shy. Just speak up, loudly and firmly. Tell him what's what. The old buzzard won't ignore you then!"

It is possible that our desire to pass on our knowledge springs in part from the fact that such activity places us, for the time being, in the superior position. From our earliest beginnings there have been people around to tell *us* what to do, to pass on to us their experience and wisdom. There is no little gratification in turning the tables. For a while we will be the parents and someone else can be the child. It is only necessary to listen to a six-year-old lecturing a three-year-old to see vividly the strength of this pleasure.

Teachers, since it is their avowed objective to extend the knowledge boundaries of others, are particularly beset by the temptation to tell what they know—to point out right paths of thought and action. The areas in which their help is called for are ones they have penetrated many times. They have reflected, presumably, upon their subjects from all angles. They feel that they know the answers and, with unselfish abandon, they are willing to tell all. Their students thus will be saved all the time and effort it would have taken them to work things out for themselves, even granting they ever could work out such excellent answers.

Yet no amount of information, whether of theory or of fact, in itself improves insight and judgment or increases ability to act wisely under conditions of responsibility. The same statistical tables covering all aspects of a business may be available to every officer of the organization. Nevertheless, it does not follow that it makes no difference to the business which officer makes the decisions. Likewise, the whole body of generally accepted business theory may be equally familiar to all executives, yet the decisions reached by the various individuals are unlikely to be the same or to have equal merit.

We cannot effectively use the insight and knowledge of others; it must be our own knowledge and insight that we use. If our friend, acting solely on our advice, undertakes to tell the president what is what, the chances are he will make himself conspicuous but not impressive. For him to use our words effectively, granting our diagnosis of the situation is sound, they must become his own through a process of active thought and feeling on his part. Then, if he agrees with us, he will be able to act as we suggest, not on our advice, but from his own heart. The outstanding virtue of the case system is that it is suited to inspiring activity, under realistic conditions, on the part of the students; it takes them out of the role of passive absorbers and makes them partners in the joint processes of learning and of furthering learning.

The case plan of instruction may be described as democratic in distinction to the telling method, which is in effect dictatorial or patriarchal. With the case method, all members of the academic group, teacher *and* students, are in possession of the same basic materials in the light of which analyses are to be made and decisions arrived at. Each, therefore, has an identical opportunity to make a contribution to the body of principles governing business practice and policy. Business is not, at least not yet, an exact science. There is no single, demonstrably right answer to a business problem. For the student or businessman it cannot be a matter of peeking in the back of a book to see if he has arrived at the right solution. In every business situation, there is always a reasonable possibility that the best answer has not yet been found—even by teachers.

Exercise of mature judgment obviously is inconsistent with a program of blindly carrying out someone else's instructions. Moreover, no matter how worthy those instructions may be, they cannot cover every exigency. Tommy's mother says: "On your way home from school, never cross the street until the policeman tells you to, and, when he does tell you to, run." Perhaps one day no policeman is there. Is Tommy to wait forever? Or perhaps a driver fails to observe the policeman's signals. Is Tommy to dash under the speeding wheels?

So far as responsible activity in the business world is concerned, it is clear that a fund of ready-made answers can be of little avail. Each situation is a new situation, requiring imaginative understanding as a prelude to sound judgment and action. The following sad limerick, aimed at describing what might happen to business students without benefit of cases, has been contributed by a friend who prefers to remain anonymous.

> A student of business with tact
> Absorbed many answers he lacked.
> But acquiring a job,
> He said with a sob,
> "How *does* one fit answer to fact?"

A significant aspect of democracy in the classroom is that it provides a new axis for personal relations. No longer is the situation that of the teacher on the one hand and a body of students on the other. The focus of the students' attention is transferred from the teacher to each other, their contemporaries. It is not a question of dealing more or less en masse with an elder; it is a question of dealing with a rather large number of equals whose criticisms must be faced and whose contributions need to be comprehended and used. Everyone is on a par and everyone is in competition. The basis is provided for strong give-and-take both inside and outside the classroom. The valuable art of exchanging ideas with the object of building up some mutually satisfactory and superior notion is cultivated. Such an exchange stimulates thought, provides a lesson in how to learn from others, and also gives experience in effective transmission of one's own ideas.

Under the case system, the instructor's role is to assign the cases for discussion, to act as a responsible member of the group delegated to provoke argumentative thinking, and to guide discussion by his own contributions and questions toward points of major importance; and, if he chooses, to take a final position on the viewpoints which have been threshed out before him. The more powerful are the student arguments, the heavier is the burden on the instructor; he must understand and evaluate each contribution, many of which are new to him, regardless of how thoroughly he has studied the cases or how many times he has used them with previous classes. To the instructor, every class meeting is a new problem and a new opportunity both to learn and to help others to learn. The important question under these circumstances is not whether the student pleases the instructor, but whether he can either support his views against the counterattacks and disagreements of others in the group, or, failing to do so, can accept coöperatively the merits of his antagonists' reasoning.

For both teachers and students, the disciplines of the case method of learning are severe. Sometimes the shock is devastating to young men who previously have been dominated by authority and thus have been faced merely with the relatively simple task of more or less verbatim reception and repetition of facts and ideas. Not all students can bear the strain of thinking actively, of making independent judgments which may be challenged vigorously by their contemporaries. Many people will always prefer to have answers handed to them. Teachers, for their part, particularly those unused to the system, sometimes find it straining to leave the safe haven of dogmatism and meet their students on a democratic plane. The inherently dramatic and challenging character of the case system, however, although it may produce anxiety and confusion for the newcomer, also arouses his deep interest and leads him to make the effort required for adjustment.

In making the adjustment to the democratic disciplines of the case system, a student typically passes through at least three objectively discernible phases. The first phase is that of discovering his inability to think of everything that his fellow students can think of. In many instances, to be sure, the challenge to original thought is pleasing from the first. Yet perhaps more often confusion and a feeling of helplessness set in: "But it's so discouraging to prepare a case as well as I can and then listen for an hour in class to other students bringing out all sorts of interpretations and arguments that I had never thought of."

The second phase is that of accepting easily and without fear the need for coöperative help. During the last half of the first year and the first half of the second year, students learn to draw more and more fully upon each other's ideas in the working out of problems. Competition for high academic standing grows more keen, to be sure, but the mutual giving and taking of assistance ceases to be a matter of secret anguish. The young men are making common cause and thereby learning the pleasure of group pooling of intellectual efforts.

The third and final phase in the march toward maturity usually comes well on in the second year with the recognition that the instructors do not always or necessarily know the "best" answers and that, even when they do seem to know them, each student is free to present and hold to his own views. When this phase is reached, the student is ready to make independent progress and to break new ground on his own account. He is operating as a responsible member of the community, taking help, to be sure, from both contemporaries and elders, but making his own decisions without fear of disapproval or search for an authoritative crutch to lean upon.

This sequence of student development is not peculiar to the use of business cases. Other schools using the case system apparently have a similar experience so far as initial confusion among students is concerned. For instance, Dr. Josef Redlich, Professor of Law at the University of Vienna, after investigating the case system of teaching law for the Carnegie Foundation, reported, in part, as follows:

> I am just as positive that, if all first attempts are difficult, this is especially true of legal education according to the case method. Eminent professors of law have repeatedly explained to me that it takes a long time before the excellent effects of instruction by law cases are evident. The beginners are, as a rule, rather confused by what is demanded of them in class, and usually for a considerable period only the particularly quick or talented students take part in the debate; but after some weeks or months, things become clearer to the others also . . . and there soon follows the hearty coöperation of the majority.[1]

An outstanding effect of the case system, in other words, is to put upon students the burden of independent thinking. The initial impact of such mental activity upon a mind not used to it has been described by Chekhov in the words of one of his characters in the story, *Lights:*

[1] Quoted by C. F. Allen in "The Case System for the Study of Law," from the *Proceedings of the Society for the Promotion of Engineering Education*, XXVII (1919), p. 55.

It appeared that I . . . had not mastered the technique of thinking, and that I was no more capable of managing my own brain than mending a watch . . .

For the first time in my life I was really thinking eagerly and intensely, and that seemed to me so monstrous that I said to myself, "I am going off my head."

No method is foolproof. A badly handled case system cannot but be an academic horror. Improperly handled, a case is merely an elaborate means for confusing and boring students. If, moreover, the teacher insists on being a patriarch—if he is sure he has the right and only answers and visualizes his task as one of forcing the students, the case facts, and *his* answers into an affectionate rapport—it will be found that the out-and-out lecture system is infinitely less costly and less straining to everyone concerned. Such use of cases perverts the unique characteristics of the system. The opportunity which this system provides the students of reaching responsible judgments on the basis of an original analysis of the facts is sacrificed.

In addition to the possibility that the case system will be misused, and so become merely a wasteful way of telling the students what the teacher thinks, it must be recognized that the case does not provide a perfect replica of a business situation. In the properly conducted class using business cases, the students are put in the position of the executives who must arrive at definite conclusions to be followed by specific actions whose merits will be tested by resulting developments. There is no escaping the fact that the students' decisions are not tested in this way. As Winston Churchill is reported to have remarked recently, there is a great deal of difference between being responsible for an order which may lose several valuable ships and expressing an opinion without such responsibility. It is too much to expect that anything except experience can be exactly like experience.

Nevertheless, a training period which allows students this relative irresponsibility has great advantages. The serious student gets the essential background for responsible decisions without the risks to himself and to his industry which are inseparable from amateurish action. He is led to active consideration of a tremendous number of diverse and related real situations, which it would take him at least a lifetime of experience to encounter, and he is thus given a basis for comparison and analysis when he enters upon his career of business action.

The case system, properly used, initiates students into the ways of independent thought and responsible judgment. It faces them with situations which are not hypothetical but real. It places them in the active role, open to criticism from all sides. It puts the burden of understanding and judgment upon them. It provides them with the occasion to deal constructively with their contemporaries and their elders. And, at least in the area of business, it gives them the stimulating opportunity to make contributions to learning. In short, the student, if he wishes, can act as an adult member of a democratic community.

As for the teacher, the case method of instruction provides him richly with the basic means of research. Not only does the existence of a stream of recorded business experiences enable him to keep in touch with business life and to make continuous necessary modifications in his inductions and general conclusions. In addition, the relations which the case system sets up between himself and his students give the teacher the continual benefit of fresh, imaginative points of view which always hold the possibility of true advance.

Some Comments on Teaching by the Case Method

JOHN D. GLOVER AND RALPH M. HOWER

THERE IS NO FORMULA

This may be disconcerting for the person who wishes to teach by the case method, and also for anyone who wishes to write about it. However much he may desire to be helpful, the experienced instructor finds it difficult to tell the inexperienced instructor very much about how he really conducts classes. In part the difficulty stems from the problem of verbalizing what is, inevitably, a very dynamic process—and especially so when the instructor responds to the situation before him rather than attempting to force it into patterns conceived by him either before class or during the course of the discussion. And in part the difficulty arises from the fact that any verbal statement which the experienced instructor might finally achieve seems to have little real meaning for anyone except a person with considerable firsthand experience in teaching by the case method. This barrier is somewhat less bothersome when two people can sit down together and discuss at length various aspects of teaching; but when one person tries to put down his ideas on paper for other people in a one-way communicative effort, the obstacles to understanding are almost insurmountable.

If the reader will bear these caveats in mind, the following material may be of some help; it is offered as food for thought, not as rules for procedure or a complete statement on the subject. Let the reader bear in mind, too, that the views expressed here are our own opinion on how to use the case material in *The Administrator;* they are not offered as having any necessary relevance to other casebooks.

IMPORTANCE OF ATMOSPHERE ESTABLISHED BY THE INSTRUCTOR

As a number of us conceive it, teaching by the case method consists of considerably more than the assignment of cases and the application of techniques for conducting discussion. A large part of its success (or failure) depends upon the relation which obtains between the instructor and the students. This is particularly true of a course like "Administrative Practices." One of the instructor's main concerns, therefore, will be rapport with the class. This ultimately will depend upon the instructor's intelligence, patience, tolerance, and understanding as actually manifested by his daily behavior; but he can at least think in advance of the kind of atmosphere which he will strive to maintain during discussions.

Clearly, if the students are to take responsibility for analyzing and discussing cases, they need a favorable climate for doing so. This means a permissive atmosphere in which they feel free to put forth their ideas and their questions without the instructor's reacting in the form of rejection, derision, blame, or authoritarian injunctions to think along certain other lines preferred by the instructor at that moment. This free atmosphere will be fostered if the instructor makes up his mind to hear and to try to understand what students have to say, and encourages others to do the same. At times he may have to ask for amplification or restatement, and certainly what students say will often seem wrong or absurd; but in any event, he will try to grasp and respect whatever views the student tries to express.

Behind such behavior will be a feeling of equals collaborating in the struggle for enlightenment. Whether or not the instructor agrees with what the student has said, he will want to explore further in a joint effort to find out where such views lead. And he will want to hear what other students think, too. On occasion (usually when asked) he will put forth ideas of his own; but he will do so with the explicit understanding that his ideas are to be scrutinized, discussed, criticized, accepted, or rejected with the same freedom that is accorded those of anyone else in the class. Even the wisest instructor has no monopoly on ideas. In short, he will try to regard, and therefore treat, his students as adults, with the respect, tolerance, and will to understand which goes with mature relationships.

With such an attitude and in the atmosphere which results from it, there is a better chance that students will learn to express their ideas and gain familiarity with the difficulties in reaching conclusions and communicating to others what they think. They will gradually increase their respect for the views of others and acquire experience in the process of understanding other people. They tend to gain, too, a deeper understanding of the complexities of administrative situations and of the elusive nature of wisdom and truth. With this increased understanding, moreover, they usually acquire greater skill in thinking, in communication, in integrating divergent ideas, and in the general process of working with others. Not unnaturally, the instructor, in our experience, makes similar gains.

CAREFUL ANALYSIS OF CASE DATA COMES FIRST

Another basic point in teaching through cases is the careful, step-by-step analysis of case facts as a prelude to discussion. Many students are tempted to read cases through quickly as a kind of story and then to engage in a rather haphazard, easygoing "bull session," so general and abstract as to be of little value. The remedy for this, we think, does not lie in rigid censorship over what students can say, for that is likely to kill all exploratory discussion. Rather, the solution seems to be for the instructor to have the details well in mind, to ask questions which continually relate back to the case data, and to check with other members of the class on the accuracy, completeness, and relevance of a student's references. Indeed, a moderate amount of drill in the painstaking analysis of cases seems to be desirable at the beginning of the course in order to give students adequate grounding in appraisal of specific situations, including an orderly cataloguing of alternative interpretations and choices of action at various points. Much of the value of discussion will be lost unless students form the habit of directing their remarks to the specific situation before them, thus having to formulate their proposals in the light of the particular set of objective facts and the conflicting interests, principles, and sentiments which they encounter among those facts. Initially students usually complain that they need more information than the case provides; but the simple question, "Have you made good use of the facts you do have?" is likely to induce a new attack on analysis.

This drill is not easy to manage without boring or frustrating the class and stifling all initiative. An oral quizzing which leads to a mere repetition of case facts is likely to be disastrous. We do not ask that students memorize the case, for there is no point in doing so; they have the printed case in front of them for easy reference. We do assume that everyone has read and tried to grasp the facts of the case. Although we are sometimes disappointed in this assumption, we do not care to stultify the whole class by a disciplinary approach. We quickly pass on to a student who is prepared to participate in discussion by being familiar with the case.

Cases like the Jim McFee, the Superior Slate Quarry, and the Joseph Longman cases particularly lend themselves to early drill in a thorough-going analysis of this sort, for each has two or three separate stages which need to be compared for items of similarity and of difference. One useful approach is to sort out (in the order of happening if the sequence seems to be of significance) the *activities* which are described in a given situation, then the *relations* between the people concerned in them, and lastly the *sentiments and beliefs* which are revealed by remarks or behavior in connection with the activities and relations. One is then in a better position to determine concretely the impact of change upon these aspects of the situation, as a basis for evaluating possible consequences, need for action of some sort, and so on.

If the instructor can continually focus upon the significance of case details—their relations to one another and their implications for administrative action—and if he can induce students to raise questions of their own along such lines, he will probably find not only acceptance of the step-by-step analysis as a necessary phase but also real and growing interest in the process on the part of the students. The likelihood of this result taking place will be improved if the instructor, while possessing ideas of his own to start with, feels and shows a genuine interest in the views put forward by others. By such means he whets normal curiosity and provides an incentive for the use of imagination in achieving new interpretations and syntheses. Moreover, he thereby encourages the free exchange of interpretations and proposals out of which a more satisfying treatment is likely to develop.

As a part of the case analysis, the instructor will want to be alert, both in reading the case and in listening to discussion about it, to errors resulting from a failure to discriminate between objective facts and personal evaluation of those facts. This error is extremely common, of course; but possibly it is harder to avoid than is generally realized. Thus, Jim McFee's statement, "It seems unreasonable to expect anyone to produce 35 units per hour," may be accepted as a factual statement of Jim's feelings; whether this expectation is objectively "unreasonable" is another question, and one which is, to a large extent, irrelevant. Certainly, discussion is desirable as to why Jim felt that way. The latter issue seems to lead to pure speculation; yet, by digging back among the case details, one can assemble a number of possibilities as to the answer, supported by fragments of evidence of the kind which we usually have to work with in real life. Learning in this instance comes from formulating the array of possibilities and then striving to appraise their implications for management.

Gradually the students (and the instructor) increase their ability to discern that apparently simple situations are usually complex; that there are various ways of looking at the facts, and each of them may be valid for its purpose; and that each person evaluates the facts differently because of what he brings to the case from his own past experience and current preoccupations. Once the class has struggled through confusion and frustration to this stage, it can proceed with less difficulty to the task of integrating various points of view and working toward acceptable solutions.

CASES GROW AND CHANGE DURING THE DISCUSSION

Many instructors approaching the case method for the first time need to be forewarned that, from the moment a discussion starts, they will not be dealing with a case having an objective existence of its own, a collection of printed material which provides a secure base for reference whenever a difference of opinion emerges. Each person deals with the case as it appears to him. One student identifies himself with a character in the case; another projects his own feelings and attitudes into the situation; a third deals with stereotypes rather than with the people described; still another is responding more to his feelings toward the instructor than to the case situation; another seemingly says what he thinks the instructor wants to hear, or else what the majority of the class will approve, rather than advancing his own inner thoughts. Some talk principally in terms of reaction to other students' views rather than to case material; some go off on what appear to be irrelevancies; and some repeat ideas which have already been discussed, quite as if they were wholly fresh contributions. Students' views (and those of the instructor) change in the course of discussion—indeed, sometimes during the very act of speaking. Such phenomena are typical, and they cannot be ignored or rebuffed without doing damage to rapport and to the learning which might take place if students were helped to recognize and discuss what is happening in the classroom.

If the instructor can maintain the view that he is offering help to students rather than teaching substantive material, he will deal patiently with the case as it develops in the classroom. That is to say, he will ask the students to tell more about how they reached their conclusions. He may call the attention of the class to what is going on (for example, that members of the class are really altering the case facts, and so on) and make this a subject of discussion. When students complain, as they will, about the number of factors to be related and the differences of opinion that emerge, he may frankly ask (as a means of trying to encourage students to struggle on through the doubts and frustrations) such questions as the following: What should we do about these complexities? What should we do about the points of view with which we disagree, or which we cannot understand? What are the possible consequences if we do? Do you really want the instructor to decide which students are making relevant and useful contributions and to ask the others to be silent?

By such means the students usually become aware of what is going on and consequently gain maturity in thought and behavior. Some students seem to make no progress whatever in their thinking. Some even appear to lose ground. But those who progress the most are not always the most articulate. Indeed, one of the disturbing discoveries one inevitably has to make is that sometimes a student who can verbalize impressively turns out to be wholly superficial and ultimately to show very little genuine understanding. On the other hand, we have repeatedly had students who seemed to get very little out of the discussions at the time and yet later experienced a kind of delayed reaction, indicating considerable insight and growth.

It takes time and patience to weather the periods of difficulty; but if the instructor will try to concentrate on helping students develop points raised by themselves and will encourage free discussion of bothersome issues, the students, both individually and as a group, will usually begin to show progress. Even experienced instructors are sometimes tempted to cut the discussion short; to rule embarrassing questions out of order; to deliver caustic lectures about students who do not pay attention, or fail to think systematically, or are talking too much; and to decide for the students as to right and wrong answers. To yield, however—far from hastening the learning process—is to *impede* it.

This view of teaching by the case method rejects the idea that the instructor can, or should, anticipate the course of discussion and devise ways of guiding or leading students around to what he or some other "authority" has decided are the important aspects of the case. To guide the discussion, we think, sets the wrong tone at the outset and takes from the students responsibility that they must have if they are really going to learn to think for themselves and to bear responsibility for their conclusions. The instructor should, of course, work up ideas and be prepared to ask all sorts of questions about points raised by the students; but he should try to come with an open mind—not only prepared for the possibility of hearing something new from the class but actually expecting to do so. In addition, he will recognize, and help his students to see, that a case discussion is not a series of bilateral interchanges between the instructor and individual students but is in truth a group discussion in which the instructor plays an important but not dominating role and in which also the reactions and interactions among the students are a proper subject for thought and discussion.

A FEW POINTERS

Effective teaching, we believe, is not achieved through mechanical routine; the great teacher is not distinguished by some procedural trick which anyone can imitate to produce the same results. Some of us who have tried to copy what we took to be the teaching techniques of some of our older and more experienced colleagues have inevitably "come a cropper." We have found that, for better or worse, we have to be ourselves; and "technique," we now hold, must be a manifestation of one's true self—in teaching and in administration alike. If it is a kind of synthetic overlay without integral relation to the man, it can hardly be otherwise than uncomfortable, ineffective, and ridiculous.

Some instructors will understand immediately what it is we have in mind; some of them, undoubtedly, could express themselves better than we. But, very likely the "tone" or attitude we are speaking of will be alien or downright unacceptable to some individuals. In these men, the "tone" which we think is generally desirable may be, in varying degrees, incompatible with their present general outlook on life and accustomed approach to teaching. Such a person, we think, would make an error if he tried, overnight as it were, to assume without much faith or conviction the sort of approach we have in mind. For some of us it has taken time and struggle to reach our present stage of thinking, and we have come to feel that no matter how much progress any of us makes there will always be opportunity, and need, for more. The instructor must be himself, and must progress, if at all, toward this kind of attitude over a period of time in his own way. "Let him combat and persuade himself before trying to persuade or combat others. Let him, by all means at his disposal, concentrate his will on the construction of an unshakeable faith even though it be only a faith in the dignity and destiny of man. The method he employs is of no importance. We have said it before: no matter what road is chosen the travelers who started from different valleys will all meet on top of the mountain, provided they keep on ascending. No one must pride himself on having chosen the best route nor force his neighbor to follow him. Everyone takes the path which suits him best, imposed by the structure of the brain, by heredity, by traditions. One can offer support, enlightenment, help. But what succeeds with one may fail with others, and every man must wage his own fight without which he cannot progress." [1]

We are also reminded, at this point, of the words of Francis Bacon, speaking of his own work: "I do not endeavor either by triumphs of confutation, or pleading of antiquity, or assumption of authority, or even by the veil of obscurity, to invest these inventions of mine with any majesty . . . I have not sought nor do I seek either to force or ensnare men's judgments, but I lead them to things themselves and the concordances of things, that they may see for themselves what they have, what they can dispute, what they can add and contribute to the common stock." [2]

Accordingly, the following suggestions are offered as an indication of tone or flavor—as manifestations of what we think is an appropriate atti-

---

[1] As quoted in Glover and Hower, *The Administrator* (p. 67), from Lecomte du Noüy, *Human Destiny* (New York: Longmans, Green, 1947).
[2] From the Preface to *The Great Instauration*.

tude of the teacher toward his students, his subjects, and himself. We do not know of any prescriptions for "sure-fire" teaching.

We have found that it is helpful, especially early in the term, to start the discussion with questions like "Do you see a problem in the case? What do you think it is?" Disentangling a problem or problems is sometimes the most difficult phase of dealing with a case. Needless to say, such a "diagnosis" must be made before any very satisfactory progress can be achieved in discussing possible lines of action. Within a short time it will be possible to begin the discussion by simply asking, "Who wants to start?" or "Who is willing to open up the case?"

It is frequently useful to summarize what a student has just said as a means of verifying (a) whether you and others in the group understood what he said and (b) whether he said what he meant (that is, whether he expressed adequately in words what he was trying to say). The student may then make corrections in the statement if he desires, and the discussion can proceed without too much misunderstanding. Thus, the instructor will find himself saying such things as:

"Let me summarize what I think I heard you say, to see if I caught what you are driving at."

"Would you mind elaborating that? I'm not sure it is clear to most of us."

"Is this what you mean? . . ."

"I think I see your point, but I am having difficulty relating it to your previous interpretation (or to what Mr. —— has just said, or to the situation as developed in the discussion so far)."

The instructor, like any participant in any conference, will assist well-tempered, thorough, and fruitful discussion if he refrains from rejecting forthwith a view with which he disagrees and also from accepting immediately a view with which he is in accord. He may want to ask questions of the speaker which probe further into the validity or consequences of the views, or he may refer the matter to the rest of the class (if no one voluntarily agrees or challenges) by saying something like "Does anyone care to comment on what Mr. —— has just said?" In this way the class, rather than the instructor alone, will be induced to judge the merits of the contribution.

When the student asks a question, the instructor frequently will turn it back by saying in effect, "That is an interesting question. Do you yourself have some views on it?" Or, "Does anyone want to propose an answer to Mr. ——'s question?" Or, "Well, here is my own opinion . . . But what *should* I think?" Or, "Do you see anything in the case which might throw light on that point?"

Occasionally the instructor may try to pull together a number of the views expressed, both as a means of reminding the students about what has been said and as a basis for proceeding to new issues or new proposals. From time to time, too, the instructor may feel impelled to outline a number of points not touched upon by the class, or to suggest alternate interpretations or proposals—not by way of saying, "This is the answer," but rather to indicate room for further analysis and reflection. This must be done with caution, especially in the early part of the term before the students have come to understand and appreciate the independence of thought which they are encouraged to have. Otherwise it may encourage too many students to depend upon the instructor for ideas.

The objective is to help the student develop ways of thinking and grow in the maturity and depth of his point of view, rather than to give a specific "best answer" to a series of situations, none of which will ever recur in the same way. To do this the instructor has to achieve the attitude that his role is to help students *to recognize for themselves* the various elements in the situation before them, rather than to try to tell them what he thinks they ought to think. It is a form of learning by doing, of course; and the wise instructor will, though often sorely tempted, resist the desire "to put the students straight" by telling them what they should think. He is concerned with developing their perception, not with deriving formulas; with enhancing their powers of discrimination rather than their ability to generalize uniformities from a base which is essentially unique.

Just as the discussion should focus on the case situation as it develops in class, so the instructor should concentrate upon the points that are of particular interest to students. This sounds easy, and yet it is difficult; for students who are accustomed to normal classroom procedure tend to concern themselves with what they think the instructor wants, so as to be able to hand back—unassimilated and unchanged—*his* ideas when required, and so earn a good grade. Hence they are likely to be diffident at first about bringing up questions of personal interest. There are so many issues about which we rarely dare to expose our doubts, our ignorance, or our curiosity, just because we are afraid of being considered ignorant or unorthodox!

If the instructor habitually deals with those aspects of the case (or questions arising out of the case discussion) which are of particular interest or significance to the students at the particular time, he and the students will both gain. They will then be able to deal with a problem when it is meaningful to them and at a level at which they can effectively deal with it, rather than being obliged to try to cope with something which they find boring or irrelevant or incomprehensible. The instructor should endeavor to stay with points of interest until the class as a whole (though not necessarily every person in it) has achieved some understanding. This process is definitely helpful in encouraging students to acquire ways of thinking and acting which are personally useful to them in relation to their own problems. And, after all, it is precisely the increased effectiveness of each man in dealing with his own problems that is the basic objective of the course.

Initially the instructor is likely to find the discussion taking the form of a series of discrete monologues, each student dealing with the case as it appears to him, with little or no relation to what has been said by others previously in the discussion. Fortunately, students soon note what is happening; they may even complain about it! When they do, there is opportunity for talking about the discussion process, the difficulty of paying attention to what others are saying, the problem of weaving it into one's own thinking, and so on.

The instructor will also find many unstated (and sometimes unintended) assumptions embodied in the discussion, and he will help students learn a great deal by lifting these assumptions up for recognition and examination. For example, in the John Edwards case, students frequently assume that the three men who protested the promotion of Edwards did so because each of them felt entitled to the position. One must first identify this view as an assumption, rather than a case "fact"; and then one must ask whether it is necessarily valid, or whether other assumptions might reasonably be made which could lead to different conclusions.

Far more difficult than recognizing the unstated and unconscious assumptions of others is recognizing assumptions of one's own. Beyond the phase of recognizing one's own assumptions in particular cases lies that of becoming aware of the assumptions by which one guides one's own life and interprets it and the world about him. Still farther beyond lies the pensive reëxamination of these assumptions and values. From this reexamination comes emotional, as well as logical, qualification, rejection, or reaffirmation of these foundations of attitude and outlook. In this never-ending process of growth and maturation, the instructor—if he does not prevent such development, and if he strives to keep open his eyes, ears, and mind—can receive help from the students. They, more than he, will recognize his assumptions and examine their validity. In a democratic and permissive atmosphere, the students will tell him of their observations and doubts. In an authoritarian atmosphere, the instructor will have to make his progress, if any, without this help.

As the term goes on, both instructor and student will find it convenient to refer back to something in a previous case, or in the discussion of it by the class, as a kind of bench mark or background for current comment. Used in this way, cases may well serve as illustrations, provided they have been well discussed and provided they are used as such with students who took part in the discussion. When the Marshall Company cases have been discussed by the end of the first term, for example, we have found that students refer back to the series and to various people in the cases with almost daily frequency. And we have encountered students who, long after they have finished the course, have told us of situations they have observed, illustrating by saying, "It was very much like A in the XYZ case."

Apart from such instances, the cases in *The Administrator* are not intended to be illustrations of principles or theories or "typical" situations. Each individual case involves many things deserving of analysis and study, and each is intended for consideration in the classroom (as it actually occurred in life) as a total situation resulting from many interacting and often interdependent factors. No case has been selected on such grounds as "This case shows how to (or how not to) handle women industrial workers in wartime"; or "This case shows how to deal with salesmen in a small company selling consumer goods in a buyers' market"; or anything of the sort.

Neither are these cases intended as springboards for lectures by the instructor. They were selected for their merits as bases for the discussion of administrative problems involving people. To be sure, a number of us deliver an impromptu "lecturette" from time to time on some aspect of a given case or some phase of administration. But such messages usually originate as a response to a classroom situation (particularly to questions) rather than as part of a preconceived plan. The essence of teaching by the case method is to let the student carry the main load. Only by this means can we realize the ancient goal of having the teacher teach less and the learner learn more.

The inexperienced instructor (and, indeed, many of the old hands) may feel a great sense of insecurity under the case method, since he must, to a large extent, "play by ear." He will feel a strong sense of frustration, too, because points that seem obvious to him will provide stumbling blocks for his students, and he will be sorely tempted to try to put them right. This temptation will be especially strong about two months after the start, when the students become conscious of the fact that their discussions, so interesting and lively, have not been supplying them with formulas they can put down for memorizing. They then begin to bombard the instructor with demands for answers.

If by any chance the instructor does try to "tell them," he may find, to his consternation, that he has not helped matters; for any verbalizations that he can produce will, at best, usually fail to satisfy more than momentarily. Moreover, he will probably find that whatever he says—above all, as regards any particular case—is likely to bring on a chorus of disagreement.

And the disagreement will usually increase in scope and intensity if the instructor dogmatically insists on his own views. By about the middle of the first term, the students will have had enough exposure to concrete and analytical thinking to be dissatisfied with broad general statements, while they will, at the same time, have formed the habit of criticizing the shortcomings of any more detailed proposals for action. Learning takes time, and the instructor must not expect too much too soon; but the period of confusion and frustration usually gives way eventually to new insight. About the only step that helps during this phase is a frank discussion of the problem, encouraging the class to state its desires and expectations and then asking it to help in working out solutions for its difficulties.

From time to time, the instructor almost surely will feel, possibly quite correctly, that there is a point which the students simply *must* see, something they *must* think about and discuss. At these times, he will probably try to insist upon discussion; very possibly he will deliver himself of a lecture. He may, if he is like us, become impatient or discouraged in spite of himself and his intentions. In any group of students there may be a few who will try, with some success, to get his point. There may be none. Probably he can be sure that not *all* have really gotten the point and made it their own. What then? Well, he can come back to this point another day in another way. He will probably find, however, that no matter what he or members of the class may do or not do, there will always be some upon whom the whole experience—even over a whole academic year—has had little visible effect. A few, for all that has gone on in the class, may have suffered regression, rather than enjoyed growth, as a result of the experience. Some may have only a brittle and superficial verbal facility which shatters with the impact of concrete problems. We have found that a good antidote to our depression when we consider how little progress some men seem to make, in spite of their opportunity—and, of course, in spite of what *we* do—is to reread the Sermon on the Mount, or even that gem from Du Noüy. We know from experience that it is well-nigh impossible constantly and without fail to bear in one's mind and in one's spirit the truth which is contained in the old saw: "You can lead a horse to water, but you can't make him drink."

Perhaps all the foregoing suggestions sound difficult to carry out, and the task is not an easy one, especially for those of us trained in unilateral teaching, whereby the instructors propound dicta which the students are expected to accept with little or no question. Each instructor has to learn by doing, pondering his own experiences, adapting his own methods to his situation, and developing a style of teaching which will be inevitably his own. If it were otherwise, good teaching would not be so rare. Initially it is a tough assignment, but generally it becomes easier. Many of us have found it a rewarding one.

The Case Method

D AVID N. ULRICH

In the area of Administrative Practices and Human Relations, the objective is to develop student capacity to deal with specific problems of human relations in an infinitely complex and continually changing environment. This capacity involves both intellectual and emotional maturity. In other words, the objective is to enable the students to grow.

To achieve the objective of student growth, teachers have found that they also must grow. They try to practice approved techniques of teaching until these techniques become habitual skills backed by an increasing personal conviction of their value. At the same time, each individual seeks to adapt these techniques to his own personality so that he may handle discussion with students in the way most effective for himself. Anyone familiar with this process appreciates what it may demand in live interest, patience, and self-knowledge. In the last analysis, then, the answer to the question, "How can I write cases and teach them?" will come only from the person asking it.

Yet there are some answers. We can identify certain assumptions about the case method that underlie its use; we can discuss what actually occurs in the classroom and show how this process may be utilized to create opportunities for learning; we can go into the nature of the case material that plays a part in the process. This paper will cover these basic points.

UNDERLYING ASSUMPTIONS ABOUT PRINCIPLES, KNOWLEDGE, AND SOCIAL VALUES

Principles. Persons unacquainted with the case method often find it hard to realize that the cases are not used primarily as illustrations of "principles," "rules," or "points."

Most students come to the Business School accustomed to dealing with theories, principles, rules, and other logical or quasi-logical equipment.

But they have not developed a capacity to see specific problems clearly. Instead the majority responds to each case problem according to some stereotyped approach. So the teachers have found that they must help above all else to develop the ability of the student to make careful discriminations. If the student seeks to apply principles, he must know how to test their relevance and he must know their limits. Only upon such a foundation may the teacher build useful generalizations for the student or encourage him to develop generalizations and principles of his own where he may personally feel they are needed.

Knowledge. Another basic aspect of the case method is its treatment of "knowledge" or "content." In the study of cases, teachers can and do transfer much knowledge or content to students. They deal with this knowledge in the context of its use by the *specific people* in the cases and in the classroom to meet the needs of an active situation. For most students, the case approach creates an incentive to acquire knowledge, since the student can continually perceive his need for knowledge in dealing with problems requiring action.

Social Values. A third broad consideration about the case method is its relation to problems of social values. Few cases can be unraveled very far before matters of objectively established fact lead to questions of interpretation and judgment. Interpretation and judgment in turn depend upon the underlying social values held by the person studying the case. Critics of the case method say that, since it deals with only one case situation at a time, it offers the student no opportunity to recognize the general social problems implicit in the whole series.

This limitation is not inherent in the case method. To be sure, the student will have no opportunity to raise questions about social value, if the teacher feels that such questions lie outside the scope of discussion. In turn, the teacher's willingness to hear the students depends on his willingness to subject his own values to critical scrutiny. The stimulus for deeper social thinking by the student may come from either student or teacher, but it must be accepted by the teacher within the working context of the course. With skilled instructors, a student may bring his preoccupations about social values to bear upon virtually any case. He may recognize the limits to his own perspective and acquire deeper insights. Thus he can relate questions of value to problems of action, instead of dealing with them in a vacuum.

PROCESS IN THE CLASSROOM

Fundamental to the classroom activity is the fact that it is student-centered. From the outset, through the exercise of teaching skills reinforced by his own attitudes toward teaching, the experienced teacher makes it clear that the students themselves are responsible for working through the case problems.

Impediments to Learning. From the first class period on, the teacher needs to recognize that students will not acquire new understanding until they are ready to do so. *They cannot superimpose new attitudes upon existing ones.* The process requires change of the existing structure. Change must occur especially in certain attitudes that function as obstacles to learning. These attitudes take many forms, according to the personality of the individual student.

The presence of the teacher upon the lecture platform, equipped with symbols of status and control (such as the platform itself, the call list, the grade sheet) causes many students to feel defensive, and their reactions may take the form of confusion, a withdrawal into silence, or overaggressiveness. Furthermore, students may tend to direct their attention toward "casing" the instructor as thoroughly as possible, picking up his attitudes and his likes and dislikes, as a guide to reciting well and writing good reports and examinations. This dependent attitude blocks learning; conversely, outgrowing it is an aspect of achieving maturity. Of course, the student cannot be blamed for orienting himself to the grade sheet, rather than to the case problem itself, if the instructor (and the institution generally) behaves as if the student's future, in terms of job opportunities and other rewards, depends on his grades rather than on his development as a mature individual. This is a basic problem in educational policy which has not yet received enough attention.

Another common obstacle takes an intellectual form. Many students, instead of trying to perceive the internal relations in a given situation, seize upon some of the facts presented as mere illustrations of some theory or concept. For example, a student may write, "This is an example of monotony resulting from repetitive work." Having thus broadly classified the material, he rests satisfied, unaware that instead of effectively dealing with the problem he has merely found a label for it.

Another characteristic response is the erection of dichotomies. In discussing possible courses of action, the student will outline the two most contrasting extremes and then try to choose between them. This approach creates many opportunities for clever wordplay, for devastating arguments pro and con, for the release of intense positive and negative attitudes, and for a false sense of certainty about the answer selected. Such an approach tends to prevent the student from perceiving the complexities of the situation he is studying.

A related response is the effort to find one cause to which a number of consequences can be ascribed. Simple cause-to-effect reasoning leads many students to such conclusions as, "If the company isn't running well, get rid of the president."

Another common student reaction is an unwillingness to look calmly at a situation that has symbolic significance—for example, a high-ranking military officer or a union shop steward.

Obviously all of these responses have much in common. The student's response to any case tends to take shape according to his basic attitudes, particularly those involving authority and independence. He also tends to respond according to characteristic stereotyped ways of thinking that have developed in harmony with his deepest attitudes. Much liberal arts education, by encouraging classifying and theorizing at a level well removed from the complexities of firsthand experience, encourages these stereotypes. By challenging them, the case method of instruction plunges the thinking student into many uncertainties. The frequent response of the student, in an effort to ward off such uncertainties, is a continual demand for answers, together with criticisms of the instructor who will not or cannot give them.

Because of the many obstacles to learning the students bring with them, because the case method of instruction is unfamiliar to most of them, and because they have a wide variety of expectation about the objectives of the course, the first months of a course are likely to produce a good deal of confusion and frustration. The teacher is of course the most likely target for these negative feelings. Only the most experienced teacher can get through this period without strain and self-doubts.

Classroom Objectives. Efforts at prompt clarification of the purpose of the course and of the students' part in it are futile. The common experience of working together through the term is necessary to bring understanding of a joint purpose. At the outset, the most effective procedure is to bring conflicting student expectations to the surface as quickly as possible by raising questions about them. Meanwhile, the teacher is working toward an objective which for analysis can be divided in two aspects: the teaching of a useful point of view toward the material, and the development of a working rapport with the students which will give them adequate leadership and yet leave them free to progress toward the independent exercise of judgment.

The point of view brought to bear upon the case material has certain definable characteristics. In the first place, the discipline of analyzing cases requires teacher and students to avoid the easy pitfall of pseudo omniscience. The teacher does not encourage the student to approach problems with such statements as, "Now, the management of this company should realize . . ." Instead, the student will be asked to specify concretely from what position he is looking at the problem and how a person in that position might effectively get specific members of **management** to recognize a certain problem.

Closely related to this adherence to a point of view is the implicit realization that points of view are relative and that total objectivity or impartiality is a myth. The student is encouraged to speak not as a judge but as a participant who recognizes the part he is playing.

Another basic aspect of the point of view is its continual recognition of the mutual interdependence of the factors that go to make up any human situation. Asking, "What is going on here?" the teacher seeks to draw his students beyond the stages of moralizing, theorizing, and witch-hunting and to bring their attention again and again to careful analysis of all the known relations in the events under study.

In particular, he invites the students to look at the intangibles that influence human behavior in specific situations. Ultimately, he encourages the student to understand the nature of his own relations to others. The application of this point of view to the case material requires patience, close attention to factual detail, and a continual effort to develop fresh insights penetrating the limits of old attitudes.

Developing rapport with the class is not essentially a matter of getting on good terms with the students. Rather it is the deliberate creation of an environment in which the students can learn. To accomplish this objective, the teacher from the outset of the first meeting designs his questions not to elicit responses to predetermined "points" but to develop points raised by students. He resists student pressure to give answers until the group has developed enough mutual confidence so that the students will not feel any compulsion to attach more importance to his answers than they appear to be worth.

When the students do not promptly bring up the points he considers important, he resists the temptation to "let go" and lecture at them, for he recognizes that they can learn only at the level where they are, not at the level where he would like them to be. He remains sensitive to class moods, continually judging where to turn his attention next among the students, when to develop or drop a subject under discussion, and when to drop one case for another. With the proper leadership, student-to-teacher recitation should give way to more and more frequent discussions among students, with the instructor acting as a participant or as an observer of the discussion process.

If the instructor is working to create a "learning environment," rather than merely to get some points and lessons across, he will have frequent recourse to expressions such as, "Is this what you meant?" "How do we apply this idea?" "You said this; may I add this?" "What did the rest of you hear?" "I'm confused about this point."

Classroom Results. During the first few months, students who are thus encouraged toward self-expression will make at least two discoveries. One is that each of them sees something different in each case, and that this difference is due not to what is in the case but to what each of them brings to the case from his own background. The other is that trying to understand one another is more difficult than conducting monologues designed to catch the teacher's attention.

Before the students have devoted many class periods to the analysis of cases, they become eager to find solutions—to get action. Characteristically they wish to plan specific "solutions" for each case. The recognition dawns only gradually that administrative action occurs in a never-ending continuum of events and that few problems involving human behavior end in pat solutions.

The case method has a basic limitation in that it cannot readily reproduce the unfolding quality of actual events. Yet the students are eager to speculate on what actions would be appropriate to a given situation, and as a criterion of action they combine systematic analysis of the case with their own intuitive sense of what would or would not "work."

While classroom discussion undoubtedly brings about changes in students' attitudes and increases their capacity for discriminating insights and judgments, it is difficult to identify any direct connection between these changes and the students' actual skill in situations requiring administrative action. If the student makes a conscious effort to bring newly gained understanding to bear upon events outside the classroom, he can modify and adapt his behavior accordingly. On the other hand, it is possible for a student to keep what he has obtained in class at a purely verbal level and to continue with his pattern of responses to actual events unchanged. Much more needs to be known about the factors motivating actual change in behavior as a result of education in this area. Essentially, there is no doubt that change depends on students' sensing the need for it and recognizing its promise.

The process that occurs in class during the life of a student group can be summed up as follows. Particularly at the beginning of the year but continuing throughout the year, the students will be stumbling over their own resistances to learning and gradually working past some of these blocks. In a fumbling way at first, but more surely later, they will learn to approach the case problems from a more systematic, analytical point of view. As the year goes on, they will pick up considerable factual knowledge and some useful concepts and generalizations. Finally, many of them will find ways of using this progress in their own behavior outside the classroom.

THE CASE MATERIAL

Variety. One of the outstanding features of the case method is the infinite variety of material that can be adapted to it. At the same time, efforts to impose any specific form or any particular arrangement of cases are likely to yield extremely elusive results.

Within the scope of such a course, the instructor may wish to cover specific areas such as studies of face-to-face relations between persons at different organizational levels, or studies of interaction patterns throughout large-scale organizations. He may wish to introduce particular generalizations in connection with these studies. He may wish to emphasize particular aspects of them, such as the nature of the administrative process. Generally speaking, these efforts at "teaching" should come when the students have shown a capacity to take the course in their stride. If the teaching is intended to communicate knowledge or to help the student develop a more or less general point of view, it will have a good chance of success. If, however, it is intended to produce specific changes in the ways students feel about or look at certain problems, the instructor will usually find by the end of the year that he has accomplished much less than he hoped to. With surprising tenacity the pace of learning is set by the students themselves.

Role of Case Writers. One characteristic common to all cases written in this area at the Business School is their strict adherence to a consistent point of view. When the case writer has interviewed a number of persons in an organization, he does not report, "A thought so-and-so and B thought so-and-so." He may write, "A told X so-and-so, X heard A tell B so-and-so, or it appeared to X that A and B thought so-and-so," X being of necessity the case writer. This limitation of point of view is useful in helping the student see the case as a participant rather than as an omniscient and detached judge. It is also necessary, in order to avoid distortion in the writing of the case.

To enrich cases for the Human Relations and Administrative Practices area, the case writer may include conversations recorded as nearly verbatim as possible and also his own observations on aspects of events not usually noticed by the persons the case writer is describing. In general, those whom the case writer observes are likely to be so preoccupied with getting things done that they regard the accompanying emotions, attitudes, and values as unreal or irrelevant. The case writer looks not only at the active, instrumental elements of the situation but at the process by which the action takes place—process in terms of (1) interactions among people, and (2) the behaved or verbalized expressions by these people of their emotions, attitudes, values, and opinions, with regard to one another and their work.

To be an effective observer, the case writer must be aware not only of his own bias but also of the effect he has on the people he is studying, for both of these factors are invariably present. Such awareness does not come easily or quickly. The case writer is himself a specialist, with a specialist's point of view toward the situation he studies. The parallel between the case writer's point of view toward his research and the instructor's point of view toward the class should be apparent. It is this point of view which, it is hoped, the students also will learn to employ toward situations both inside and outside the classroom.

A researcher is ready to start in the field the day he finishes taking the course for which he will do research. His training will come through work in the field, discussion of his field activities with an experienced supervisor, participation in departmental meetings and seminars, reading, and, if possible, practice in interviewing under controlled conditions.

When a case writer seriously begins the work of case collection, he is subject to numerous pressures which it is well to recognize because of their inevitable effect on his work. He will feel a compulsion to be "objective," matched by increasing doubts about the objectivity of any of his observations. He will be uncertain and confused about how to proceed and what to look for. He may feel a strong compulsion to "bring home the bacon" which will force him to make invalid findings; this attitude depends to a large extent upon his superior's attitudes. He may feel that the people whom he is studying regard him as something of a curiosity because his work and manner of approach are foreign to their everyday experience. Many of these feelings are inevitable, and one of the functions of an effective supervisor is to let the case writer get some of them off his chest. Here again, it is desirable for the supervisor to wait for the case writer to raise questions of research method rather than to crowd him with advice.

To overcome the strangeness of new situations and new contacts, the case writer's normal social response is to talk about common interests and common acquaintances, to offer statements of purpose, and to bring forth his own knowledge of the other person's situation, not to mention falling back upon his personal resources of wit and charm, whatever these may be. While a certain amount of small talk is essential to any contact, too much reliance upon social give-and-take will draw the researcher too far into the situation and blur his role as observer.

Careful statements of the purpose of a research study at the beginning of a contact are usually misunderstood. A description of the way the material will be used in class is frequently helpful. The possibility of disguising the material may be discussed. The researcher should reassure the other person that he will hold what he learns in confidence and use any of it only following a signed release. If the researcher obtains material from a number of persons in the organization under study, he should repeat the explanation regarding confidence to each one, and if any of the material reflects unfavorably upon someone in the organization, he should secure individual releases before proceeding to the official release. It is not unheard of for releases to be withheld after the researcher has made a long and careful study.

The case writer can expect a wide variety of reactions from a person not thoroughly familiar with the classroom process. The other person may believe that the researcher is anything from a curiosity to a source of expert advice. Many persons are quite uneasy about being studied "like guinea pigs," although they seldom refuse contact on this account alone. Some persons are afraid of leaks back to their own superiors, or are unwilling for other reasons to divulge information. The researcher must not attempt to force their confidence by a show of delegated authority. He may clear up cases of obvious misunderstanding of his purpose but should not press further.

Most people seek to use the researcher as a source of information and opinions they cannot otherwise get about their own organization. Most of this interest is perfectly legitimate. The case writer is wise not to let himself be drawn into discussions, however, until he is finished with his observations. If he finds himself under pressure to discuss things, a request to postpone the discussion will invariably be respected. Often questions asked of the researcher are not so much information-seeking as they are expressive of the preoccupations of the questioner. In these cases, a restatement of the question is enough to send the person asking it off on a fresh tack.

The case writer will be repeatedly surprised at the number of people who will grasp his purpose easily, talk freely, and help with introductions to other members of their organization.

After the initial contact with an organization, useful ways of getting started are touring the plant, meeting people, looking at the formal organization chart if there is one, and following any other procedures that are easy to understand and arrange. The case writer should be careful not to speak to anyone at lower echelons without clearing through supervisors up to the level of his initial contact. He should also be careful to keep the initial contact informed of his activities.

To be an effective observer, the researcher should make it clear by his own behavior that he is not present to talk about himself, to offer advice or information, to argue, or in any way to press his own interests save for his interest in the situation under study. He should refrain from asking predetermined questions which will condition the other person's responses and prevent the other from giving the picture as he sees it. He should be ready to listen with full attention, discerning the pattern of the other's remarks as best he can so that he can ask relevant questions. Most difficult of all, he should accept what he hears not as "good" or "bad," "right" or "wrong," "true" or "false," for these imply judgment by the listener, but rather as symptomatic of the other person's point of view, as related to the other's personal history and present situation. This behavior is essential if the researcher is to obtain an accurate picture of the other person's world.

The observer role obviously requires a good deal of self-discipline until the researcher learns to relax and "play it by ear." The researcher's self-confidence properly depends not on impressing the other person with himself or what he knows but with his interest, willingness to learn, and ability to learn. It is quite safe for the researcher to say, "I don't know—what do you think about this?"

When the case writer comes eventually to make a case from his observation of relations, this behavior and this attitude enable him to make a fruitful addition to course materials. By producing cases he makes learning possible.

A Classroom Evaluation of the Case Method

JOSEPH C. BAILEY

The following memorandum was condensed from some ten to twelve pages of notes set down by me immediately after the close of the class session. The purpose of the memorandum was to report as literally, yet as briefly, as possible the principal ideas and feelings that had been expressed. The memorandum as here printed was shown later to nearly a score of those who became the active leaders of the hundred men who composed Section E, and they were asked to add whatever they felt had been omitted from this record of the session, or to strike out what was unimportant or misinterpreted in order to give the account the greatest accuracy. Agreement was general that the reporting followed the themes of the discussion very closely; the only uncertainty expressed was whether the intensity of feeling on the part of the group or of most of its members was underscored sufficiently so that a reader might sense it.

Readers familiar with the case method of discussion do not need to be reminded that the apparent crisis exhibited in the memorandum is only one phase of a continuing process—the process of learning. Teachers learn to expect confusion, frustration, and hostility on the part of students when they are required to begin at last their own problem solving. Once they do begin it, usually after some incipient rebellion of the sort shown here, then a teacher is free, finally, to work with his students and to learn with them as an integrated team working together on common problems.

After experiencing the emotion, as well as facing the hard, intellectual fact that they are really on their own, students bit by bit relinquish their long conditioning toward a teacher as a person who has the word or the answer for the problems presented by a case (which is a report on someone else's real-life problems). Bit by bit, in the slowly reassuring solidarity of other student weanlings, case students move on to other phases in the process of learning and come to relish the challenge of doing the work themselves; come to regard the teacher as one who is able and willing to help them work out their answers, not give them answers which don't exist; and at last to take pride in their self-sufficiency and in what they have proved to themselves they are able to do. At this point they are free of a need for a teacher—as they should be—but there seems to be no way of gaining such freedom except by personally experiencing the struggle to attain it.

MEMORANDUM

On Wednesday, October 27, 1948, Section E in Administrative Practices, shortly after class began at 2:10 P.M., chose to launch an inquiry into the function or responsibility of their teacher, Bailey, to their class, Section E. As the inquiry was in full tide at 3:30 P.M., the bulk of the class, as well as I, elected to continue until 4:30 P.M., at which time substantially all the issues raised and feelings expressed seemed to have been sufficiently ventilated. Adjournment was by common consent.

The views expressed most frequently, when clarified, follow hereafter in summary form. Once these views were clarified and accepted by the student speaker or speakers, I then raised the *un*expressed inference. The usual reaction was for a few students to fall silent, perhaps to think. A larger number would, almost as a reflex, embrace the inference raised. The clear majority would mill about until a new issue was found and use it to return to their chief interest, my responsibility to them.

The view expressed (by students)	*The inference unexpressed (except by me)*
1. Many students waste time in class with irrelevant or repetitious or mistaken contributions.	You (the teacher) ought to stop it.
2. The class may leave a case with many points of importance undetected and undiscussed.	You should point them out to us.
3. Class discussion often ends with our conclusions confused, scattered, unassorted.	You should put them together for us.
4. We often may be reasoning wrongly and arriving at erroneous estimates.	You should put us right.
5. We may be too inexperienced personally or without the learning needed to appraise the merits of the judgments we offer.	You should supply our shortcomings from your superior knowledge.

6. Your acquaintance with the pertinent literature is wider and sounder than ours.

You should tell us what to read and what each reading is worth.

7. Many students tend to express "feelings" about these cases, feelings we don't share, don't care to listen to, and often find annoying.

You should stop them by pointing out that they are merely expressing personal feelings which most of us find tiresome.

In the periods of discussion that followed *after* the inference had been raised for them by me, the issue at hand was abandoned, usually after I had raised the further questions below:

1. If I tell a student (nicely, of course) that he is wasting class time and he tells me that *he* doesn't think so, what should I do next?

2. If I think the class has missed many points in the case that I consider interesting, should I say so when they think they are finished and ask them to begin again? Or, if I tell them what I think they missed, will they come to rely upon me to do this, and do they wish to so rely? Then upon whom will they rely for points missed in the day's problems following graduation from these ivied walls in June 1950?

3. If discussion often leaves cases scattered about in bits and pieces, conclusions uncertain and interpretations contradictory, who should put them together? Who put them together for poor Henry Carlow? [1]

4. If you seem to me to be reasoning wrongly, should I merely say so? Or, should I then go on to reason correctly for you? What should I do if my reasoning fails to convince certain students, inform them they are wrong or, in the end, assure the others that my view is right?

5. If I have reason to believe you may attach more importance to what I say than my views merit when stripped of the authority of the professorial chair, how am I to govern myself in case you remember my opinions after graduation, act upon them, and discover them not to be reliable in your situation? (*a*) Will you blame me for the consequences? (*b*) Will you blame yourselves for listening to me? (*c*) Will you blame yourselves for asking me to tell you?

6. If I am to put reading before you that may prove helpful, how should I do it? On a conventional reading list? (Widespread dissent.) I have already recommended five references I think applicable. How many men have looked at so much as one out of five? (Eighteen hands showed.) Do you wish me to reward these eighteen and penalize the rest?

7. If there is one lesson this section seems to agree on it is that you have learned from *all* the cases we are now reviewing that workers, and even executives, have feelings; that they want those feelings recognized and respected; that they wish to be treated as people of some value to the group with which they are working. Now, do you wish me to tell a student expressing feelings that seem important to him that he is wasting our time and we wish him to stop?

[1] Henry Carlow is the distraught young man in "Daycomb Company," a case in Glover and Hower, *The Administrator*, pp. 255–256.

Additional issues raised are set forth below, not because they claimed less student interest, but rather because they were clarified by one or two students in place of one or two dozen. Thus, these were dealt with, as it were, in the interstices between the longer, louder discussions proceeding simultaneously on the more confusing issues.

The view expressed plus that implied

The response which returned the problem for the students' further reflection

1. You possess "knowledge" invaluable to us. You probably have "the right answer" to every one of these cases. If you didn't, you wouldn't be up there on that platform. We've paid our money and are entitled to every grain of wisdom you possess, especially and specifically "the right answers" to our problems.

Will students gain as much from whatever experience I may possess if I strive to convey it in the form of questions as if I put it into the form of statements, lectures, or answers?

2. We're entitled to know what the Faculty thinks about these problems and cases. You represent the Faculty. It's your obligation to give us their opinions.

What would this section think if it could oversee and overhear the Faculty occupying the students' seats in this room, discussing one of their cases, expressing as much diversity of view, disagreeing as much over meanings, and arriving at incompatible interpretations of the meanings discovered? Would that reassure them?

As the session wore on toward its close certain students ventured expressions of faith that they were going to learn something. Dean David had forewarned them of confusion coming, but thereafter, illumination; second-year men told them it would clear up one of these days; a reasonable number of students did seem to graduate annually; etc. Some men went further. One said he left the classroom with only questions in his mind, but that he liked that. Another confessed that he "felt scared." For sixteen years he had been told answers. He had big notebooks full of them, and bigger textbooks still fuller, and the teachers ready to supply anything he couldn't find. The case method was wholly unfamiliar and he didn't know what to hang on to. (Only fifteen men, it developed, had ever had even one case course before.) Though scared, he liked it and wanted to go on trying to puzzle out his own answers.

Judging from the tones of such comments that the vigor, not to say the rigor, of their inquisition was slackening, I concluded the session with the reminder that they, as executives and managers, would often find themselves in my shoes, a teacher and trainer to their subordinates. How did they propose to go about that task? Would they choose to "tell" their students the "right answers"? Or what?

At the following session of the class I began with the remark that we had explored, or started to explore, some very far-reaching questions. I felt that we had given them a good start, possibly as much as we were able to give just now. They would find, I thought, that some of the issues raised would develop in their minds in chain-reaction fashion. In any case, let's wait and see. Meanwhile I would put on the board a couple of my own overnight recapitulations.

Function or $\longrightarrow$ Function or
responsibility of the teacher $\longleftarrow$ responsibility of the student

The class had raised the first. I had raised the second, because the first could not be determined without inquiring closely into the second. Roughly speaking, there also appeared to be at least two types of educational endeavor distinguishable as follows:

CLASSROOM EVALUATION

Type of School:	A. Liberal Arts colleges: graduate, and undergraduate	B. Professional schools: law, medicine, business, etc.
Objectives:	"Knowledge," learning, scholarship, etc.	Ways of solving selected kinds of problems. Useful ways of thinking
Techniques:	Lectures: teacher talks; student listens, takes notes, reads, etc.	Class discussion: teacher listens; student talks, pits his way of solving problems against classmates; teacher asks questions
Tools:	Textbook, libraries, research—individual work	Cases: Analysis and diagnosis thereof, in study groups, in classroom, clinic, or laboratory
Product:	Scholars, teachers, research workers, etc.	Doctors, lawyers, administrators, et al.: those who must prepare to accept responsibility for actions and decisions involving other people
Evaluation of Product:	Breadth and depth of "knowledge," learning, scholarship. Output of research inquiries. Training of younger scholars	Skills, or the quality of performance, required to reach successful judgments and initiate successful action in problems involving other persons

I observed that most of the class seemed busy copying the equation and its accompanying classification while I was putting it on the board. We began, however, discussion of the next case as soon as I had finished writing.

A Note on Counseling as an Adjunct of the Case Method

JOHN B. FOX

I should like to try to describe, from the vantage points I have occupied, the kinds of problems encountered by students during their course of instruction. Some of these problems obviously are similar to those encountered in any educational institution, or, for that matter, in any other organization. But some others, I think, are quite uniquely related to the case method of instruction; it is these I believe to be worth some special attention. Improved methods of selecting students for admission to the Business School can, to a considerable extent, decrease the numbers of individuals having problems and also can decrease the intensity of the problems which occur later. I would also maintain that the degree of maturity and practical experience that our successful applicants have has a very direct bearing on the incidence of problems of adjustment. Our experience with the first postwar classes confirms this.

We have never made a careful statistical analysis of one of our first-year classes from the point of view of estimating the degree of maturity attained by our students, but I think it would be possible to gain considerable acceptance to these rough figures. Of an entering class of 600, almost a third apparently adjust to work at the School adequately. Within this third I think it would be found that the adjustment of half this number is to all intents and purposes complete. Any further breakdown of these hundred men would, I predict, reveal two or three traits which might or might not have been reflected by the individual's previous academic record. All of these men, incidentally, would be found to have unusual capacity to handle comparatively simple arithmetical problems, to express themselves clearly both orally and on paper, and to learn from experience.

The balance of this first group might benefit from discussions with either faculty or administrative people, but, by and large, discussions with other students are sufficient for these men. I do not mean that these first two hundred men go through the School with no faculty or administrative attention. Obviously, these men develop relations with many people, but they come to us prepared from the start to take advantage of the case method, and from the start begin to grow both emotionally and intellectually.

The second group amounts to about three hundred men. Most of this group, I would estimate, require between five and ten hours of faculty and administrative officers' time. With all but a very few of these men it would make very little difference whether they discussed their progress or lack of it with either faculty or administrative people. Many of the problems facing this group are largely problems of failure to understand certain academic concepts, as contrasted with more fundamental problems of difficulty in grasping the purposes of the case method itself, or the most difficult problems of all, those of personal adjustments. Unfortunately, however, there are always a few members of this group whose difficulties do not come to the attention of any members of the staff and who find themselves in academic difficulty either at midyears or at the end of their first year's work. But my belief in looking at this group as a whole is that the great majority of them are able to diagnose their shortcomings themselves.

Up to this point I have consciously avoided any reference to the relative capacity of these men as measured by our grading system. In the first group of a hundred one might expect to find some concentration of high-distinction men; in all the other groups one would expect a normal scattering of academic prowess. I would even go so far as to maintain that in the last group of a hundred there might also be found a larger proportion of high-distinction men than many would at first suspect.

We need not concern ourselves unduly with the ten or fifteen men in the final group of one hundred whose situation requires psychiatric attention. I would not go so far, however, as to admit that all of this group should not have been allowed to attend the School, although there are always one or two cases of great intensity that probably should be classed as errors of admission.

But the rest of this group, eighty or so in number, have problems which might be termed nonmedical difficulties of social orientation. They find themselves, usually within the first six weeks of school, failing to advance with their class, aware of this failure in varying degrees, but almost without exception bewildered and disturbed. Occasionally one of these students finds great help and benefit as a result of discussing his lack of growth with a faculty member—even, in rare instances, with an instructor who has him as a student. In most cases, however, the time required to help this student reorient himself is more than a faculty member feels he should extend to a single student. Furthermore, it has been my experience that the interference with normal growth that a student complains about is related in his mind at the start quite specifically with the personalities of certain of the faculty, and accordingly the student is more reluctant to discuss these difficulties with another faculty member than he is with someone in the administrative group.

One of these students is usually 22 or 23 years of age and has come to the Business School directly from college. What his major has been is unimportant. But he does come to the School with the idea that there he will be taught business methods and practices, and he arrives in an optimistic mood, anxious to receive the wisdom which he has been led to expect will be delivered to him during his two years. He also usually assumes that there is a direct connection between the number of hours he puts in on a given assignment and the grade he receives. Perhaps at the end of his first month he pauses to try to take stock of his progress. He will look at his grades, peruse his notes, thumb through his cases, and then perhaps try to reflect what has happened to him so far. Usually the results dismay and perhaps even frighten him. In contrast to college, he finds little that he can point to, saying to himself, "This ground I have covered, can remember, and could report back on a test or examination."

He returns to his studies, hoping that longer hours, more note taking, and closer study of the cases will show him the way out. But usually at the end of two weeks he is more confused than before. At this moment he begins to realize that his difficulties are not confined to a single course. It is left up to him what course of action he takes and there is a wide variety of assistance open to him. But if the administrative officers have done their job adequately, this student will know that he may turn to one of them for help.

The first task of the administrative officer is to determine whether this student is one of the rare instances I mentioned earlier of someone needing psychiatric help. Should that be the case, it is that administrative officer's duty to urge that the student consult the School's medical officer, who in turn will decide whether this is a situation which he prefers to handle himself or to turn over to one of the psychiatrists in the University's Department of Hygiene. But it has been our experience that, if the student is not one of the few who is really mentally ill, he can be helped more effectively by an administrative officer than by anyone else. One of his basic difficulties is found as a rule to be his failure to realize that the case method is attempting to increase his power of analysis and simultaneously is requiring that he come to know his own strengths and limitations. In this process the instructors are not fulfilling the role that he expects of them, namely, sorting out the important from the unimportant. Rather, they are asking him and his classmates to examine a whole range of areas and reach their own conclusions.

Often the student is especially upset by the way one or two instructors conduct their classes, claiming that these men never give them any answers at all. The student is usually also bothered by what he calls the amount of class time wasted by his fellow students, and raises the question why the School permits this to happen. The amount of time that is required to reorient successfully the men in this group varies widely, but the minimum is between ten and fifteen hours and some cases may require up to thirty hours. Without this attention we know that these men not only will fail to develop themselves as they should but in many instances will begin to retard the growth of some of their fellow students, and it has been known that they have adversely affected the progress of a whole section.

The student who is capable of reorienting his thoughts finds the process a rigorous one, but in most cases, with the new insight acquired, he is able to progress with his classmates. It has been my experience that the grade distribution for men who have encountered difficulties such as these is slightly above the average of the class as a whole. It is obvious that the administrative officials who carry on such work as this require special skills and training, and it should be reëmphasized that for the student the task of readjustment is arduous.

So far as I know, no study has ever been made comparing the problems of adjustment of students studying under the lecture method with those of students studying under the case method. The difficulties of making a useful study of this kind are enormous. I would maintain, though, that the case method does tend to bring out what I call basic inadequacies for successful living to a greater degree than would be possible under the lecture method. The responsibility of an educational institution using the case method to be prepared to treat those individuals who are not progressing satisfactorily is clear. Most people today, I think, agree that under either system it is naïve to assume that a process of intellectual growth is taking place among all the students merely because there are a group of students gathered together in a room with an instructor present, no matter what teaching methods the instructor may be using. Those students who are failing to develop in an institution where careful selection has preceded their admission should be given the opportunity to reorient themselves so that they can take full advantage of the program of study. Some of them, it will be discovered, lack the capacity for further growth, but so long as our society is operated on the assumption that each individual should be afforded the opportunity to make his maximum contribution we cannot afford to slough off those who find themselves in difficulty and seek help.

I hope it is clear that I do not maintain that every student at the Harvard Business School requires guidance and counseling either from a faculty member or an administrative officer. But I also hope that I have made clear that under the case method of instruction, it has been my experience to date that between a sixth and a third of every class, no matter how carefully selected, can derive much benefit from conversations with either instructors or assistant deans, and that in certain classes of individuals real development would not take place without the opportunity for reorientation which the administrative officials can provide.

What One Student Learned

HARRIET O. RONKEN

I have been doing some thinking along the lines you taught. Although I have not yet passed the acid test, which is to use these insights in my own personal life, at least I am getting some insights." So wrote an undergraduate to his instructor almost two years after completing a term of case discussion in a course called Human Relations.

"I only took this course because I needed the distribution," he had said at the time.

In the six weeks of group discussion, that student had learned something about individual motivation, the nature of group formation, social equilibrium, obsessive thinking, the role of semantics in face-to-face relationships, situational thinking, and the clinical method. He might have become much more fluent about these concepts had the instructor spent the class hours lecturing logically and systematically. But if that had been done, a boy who was once hissed by other members of his class would not have learned to get along with his classmates well enough so that he could invite them to his room and expect them to come.

THE CLASS—OPENING WEEKS

This is the story of that class and of one student who, in particular, found it an experience from which he could learn. The summer-school version of the regular course in "Human Relations" met for one hour, five days a week. The course carried 3 semester credits in the social sciences. During the regular terms it was open to sophomores, juniors, and seniors, but in summer sessions freshmen and graduate students could also enroll. The class consisted of 25 students, most of whom had never seen one another before they walked into the room for the first meeting. They ranged in age from 18 to 40 (the majority were in their twenties) and in formal education from four years of high school to five years of college. The undergraduates represented a broad cross section of departmental "majors." Some took the course because they needed distribution credit in the social sciences; some in the social sciences needed an additional course related to their special fields. A few took it because they had to go to summer school and this course did not threaten their extracurricular activities. On the whole, however, they seemed a serious lot, if somewhat miscellaneous in origin and attitude.

With such variations in what they brought to the class, shaping what they saw in the cases, the students at first did not really have even the class in common. During the first two weeks, interaction between members of the class was at a minimum; "discussion" was largely a collective monologue. A case, it is frequently said, gives students a common problem or common subject upon which they can focus, but dealing with a case in such a way that it remains "common" is an acquired skill. At first the case was treated as a stimulus to free association, or simply as an example of an abstraction which they assumed must be the real topic of the day. In this they were like other groups new to cases. A new class will go from "Joe Longman," [1] the individual, to "technological change," the high abstraction which describes his situation, in one easy step, whereas it will take more experienced students a very much longer time to cover that distance. This class was fond of generalities like "people" or "unions" or "coöperation," but they did not know how to look at the actual people in the cases and *consider what unions meant to those people or what constituted coöperation in those specific situations.* The instructor at no time felt resistance in the group; their state of mind was rather bewilderment before a technique new to them.

One device which helped to create a common focus and mark out an approach to a case was the blackboard. As the students recited, I used the board to organize the material, to show the interconnection of the observations made, to draw diagrams, and to list the attitudes mentioned. In addition, I responded to generalizations by pinning students down to the case with a specific question. Stories out of their own experience were related to the case at hand by asking, "What do you see in the experience you reported that helps you to understand the situation in this case?" Much drill was necessary in distinguishing fact from interpretation and in keeping the facts straight so that the students knew what they were interpreting. For instance, they at first used one event to explain another in a direct cause-and-effect relation, whereas a simple question to bring out

---

[1] Joseph Longman appears in the case of the same name in Glover and Hower, *The Administrator,* pp. 111–120.

the time span involved would sometimes demonstrate the fallacy of such reasoning.

Thinking it might appeal to the students in view of their taste for generalizations, I frequently brought concepts from the assigned reading into class discussions. My aim was in part to help them see some ways in which theoretical reading could be applied to specific cases and in part to intrigue them into completing their reading assignments on time. At first every attempt in this respect drew a blank. There were no questions and little evidence of "hearing" the reading discussions. The students did not appear to be interested in playing on the conceptual level.

The changes that were slowly occurring in the approach used by the class may be illustrated by several examples from the discussions during this first period.

From the first meeting, discussion was lively. The initial case reported a simple interaction among three people, together with a brief history of their relationship as told by one of the people in the case, Kay. Consisting of less three mimeographed pages, the case was handed out in class and read aloud. The opening question was, "What kind of picture do you get of these people?" Everyone in the room wanted to answer that question. After some 15 minutes in which the class had concentrated on Kay, I began putting on the board the key word or words from each student's "description" of her. A list of about 20 expressions was quickly accumulated. The first eight, which were all that the recorder had time to note down, were "erratic, lazy, homesick, extravert, in revolt against family, stable, go-getter, dependent." At that point the instructor read the list and asked, "What have we been doing?" One student replied, "These are all interpretations in the light of the experiences of the person making them." When this point had been developed by class discussion, the members agreed to go back and look at the facts available before judging the girl. This was a dramatic illustration, but it was a lesson the class needed to have repeated often.

On the second day, the class was considering the case of a recently discharged veteran who, with no capital assets, bought a house, furnished it with the aid of an interior decorator, became a father, and, having accumulated a $15,000 debt, threw up his $50-a-week job, all within a year's time.

Student 1: "One thing the veterans' counselor might do is to write Ralph's family and see what they could do. After all, they're responsible; they brought their son up this way."

Student 2: "I think we have to leave his family out of this. They are in California and he is on the East Coast. What the counselor has to do is to make him assume adult status and accept his responsibilities."

Instructor: "How would she do that?"

Student 2: "He'd have no choice; he'd *have* to do it."

The following week the case concerned a boy who failed to get into the fraternity on which he had set his heart. The class had been discussing whether the boy's roommate, a new member, should try to get him in. Finally, this exchange occurred:

Student 1: "Getting Dan into the fraternity is going to be no solution for him. He will still have that class consciousness that kept him from making friends there in the first place. He will have to realize his own deficiencies and do something about them before he can make friends."

Student 2: "At prep school Danny felt he was below the rest of the group; at home, he felt above the others. He has had no place where he felt equal to everyone else."

ALLEN PRICE'S BEHAVIOR

The student who particularly came to the instructor's attention during this period was Allen Price. According to his card he had just completed his junior year in the field of political science with a *B* average, was 21 years old, and had been a "vocational counselor" in an Army Separation Center. Recognizing him when he came into the office to buy his case materials on the second day of the term, I greeted him, "Good morning, Mr. Price." He replied, "Oh, you know my name already," in a tone which sounded as though the simple gesture was meaningful to him. When he was told the price of the case book, he decided to use the library copy, explaining that he was not on the GI bill. "I'm a member of the unemployed and getting my benefits that way," he added. A week later, he returned and bought the material, but commented that an economics professor had sold his students an equal amount of mimeographed material for less than a dollar. I also noticed Mr. Price because several times he sat through the entire hour, in spite of the summer weather, without removing his raincoat.

My daybook carries no record of any particular recitations by Mr. Price during the first week, except for a notation that he was introducing red herrings. On the second day, for instance, he told a story about General Robert E. Lee and some slaves which was so far off the subject that I could not see any relation. "What conclusions do you draw from that analogy?" I asked.

"Nothing," Price replied. "I just thought it was an interesting parallel."

This story was typical of Price's contributions at that time. He went outside the case; he told stories from his own experience; he reported newspaper articles on topics like "unions"; he referred to theories he had studied in other courses which seemed to him vaguely applicable; he appealed to anything that he thought would give him grounds for an opinion except the case.

His pattern of behavior in class became clear very early and he followed it pretty consistently for the first third of the term. On one of the first days he told the instructor that he had intended to take public speaking in summer school; but when he learned that he was limited to one five-minute speech a week in that course, he decided to take Human Relations instead. The implication was that he intended to make a speech a day in Human Relations, and he fulfilled that aim. The daybook reported, "About the middle of the hour he opens with a barrage, fires all his heavy ammunition, and retires. His manner suggests that since he has laid out the case there is no point in anyone else's trying to do anything with it."

It was equally obvious that he had not prepared the case in detail. Most of his comments were concerned with either assessing blame or recommending a solution couched in the most general terms. For example, on July 9, Price said, "There are two different types of factories: those where there is a 'climate of security' and those where there is a 'climate of insecurity.' You have the latter type in this case. If employees are insecure, they won't work together. That's what is happening here. There is no promotion system. The employment routine has too much red tape. Piece work makes for competition. But the main trouble is that there is no union."

Again, on a case concerned with the Community Fund, the class was considering why the people in the socially "correct" section of town volunteered to work on the Fund drive. Price's contribution was, "For one thing it is a human instinct to help your neighbor. This was a way of salving their consciences and at the same time gaining prestige for themselves. But the real reason they volunteered was that they are trying to disprove the theory of the class structure and Americanize the scene. That's why they accepted a middle-class Irishman as chairman of the drive." Asked on what he based his reasoning, Price replied, "I haven't read the case that carefully. This is just my impression."

That last reply was one Price used almost daily whenever the instructor tried to get him to make explicit the basis for his statements. On July 13, however, the daybook reported triumphantly, "Today Price appealed to the facts of the case in support of his argument."

In addition to pinning him down, the instructor tried to handle his recitations by saying, "You have put up several different orders of problem here: 1 . . . , 2 . . . , 3 . . . Let's take a closer look at one of them." Later, as I grew to know what to expect from him, I tried to pick up a point as soon as he made it instead of allowing the monologue to continue. By doing so, I hoped in part to draw his contribution into the general discussion and in part to protect his relationship with the other students, or rather, his potential relationship with them. The attempt met at first with little success; not before the middle of the term did it begin to pay off.

On the whole the class permitted Price to talk and then resumed their discussion as though there had been no interruption. He in turn ignored them. From the beginning, however, he showed flashes of insight, and these occasionally came in response to the contribution of some other members of the class. For instance, on July 9, one of the students was talking about Catherine, a new factory worker who had been made an inspector on her third day in the department and who was having considerable trouble with the other girls. The student talked about the personal qualities which he thought an inspector ought to have in order to be successful.

Price: "That's a supervisor; an inspector doesn't need those qualifications."

Instructor: "If you think it makes a difference, why don't you tell us what an inspector does?"

Price: "It's just a technical job; it doesn't require leadership. But an inspector can send products back to the girls who made them, which means that the operators do a lot of griping about her."

Instructor: "Are you saying that Catherine was put in a position where she became the focus of resentment from the other operators before she had a chance to establish her relations with them?"

Price: "Yes."

About that time the idea was developed in class that there are two different types of communication, verbal and nonverbal; that is, that people communicate their attitudes not only by the way they talk about them but also by the way they behave. Price's sole contribution to this development was the remark, "That's a cliché." The instructor did not pick it up at the time, but an opportunity was presented several days later in reading conference. These conferences consisted of small groups of students, meeting voluntarily, to discuss the relation between the collateral reading and the cases which were handled in class. Ordinarily they met in the afternoons, but several students who were otherwise committed for their afternoons had requested a morning conference. Four students came; one of them was Price. Picking up a book from the department library, he buried his face in it and kept it there during most of the session. Toward the end, however, reference was made to the "cliché" comment. The instructor observed that it was probably true. In fact, it was so true that much of the time we take the distinction for granted and behave as though we had never heard of it. Price came out from behind his book for the only time during the conference, smiled and nodded, but said nothing.

THE CLASS REACTION TO PRICE

During the second two weeks of the course, the class began to settle down in earnest. There was considerable evidence that they were doing their collateral reading, as more and more frequently concepts or parallels to the situation under discussion were brought into class from the reading. The material in the cases was the subject matter which they dealt with in discussion. Material from other sources was brought in with less frequency or with greater relevance. Members of the class began to form little groups of twos or threes who sat together in class, talked to one another's points, and were occasionally seen together in the Yard. During this period, however, the group did not act as a whole; in other words, there was no evidence of the presence of a group larger than the small cliques, with two exceptions. One was that if there were a single focus which commanded the attention of all, they reacted to it as a group. For instance, we occasionally used what is called a swing-over chart, a large chart placed at the front of the class which presents a conversation one speech at a time, so that the students react to each separate step in an interaction. When we used that chart, the students not only responded to it but responded to one another's ideas more consistently than in the general case discussions; the latter were much more diffuse.

The second nucleus for the formation of the group was a collective activity which developed around hostility to Price. The group no longer ignored him. He began to get under their skins. As he spoke, the class became markedly restless; some students made faces to show their strong disagreement; occasionally muttered "No, no's" could be heard around the room. By the time he finished speaking there were usually a number of hands in the air. On the whole the class resisted his ideas even when they were to the point. One reason for this may have been that, since Price was the only student who attempted to utilize psychoanalytic concepts or the idea of the class structure, the others felt he was deliberately trying to shock them. Disciplining Price became such a sport that it was occasionally necessary for the instructor to referee in order to make sure that he got a chance and did not become too much alienated from the class. The climax occurred on July 14. As Price arrived 25 minutes late for the second day in succession, he was hissed by some of the other students. When he was again late the following day, he apologized to the instructor after class and added, "It won't happen again, I assure you."

Nevertheless, during the minutes that Price was absent, discussions proceeded more effectively. The students plunged immediately into the facts of the case and helped one another to put them together in such a way as to discern a pattern which "explained" them. As soon as Price joined the group, discussion became again more a matter of giving "personal opinion," and of hitting the high spots, not staying with any one fact long enough to discover its significance.

In the course of reacting against Price, however, the students went on to react to one another. All recitations were no longer addressed to the front of the room; it became increasingly common for students to provoke among themselves a discussion which went back and forth across the room for some minutes before a question, impasse, or obscurity made them turn to the instructor.

On his side, Price gradually ceased to behave as though he were trying to ignore the other members of the class. He began by defending his contributions against the attacks of other students. This tended to break down his pattern of a "five-minute speech" and presently he abandoned it. He contributed to the discussion from time to time, although at first it was any idea that the discussion suggested to him rather than a development of a line of thought that the class was working on. His three contributions to the case of Robert Kelly illustrate both the direction of his progress and his favorite rabbit holes. The case involved a son of a Dorchester truant officer who went, on scholarship, to an exclusive Eastern college for men. The action question was whether the Dean should recommend the boy for further training, and the considerations involved both his academic and his social adjustment. Price said:

"I once thought I wanted to be a college dean so I read a book on counseling college students. One of the things I learned is that the most important thing may be what is *not* said. Dean Harris needs a book like that. Kelly has given him a number of leads to things that may be bothering him but the Dean has not explored any of them."

"Robert Kelly comes from an upper-lower- or lower-middle-class origin. That class believes that there are two ways to get ahead. One is through education and the other way is by excelling in sports. Kelly is trying through education. In that way he is trying to be better than his family; in other ways, he's not. He can 'rise above himself,' as his father called it, and still maintain the family ties."

"We are being too hard on Robert Kelly. I read someplace that half the people who graduate from college enter employment which doesn't utilize their college major. Kelly isn't unstable for thinking about changing his field; he is just a normal undergraduate."

In spite of the fact that these contributions represented considerable improvement for Price, the class would have none of them. Ross, who might in some ways have seemed like a brother-under-the-skin to Price, declared after one of Price's remarks, "That's the kind of intellectual snobbery that goes on too much around this college." It was interesting to note that the first time Price explicitly recognized another student's contribution, he broke into a sharp exchange between Ross and a third student to say, "I think Ross is making sense," and developed his point. By the end of the term, Ross and Price were seeing something of one another outside of class.

In a session about the middle of the term, the class used words such as "personality" and "maladjustment" very freely. Finally the instructor asked what they meant by one of them. After considerable discussion by the group, I gave a short "lecturette" on some of the semantic problems met in class so far. It was during this "lecturette" that Price asked an "either-or" question of the type that often indicated his resistance. Not being sure how to handle it, I stalled with, "Can you separate the two?" Price replied, "No, I'm asking you because I really want to know. I'm hazy about it." Sure then that the question was in good faith, I invited the rest of the class to discuss it. That was the first time the class worked with Price rather than against him. After class he commented, "I wish we could have more classes like this. I learned more in the last ten minutes today than in all the classes so far." After another similar session he said, "I wish I had four ears."

On the following day just as class was about to begin, a stranger entered the room and under a "Please Save" sign chalked on the blackboard:

> "It *has* happened
> Where: U. S.
> What: 7 citizens arrested for communist leanings
> Protest violation of civil rights
> Mass meeting 1 o'clock Memorial Hall"

Immediately after class, Price changed the sign to read:

> "It *had* happened
> Where: Czechoslovakia
> What: 70 citizens arrested for democratic leanings
> Protest violation of civil rights
> Mass meeting 1 o'clock Memorial Hall"

Several other students stopped to watch the alterations.

On July 23, two days later, a note was entered in the daybook: "Hostility of the class toward Price not so marked. P's contributions improving."

ALLEN PRICE AND THE INSTRUCTOR

One episode involving Price, which spanned the three periods the session seemed to fall into, also indicates the stages through which he went during the term. On July 8 the students were asked to write a one-page paper on the case for the following day. The case, The Spofford Company, which was written by a member of the company's training department, reported the experiences of four new workers in a war factory, of whom three had left the company within two months. The author of the report was interested in a program to reduce turnover. Students were asked to write on the factors suggested by the experiences of these four workers which might be taken into account in such a program. Most of the students indicated the needs which the workers brought into the factory and suggested more or less specific ways in which those needs might be addressed. Price wrote his paper in the form of a memorandum from "Allen Miller Price Associates, Industrial Analysts," to "Mr. Big Capitalist," Spofford Company.

It read in part, "Our analyst, Col. Amalfio Petrosino, has completed his study of your factory. The following are the steps which must be taken immediately.

1. Install a suggestion system.
2. Encourage the formation of a union.
3. Get the union to approve piece rates for the factory.
4. Get the coöperation of your workers."

On the back of his report, the instructor wrote a memo in reply. "Dear Mr. Price, Thank you for your letter with the suggestions for reducing turnover in my factory. I have studied them with interest. At the risk of being considered slow squadron, however, I must admit that there are a few things about it which I do not understand." There followed a series of questions, all growing out of his paper, which were designed hopefully to force him to reconsider the specific facts in the case. The instructor also wanted to talk with him about his report but decided to give him ample opportunity to seek an appointment himself before asking him to come in. For a week he gave no sign of doing so. Then one day he waited until all the other students who usually gathered around the desk after class had left. He said, "You know the memo you wrote on the back of my Spofford paper, that 'slow squadron' memorandum?"

I nodded. "Well," Price went on, "I didn't quite know what to do with it, so I sent it to a handwriting analyst. I called him this morning and he said it was very interesting writing and he wanted a couple more days to work on it." Hoping that my gasp was not audible, I indicated that I would be much interested to see the results.

Two things seemed to stand out about this conversation. Price's recitations to that date had shown a heavy reliance on stereotypes. His identification of the comments as the "slow-squadron memorandum" suggested that he was thrown by an instructor who did not behave like his picture of one. It was consistent with his performance that he should be at a loss in understanding someone who stepped out of pattern. In addition, while this particular gambit was not necessarily predictable, it also seemed consistent that he should seek some gadget which would relieve him of the pressure to come to grips with the facts. A negative handwriting analysis would allow him to dismiss the course, or the comments, without seriously considering the questions raised about the case. A third possibility was that he was looking for something which would relieve him of responsibility for the flunking grade which the paper had received.

Having been told that the handwriting analysis would be in in a few days, I decided to say nothing more and wait for him to move. From that time on, there was some contact at the end of the hour, when students always gathered around the instructor to ask questions or pursue points in the discussion with which they were not yet satisfied, as well as several informal chats on meeting on the campus or the street. Even more important were the stronger relations developing inside the classroom. As a result, rapport between Price and the instructor improved so much that I began to believe the analysis gag would be dropped. On July 28, however, I walked into class to find a copy of the handwriting analysis lying on my desk. As soon as class was over, Price left the room hastily. On the following day, I asked him to come to the office some afternoon and he suggested August 4. My impression that he was putting it off as long as he dared was reinforced when he asked, "How long do I have to stay? How long will it take?"

INSTRUCTOR'S INTERVIEW WITH PRICE

When he appeared in the office at the appointed time, I expressed my interest in the handwriting analysis and talked about it a little. In particular, I was curious about why it had attracted him, what he had expected to get out of it. Price replied that he was "just interested," and then added that a friend of his on one of the large daily papers knew the analyst. "I'm losing some of my faith in it," he said, "because I got different analyses of two samples of the same handwriting with different names attached."

This part of the conversation was very halting. His responses to direct questions were brief and, when given a chance to talk otherwise, he either sat silent or made only a slight response. Presently he said, "This isn't going to work, you know."

Instructor: "What do you mean?"

Price: "I've done the collateral reading on interviewing. You can't expect me to tell you the truth."

Instructor: "In that case, let's say this interview is for my benefit. I've been interested in your performance in class. It is very uneven. I should like to talk with you to see whether I can find any way to put this up so that it makes sense to you."

Price: "I wasn't aware that I was being blocked. I only took this course because I needed some distribution."

From then on, Price talked. There was no problem of choosing a subject, no difficulty getting started, no question, except for a few sticky spots, of "interviewing"; he took care of all that, pouring out a torrent of spontaneous conversation. Although at this point he was still not sure how frank he dared be, and in fact tested the limits occasionally, he did begin to talk. The relation built up as he went along, and he proceeded steadily to increasingly central material. He started by talking about the grade of "unsatisfactory" on his Spofford paper, which he said was rather a shock to him. He said he would like A's but always got something in the B range, B— to B+; no matter how hard he tried, he never succeeded in getting over the barrier to A—, so he didn't always work very hard. He added, "Just naturally lazy, that's me. I would like to get A's, though. I'll admit that. I'm what they call a grade-chaser. I have to get good enough grades to get into graduate school. I have to go to graduate school."

Instructor: "Why do you 'have to'?"

Price: "It's expected of me."

Instructor: "Expected? By whom?"

Price: "Everyone. I guess I expect it of myself. It's just done. With my record, I have to have pretty good grades to get in."

Instructor: "What do you mean, with your record?"

Price: "Well, you see I have been at college before. I came the first time when I was 15. I was kicked out at 17. I didn't flunk out; it was for something else, but the punishment wouldn't have been so severe if I hadn't been on academic probation at the time. So when I came back here, I was determined to get grades. I have had all kinds of educational experience, everything from college to public schools in the slums. I was sent to boarding school. My father wouldn't have put it this way, but he wanted a middle-class child taught by middle-class teachers. At boarding school I was hazed unmercifully, and the result was that I developed a great physical fear. That was so strong that it carried over into the Army with me; there I pulled every string I could to avoid basic training, simply because I was afraid of it. I never did take it, and I would do the same thing again because I'd still be afraid."

After this Price went on to talk about his work at college and repeated, with several variations, the remark that he was lazy. Suddenly he stopped talking and just sat there looking at me as though expecting some comment. When none was forthcoming, he said belligerently, "Well, should I be ashamed? . . . Is that why you are looking at me?"

In view of his opening remarks about interviewing, I did not dare "reflect back to him" the feeling latent in that question. Instead I simply replied, "I was thinking how the things you have been telling me throw light on some of your performances in class."

It is difficult to judge and virtually impossible to prove, but it seemed to me that this marked a turning point in the relationship. Price sat back in his chair and relaxed physically. That he was also beginning to do so emotionally was suggested both by the things he talked about and by his subsequent relationship with the class and with the instructor.

In response to my statement, he said, "Oh, I thought you would tell me I'm maladjusted." He paused and I did not break the silence. Eventually he picked it up himself. "Anyone else would have said I was maladjusted," he went on. "I expected that from the time you asked me to come in here. I mean, well, even the handwriting analysis is not the usual thing you expect from a student."

Having gone that far he tried to change the subject, but the new topic eventually led back in the same direction. He began to talk about the class and how much more he got out of it when the instructor did the talking than when the students did. He suggested that I lecture more and use the cases simply to illustrate the conceptual scheme developed in lectures, since the students did not know enough to extract the principles themselves through case discussion. He admitted that in reading a case he felt the need of a body of principles with which to assess the situation, and further discussion developed that this was a recurrent need with him, in all the areas of his life. Finally he got to the place where he could say in effect: (1) "In every situation in which I have ever been I have felt inadequate," and (2) "I expect to be judged. Because I don't feel competent to measure up, I want to be told very clearly what I am going to be judged on. Therefore, I prefer classes in which the professor tells me in his lectures what he expects me to know and gives me explicit principles by which to evaluate the new situations that I meet." Gradually he came to see that he could not meet standards until he knew what they were but that his methods of finding out were not always effective. He saw the fallacy of his assumption that people held him to his preconceived notion of their standards. For the first time he gave evidence of seeing why, in class, we look at the *situation;* he began to understand the significance of a *way of thinking* which took account of the values existing in a situation, of the demands people were making on it, and of what they were willing to contribute in return.[2]

Although this was progress, he was still not ready to give up his quest for "principles" in the course, so we talked for a while at this level. Eventually he saw that lecturing about "tolerance" and hiring a Jew or sitting next to a Negro in a theater might be two different things. At that point, the student himself began to take the discussion back to cases.

At the end of the interview Price told two stories which cast considerable light on his preoccupations. He referred to three subjects which he said are taboo to mention in class: sex, religion, and class. In regard to the latter, he told about the family of a girl in which he was seriously interested. The family had moved economically from "middle to upper class" but were unable to "shed their bourgeois habits and attitudes." In addition to making it difficult for this family in their new, upper-class neighborhood, he felt that this made it difficult for him to gain acceptance by her family. They regarded him with some suspicion.

The other story concerned his relationship with his father, his only living relative. When he had been deliberating the problem of his future, which involved the question of where to resume his college education, he had tried to talk the matter over with his father. The father listened while he broached the subject, and then commented, "It's up to you. I'll pay tuition and board wherever you want to go for as much schooling as you want to get. I believe in education. But that's all I will do. I don't care what you do. All I am interested in is my work."

The boy interrupted this story to remark, "You know, this is a very unusual experience."

Afraid that he felt singled out by being called into the office, I smiled and replied, "This conversation? It's standard operating procedure for this department."

"No," Price explained. "I mean that I have never talked so frankly to an instructor before." Just then he noticed the time and exclaimed, "Good heavens! You have given me an hour and fifty-four minutes. This is the first time I have ever spent that much time with an instructor. I certainly appreciate it, and I'll try to have a better attitude."

"Well, if that's the way you want to put it," I replied. "I think I got some enlightenment out of this conversation. If you did, too, that's fine."

---

[2] This is best illustrated by a quotation which, while it comes from another student, shows most succinctly the distinction with which Price was struggling. The student had come in to discuss his written report on a case called "Joseph Longman." At length he said, "I see now that in analyzing the case I should have tried to be Joe Longman. Instead, I assumed that Joe was me. He talked the way I do, he felt as I do, the things that are important to me were important to him. I never really looked at Joe."

"I certainly did," Price replied, "and I'll try, as I said."

The following day Price was absent from class, but he did not miss another session during the term.

THE CLASS, ALLEN PRICE, AND THE INSTRUCTOR

I felt that Price had got several things out of the conference, chief of which was the relationship which was established. He found that someone was interested in him. A father who cared about education but not about him, schoolmates to whom his importance was negative, as an object for their practical jokes, instructors who brushed him off—all these were part of his experience, and such a large part that "an hour and fifty-four minutes" was a token of considerable importance.

That relationship enabled him to deal more effectively with the course because it convinced him of the good faith of the course. Many times he had indicated a tongue-in-cheek attitude. Even the report from the handwriting analyst had seemed to support that interpretation. So many of the comments had seemed in line with Price's own preoccupations that I once suspected that the analyst had not had to do the job "blind." In any event, there is reason to believe the results would not have been passed on if they had presented a picture of the instructor too inconsistent with Price's own. Contained in the analysis was the sentence, "Your suavity may cause others to think you are hypocritical." Now, however, he found the instructor behaving the same game she talked. His surprise at not being judged was more than he could hold. "Should I be ashamed?" he asked, determined not to be kept in suspense any longer. When he learned that the question in the instructor's mind was not, "Is this behavior right or wrong?" but, "Is this behavior effective in achieving your objectives?" he could drop his defenses and begin to take a look at his objectives.

Finally, through seeing the interdependence of so many of his own experiences and preoccupations, he began to understand what it meant for other people. From that time on in class he faced up to the issues of the particular situations involved in the cases with a directness that was in marked contrast to his earlier behavior. His recitations were concerned chiefly with trying to relate factors in the case together into a meaningful pattern. For instance, in discussing the case of a third-grader who had developed crying spells, Price said, "There were three changes that occurred in this child's life at about the same time. First, her mother changed her method of handling her and deliberately gave her less affection. Second, she had a new teacher, who was more strict and impersonal than the one she was used to. And third, she moved to a new house with new surroundings. They all meant the same thing; they made the child a stranger."

Later he commented in class, "Six weeks is a short time for absorbing such a new way of thinking."

As Price's recitations became shorter and more relevant, as he used a more conversational and less didactic tone, as he interacted wtih the rest of the class in the achievement of the common purpose of making sense out of the case at hand, his behavior began to conform more and more closely with the group codes. Accordingly, the others began to let him into the group. They listened to him, gave him support for his ideas, and became more friendly with him. While Price's own behavior was considerably modified, the class also had changed somewhat. They had begun to take an interest in the reading and in trying to tie the more theoretical material to the cases. In this they were moving more in the direction of dealing with abstractions, an area which had from the beginning interested Price. As a result Price and the class, both handling the material more effectively than at first, had established an additional common ground between them. During the last week or ten days of the term, I believed that Price had made considerable progress in learning to handle his problems and that he felt free to come in when he wanted to talk about them. Consequently I did not devote a great deal more time to him. Others had succeeded to the position of "number one problem student."

At the same time that Price's relations with the rest of the class were beginning to develop in a positive direction, the relations of the others were also strengthening. They seemed to be preparing their cases together in informal discussion groups outside of class, a practice that was encouraged whenever opportunity arose. To prepare for the final exam, a "rump session" was held. Although half of the class mentioned the session in conversation with me afterwards, none was able to tell whose idea it had been. A group "chewing the fat" together after the final class had evolved the idea spontaneously. It went out on the grapevine. The following day most of the class showed up in the regular room at the regular hour. One of the girls was selected to write on the blackboard, "but she wasn't the teacher," reports emphasized. "She was more of a secretary while everyone pitched in. We all contributed ideas but no one dominated. It took us all morning. By noon we had listed the facts, drawn lines to indicate relationships, drawn our diagrams, and decided what it all meant. Every blackboard in the room was covered. It was almost as good a class as our regular sessions. You should have been peeking through the window; you would have thought we had learned something." Twenty-five students, as diverse an assortment as I have ever met in a single class, had formed a group after all. And Price was so much a part of the group that one of the "bull sessions" on the reading assignments, in preparation for the final examination, was held in his room in the dormitory.

For his final examination, Price wrote an A— paper, doing an outstanding job, appropriately enough, on the concept of obsessive thinking.

WHAT ALLEN PRICE LEARNED

Having got Price through the course, let us see whether we can reappraise what happened to him. Between his two statements with which we began this article lay a deep gulf of resistance, confusion, conflict, and the beginning of some understanding. The resistance he brought in with him on the first day; the confusion arose when he began to see the inadequacy of his habitual way of thinking about human situations; and the conflict developed when he realized dimly that to change the terms in which he thought about the world meant to change himself. When he registered for the course, Price brought with him a way of looking at the world formed by his 21 years of experience. This way was not revolutionized in one term but certain first steps were taken. Superficially, one of the outstanding things about his world when he first came was that it was not made up of Suzy, John, his history professor, his father, and similar people, all discrete individuals reacting in characteristic, consistent, but understandable ways. Instead, he saw representatives of the middle-middle class sublimating their sexual drives into socially acceptable channels, particularly into those which led toward the acquisition of status symbols. More simply, his was a world made up of "union members," "capitalists," and "Frenchmen." This thinking in stereotypes, this application of "principles" without first making sure that they were appropriate to the particular situation, this mistaking of the map for the territory, were Price's way of keeping the world at arm's length. Not knowing real people, he knew all the most progressive theories about them and behaved in terms of those theories.

In a case course, however, this pattern was difficult to maintain. The feelings of the class in response to Price's ways of thinking and of presenting his thoughts were made abundantly clear. He could not avoid facing up to their inadequacy. Gradually, instead of talking about "security" he began to talk about what having unfamiliar surroundings, an unfamiliar teacher, and an unfamiliar response from her mother all at the same time meant to a child. He expressed less interest in "technological change" than in what mechanization did to the feelings of craftsmen who enjoyed a particular standing in the community because of their skill. That he was groping for a more satisfactory approach was also indicated by questions such as the one quoted, with the remark, "I'm asking because I really want to know; I'm hazy." At points like this, bringing in the rest of the class so that they could express their confusions and work through together to a satisfactory answer increased the group solidarity. With Price thus increasingly in the circle, his defensiveness toward the others decreased so that he could understand what was being said. Thus he not only gained more insight from the class discussion but, relieved of a little of his own internal pressure, was also able to think more constructively for himself on the questions he raised. The small, tentative modifications in his way of thinking were inevitably expressed in his behavior in class; and the results in terms of his group relations laid the groundwork for new skills of understanding and coöperation. That he continued to use and develop the understanding he gained from the experience of this course is testified to by his subsequent correspondence, even though he still has a number of unresolved problems.

Our view of Allen Price's progress through those six weeks has been largely a matter of deduction from observation. Only Price himself could tell how accurate the deductions are, and at this stage perhaps not even he knows, for surely a good deal of it was unconscious. This paper is not to defend the interpretations but to report what took place as the instructor saw it and to suggest that something was happening inside the student. Price's problems were individual and in that sense not necessarily typical, although it has been a rare class in which there have not been some students for whom discussion of cases has contributed to personal growth. For most, the process was annoying or troublesome; for many, painful; for some few, it was more than they could endure and they protected themselves by refusing to grapple with the problems, so that they "took" the course only in the most superficial sense. Price went through several of these stages, ending by coming to grips with the course material. Presenting his story is only one way of looking at a class to see whether any growth took place as a result of the pedagogical method.

THE CASE METHOD IN HUMAN RELATIONS

The case method is peculiarly applicable to a course which deals with the relations of people, regardless of context. In the very act of participating in discussion, responding to one another's ideas or ignoring them, denying their validity or helping to develop them, the students are engaging in human relations. They have therefore in the classroom a laboratory in their subject. Coöperation becomes a reality for the Human Relations students as they coöperate in analyzing a case and deciding on appropriate action. The case is the common vehicle through which each member relates himself to the group and is the topic through which individual attitudes are expressed.

This is not to say that the entire value of a course lies in the discussion. Teachers could probably be found to represent the entire continuum from the most authoritarian methods to the most permissive, but we stand some-where between the extremes. A case course is not a bull session with aca-demic credit. The content is important as well. Whatever the content, however, the method gives the student an opportunity to test the ideas he gets out of the course by exposing them to the cross fire of class discussion and to practice his developing skills in human relations in the somewhat protected atmosphere of the classroom.

In this protected atmosphere, the important thing for many students, as for Price, is the relation with the instructor. This relation helps to hold the world steady for him as he is forced, by the material itself and by the reactions of the other students, to face up to the implications for his day-to-day behavior of his present way of thinking about his world.

Psychologists have recently pointed out that learning consists in making modifications in the way the individual perceives the world. Since his con-cept of himself is central to his understanding of the world about him, learning implies alterations in the way the individual perceives his rela-tion to the world. In view of the need of the individual to maintain con-sistency in his self-concept, the learning process involves conflict. This con-flict is the beginning of understanding and the essential ingredient without which learning does not take place. Frequently the students need help in handling their conflicts. In this regard, class discussion is invaluable in letting the instructor get to know his students. When the students do the talking, the instructor not only has a daily opportunity to estimate the progress of the student but begins to see, by the pattern of recitations, where the student is blocked. If a student shows some understanding of one-one relationships but not of groups, the instructor can help him to gain some group experience by the way his recitations are handled in re-spect to the rest of the class. In the case of a student whose manner alien-ates the others in the class, the instructor can often prevent the breach from becoming irreconcilable. If a student's difficulty lies in his relation to authority, the permissive atmosphere of class discussion may assist him to a new experience with authority and thus a new understanding of its nature.

Occasionally conflicts develop which are too severe or too personal to be handled in the classroom, and individual conferences are indicated. If the aim of education is to modify behavior in the direction of greater effectiveness, then one of the primary responsibilities of the instructor is to attempt to resolve the obstacles to growth. Individual conferences thus may be an extension of the case method and are facilitated by it in two ways. First, the rapport which develops between the case instructor and his students, being permissive and student-oriented, makes it easier for most students to talk with the instructor about their problems. Anyone who has had experience teaching by the case method can recall numerous instances when a student has appeared in his office to ask a simple, factual question and stayed to discuss something that was bothering him. Secondly, even if the student does not take the initiative, the instructor may. In doing so, the instructor is responding to his acquaintance with the student developed through class discussion, which has both shown him that some help may be necessary and suggested some of the areas which the student may want to explore.

"It is more necessary to think than to know," says Prescott Lecky, "especially since it is obvious that we shall never know without thinking." One great advantage of the case method is that it is not primarily focussed on what the student knows. In Human Relations it is primarily concerned with creating an atmosphere and a set of relations in which the students can rethink their experience so as to derive more effective meanings from it and begin to make more precise discriminations in their relations with others.

General Semantics and the Case Method

IRVING J. LEE

Shamed by my golf scores, I had arranged for some lessons with a pro. He explained that the swing of the club was related to such fundamentals as grip, stance, and position of elbows and head. He believed it more important to think about where the ball is than where it is supposed to go. He suggested that I ought to give more consideration to a method designed to establish contact between club head and ball, and less consideration to swinging the club in a way I found comfortable. He intimated that my previous practice had not made anything perfect, but had perpetuated some bad habits. He had me watch him. He held my arms. And so on with remarkable patience in the face of manifest ineptness.

This experience was illuminating in another way. It helped me to see the *talking* process in the golf pro's severely practical and functional terms.

One learns to talk. The use of a language is related to a whole complex of functions, including perceiving, thinking, feeling. Along with a sense of the proprieties and taboos, a speaker develops a set of unnoticed habits, some useful, some detrimental. How am I going about it? is subordinated to how am I doing? Is the ball going into the cup? Am I saying what I want to say? Sometimes a swing ends in a hook or a slice. Sometimes an utterance leads to conflict, confusion, or misunderstanding. Tension and noncoördination in the bodily elements mean extra strokes. Distortions and disorder in describing, inferring, and concluding mean waste motion and trouble in human affairs.

The analogy seems to hold so well that this question is inevitable: Should not a man who thinks it sensible to look to a golf pro to fix up his game similarly set out for a communication pro when his talking activities are marked by disaffection and disagreement?

There is just one hitch. Communication pros are scarce and they are not always agreed on what needs correcting in the talking process. In what follows I shall try to summarize one man's opinion about it.

Alfred Korzybski was certainly not the first person to think about the things a communication pro would look for, but he may well have been the most diligently wide-ranging one. In a sense, the last 30 years of his life were spent setting up a course of study for future practitioners.

He systematized a great deal of scattered knowledge about talking difficulties and the way to go about correcting them in a discipline he called General Semantics.[1] He nowhere presumed to be creating something where nothing existed before. He was in the main explicitly stating and emphasizing anew an ancient set of necessities.

He is not easy reading—partly, I believe, because he was asking us to look at something most of us already have conclusions about, and partly because he was trying to get us to look at something we were busy doing at the precise moment we were supposed to be looking at it. He was asking us to swing a mashie and take a look at the swinging mechanism at the same time. This was not only difficult but disconcerting.

There is another reason. He built his systematization quite unsystematically. He never wrote in the fashion of the textbook or scientific article. Those of us who were accustomed to tidy statements of a problem, presentation of the available findings, and neat marshaling of conclusions were appalled at the repetitious and disjointed character of his essays. He rarely dealt with one of the talking difficulties at length. He mentioned it, went to something else, and returned to it again pages later. (This was a way of showing how interrelated everything is.) His illustrations were too few and too fugitive. (He thought readers could supply them.) His pages abound in exhortations about the importance of avoiding confusion even before his readers had time to grasp the character of what was to be avoided. (He was trying to say that he thought his notions something more than intellectual acrobatics.) He was less interested in clarity than in stating the factors which prevented it. (He was not a very good golfer himself.) And he never sought the kind of clarity which compromises the complexity of the facts involved. In short, busy students were often unprepared for the amount of creative coöperation he required.

[1] His basic writings are the following: *Manhood of Humanity* (1921) (Lakeville, Connecticut: Institute of General Semantics, 1950); *Time-Binding: The General Theory* (Two papers, 1924–1926), (Institute of General Semantics, 1949); *Science and Sanity: An Introduction to Non-Aristotelian Systems and General Semantics* (1933) (Institute of General Semantics, 1948); with M. Kendig, "The Foreword," *A Theory of Meaning Analyzed*, General Semantics Monographs, No. 3 (Institute of General Semantics, 1942); "General Semantics," *The American People's Encyclopedia* (Chicago: Spencer Press, 1948), vol. 9, pp. 352–362; "The Role of Language in the Perceptual Process," in R. R. Blake and G. V. Ramsey, ed., *Perception: An Approach to Personality* (New York: Ronald Press, 1951).

WHAT WAS KORZYBSKI GETTING AT?

It may be helpful to describe Korzybski's focus in relation to other areas of study, even though I risk oversimplification in every sentence.

How was his interest related to what was in the texts on logic? Logicians are concerned with the conditions of necessary inference. Given all the varieties of assertions, what conclusions can be derived from them without contradiction? If this is true (or false), and if that also is true (or false) then what follows? What conditions must be preserved or achieved in order to make valid inferences?

Korzybski never called either the deductive or the inductive process, as such, into question. He was interested in the statements and the assumptions behind them. He asked this question: Under what conditions were the assertions themselves (not the inferences from them) acceptable?

He did not stop there. He moved into the bailiwick of the psychologist. The literature of psychology contains descriptions of and theories about what happens in the presence of stimuli, about phenomena labeled *attending, perceiving, feeling, learning, thinking,* etc., and their interactions, variations, and clinical control when a man is alone or in a group. Korzybski set out to exploit a tangent. How was a man's behaving, thinking, knowing, feeling reflected in or linked to his ways of talking? What habitual ways of orienting oneself "psychologically" were reflected in what modes of talking? Korzybski looked not at the linguistic performance as isolated from the behaving-responding, but as they interpenetrated and affected each other.

Korzybski also caught himself up in the work of mathematicians. They, too, were engaged in symbol-manipulating activities. His father had something of an amateur's interest in the subject and the boy had been exposed very early to mathematizing processes. And again his perspective was pinpointed. He cared little about formal problems—solving equations or proving theorems. He was fascinated by the unique behavior of mathematicians—how they achieved rigor and precision, how they tried to uncover their hidden assumptions, how they revealed the implications of a hypothesis, why they were able to include all the particulars in their abstractions.

He spent 1925–1926 visiting St. Elizabeth's Hospital in Washington, D. C., where he read widely in psychiatry, and observed the behavior of the mentally deranged. These patients talked. But as he listened to their outpourings he was struck with a difference. He heard none of the search for consistency with fact which would interest a physical scientist, little of the mathematician's effort to analyze assumptions. Here were men talking, but matters of accuracy and fitness to fact were of no moment. He learned how to spot the varieties of talking in which the language and the facts were in disordered relation.

Add to all this a more than passing familiarity with a number of the languages spoken in Central and Eastern Europe, and the accompanying awareness that what could be said explicitly in some tongues could only be approached circuitously in others, that a person talked about things in partial fashion in one and in unitary modes in another, that one predisposed the speaker to distinctions that were neglected in another.

Here was indeed an intellectual stew. Korzybski had a conceptual scheme with which to talk about human affairs, but it could fit in no one place in any conventional academic departmental organization. He had evolved a set of notions about man's talking-assuming-thinking-perceiving-behaving which merged into a discipline that cut across and around the traditional subject-matter areas. In his first two papers he called it "The General Theory." Only later (when he realized he was in the middle of problems of human "meanings") did he call it General Semantics.

THE GENERAL SEMANTIC POINT OF VIEW

One could find certain patterns of emphasis in Korzybski's writings. What was known about the structure of the world around and inside us? Did our ways of talking take that structural knowledge into account? Or did they impose categories that were distorting? What habitual patterns of response tended to keep men from or dispose them toward an awareness of the structure of the world?

One can consider General Semantics in terms of a number of unifying perspectives. From the many I choose one—*Identification*, considered as any act of perceiving-assuming-feeling-talking in which one thing is seen as something else, one kind of statement made as if it were another, one linguistic form given the properties which belong to another. A man is not responding adequately and sensibly when he shows unwittingly any of the varieties of Identification. (Of course if he knows what he is doing and insists he is doing something else he is perpetrating a fraud.)

I list a few of the patterns of Identification:

1. A partial coverage of a situation is given the preferred status of a full one.

2. An ambiguous statement (one that is too meaningful) is dismissed as if it were meaningless, or an ambiguous statement is asserted as if the values were fixed and clear.

3. A statement which segments a situation is presented so as to imply that the segment has an independent existence.

4. Undesignated interpretations are assigned terms by speakers, and

listeners assume that their assigned interpretations are necessarily those of the speakers.

5. A complicating, dynamically emergent interaction is presented in terms which catch only the static and additive factors.

6. Interrelations between men, and between men and things, are glossed over by statements which highlight the separateness; the interrelations are then denied by implication.

7. Recurring, invariant relations are classified as unique ones (and vice versa) without concern for the difference.

8. Problems are discussed in high-order abstractions as if high-order abstractions necessarily permitted the rigor which belongs to lower-order abstractions.

9. Limiting conceptions are permitted to impose their restricting pictures without recognition of the restrictions.

10. Statements based on how one "feels" about a thing or person are confused with statements referring to more publicly verifiable matters, and statements which involve both are treated as if one were absent.

11. The declarative form of assertions is allowed to cloud the distinction between statements based on observation and those which involve inferences, and the latter are made as if they had the status of the former.

And so on for about 40 more.

It seems necessary to say that Korzybski's primary objective was explication, to describe the mechanisms of confusion and indicate how they might be avoided. He was not creating the kind of positivistic doctrine which said that a man had to speak factually, accurately, precisely. If one wished to speak ambiguously, vaguely, or in terms of phantasy, Korzybski would not wish to stop him. He wanted only a recognition that the one mode was not the other, and that the one should not be palmed off as if it were the other. He urged the development of a method of discrimination so that a man would know whereof he spoke, so that if he wished to do differently the means would be at hand. If a man wanted to hook or slice he ought to know the means whereby to do it, along with the probable consequences.

Korzybski was perfectly aware, for example, of the value and necessity of both high- and low-order abstractions. Without the latter, rigor and precision are extremely difficult. Without the former, we should be unable to state either principles and rules of action, or generalizations based on samplings. Without high-order abstractions we would be unable to write a constitution or a set of by-laws or instructions which provide for both administrative control and freedom. Korzybski's objective, in short, was an understanding of the varieties of assumptions and assertions along with their uses and shortcomings.

WHAT HAS GENERAL SEMANTICS TO DO WITH THE CASE METHOD?

My answer to this question is of the most tentative sort. During the Spring of 1951 I had the pleasant privilege of sitting in on some 100 hours of classes in Human Relations and Administrative Practices at the Graduate School of Business Administration in Harvard University. I read the cases, listened to the discussions, and talked to the teachers and, at some length, to 46 students outside of class. I now believe that twice as much time for observations and interviews would have been more than doubly valuable. Looking and listening with the perspective of a student of General Semantics, I had a number of impressions.

Many of the varieties of arrogance and know-it-allness are leavened under the interacting scrutiny of students who are free to question and encouraged to enlarge their understanding of real problems.

Several of the patterns of impatience and impulsiveness seem modified in a situation in which each man knows that it is better to be sure than sorry he opened his mouth too soon.

The case itself seemed to be a continuous brake on certain of those free-wheeling, ververbalized tendencies in discussions which fill the air with sound rather than insight, and which make for talk around rather than on the issues.

The continuous effort on the part of instructors to pursue the details of the case prevented and modified the oversimplifying, easy-answer impulses of those eager to dismiss or get done with the problem.

The interest (not approval) of the instructor in what each man said, manifested by his eagerness to help the students explore their own evaluations, again encouraged a look at the case as well as reflection on what was being said.

The students loved it. I have never talked with graduate students so unhesitatingly eager to discuss their class discussions and so sensitive to the values of what they were doing.

I had never before observed teachers who themselves were so teachable in the teaching situation.

In a word, the atmosphere was one which discouraged a number of the attitudes that predispose men to Identification.

Nevertheless, my notebook contains a record of several of the ordinary semantic lapses.

Students got away with declarations which sounded factual but which were manifestly inferential.

They assumed a substance behind certain words which often was not really there.

Students generalized with ease and assurance from instances presumed but not demonstrated to be typical; demonstration might not have been easy in many of the instances.

Individuals in the discussion "pegged" a person or situation in the case in terms which shut off further consideration, as if when he or it had been classified no other way of looking at him or it was possible.

Students consumed precious time defending either-or patterns of analysis as if the notion of graded variation belonged only in textbooks.

Students talked of "solutions" as if these had a unitary character, as if they did not range from the approximate to the impossibly complete.

They dealt with statements involving variables as if they were one-valued, that is, they sought to establish the truth or falsity of statements which should have been considered ambiguous.

Speakers missed a nice distinction: "The edges of the distinction between 'feel that' and 'think that' are not hard. Feeling that something is the case slides into thinking that it is the case; and we often use 'feel that' instead of 'think' as a sort of polite hypocrisy." [2]

I should be quite misleading if I gave the impression that statements involving these and other semantic lapses outnumbered the statements which adequately evaluated what was involved. In the classes I attended they did not. An Identification Index, giving the ratio between the statements which could be presumed to evaluate properly and those which misevaluated, would show, I believe, that these students were performing with a maturity not found, say, in a random sampling of radio discussion programs. This does not mean, of course, that the case method is *the* causative factor. I did, nonetheless, find that when the lapses occurred they were not without effects. They tended to turn the talk away from the issues involved. They forced efforts at clarification which took time. They oversimplified matters which had to be reconsidered later anyway, or when neglected led to feelings of confidence about the analysis not necessarily justifiable.

I can only wonder about what might have happened in a number of disagreements and analytical impasses had members of the class sought to uncover the evaluational-linguistic mechanisms at work. Would it make a difference in the discussion of a case if the participants had been sensitized ahead of time to the kinds of conflict and confusions which are rooted in semantic mechanisms? What if a communication pro had been present to call attention to what the speakers were inadvertently doing? These questions should be considered invitations to research. It would be presumptuous to suggest anything more.

WHAT VALUES MIGHT THE CASE METHOD HAVE FOR STUDENTS
OF GENERAL SEMANTICS?

Again, I write in tentative and hypothetical terms. It is possible to teach and study General Semantics as a kind of "philosophical" subject, one about which there can be discussion only. Or it can be approached as a set of norms in terms of which a man's behavior may be appraised.

[2] Gilbert Ryle, "Feelings," *The Philosophical Quarterly*, I (April 1951), p. 186.

In this view, one should not ask, "Is Mr. Black able to discourse on the rules?" but, "Does Mr. Black exemplify the rules in his talking, listening, reading, writing?" Nor can he talk about the theory of symbolic inadequacy, but can he recognize examples of it—and more important, does he evince symbolic adequacy in his interchanges with others?

Let me consider this as a teacher. And let me assume that I have been able to bring to my classes all the directive-didactic methods available for the task of imparting a knowledge of the principles of General Semantics. Let me assume that my students are of the most faithful, receptive, and homage-bearing variety. And finally let us suppose that they pass in superior fashion all the kinds of quizzes I can devise. They will then, as Elton Mayo has so sharply reminded us, have knowledge *about* the rules. We shall know little of their capacity to put that knowledge to work. In Gilbert Ryle's words, "A soldier does not become a shrewd general merely by endorsing the strategic principles of Clausewitz. He must also be competent to apply them." At this moment I know of no single procedure or technique which can so readily test students in application as can the case method. What will these students of mine do with the case and will their verbalized knowledge become operative when they discuss it? It may be wise not to expect too much. Or it may be that the case itself will serve as the proving ground on which their understanding of the principles moves from pronouncement to the penetration that comes with performance. Whether or not I overstate the case for the use of cases must await experiments.

There is yet another test which teachers and students of General Semantics might face. We start by believing that with Korzybski's formulations a host of communication and evaluating difficulties can be made explicit. We have believed that once oriented in terms of these formulations we become sensitive to facets and nuances in human relations that we had hitherto missed or that we had been mistaken about. It should be possible to test these beliefs. Would any of us see anything in any of the Harvard Business School cases ordinarily neglected by the candidates for the MBA? Would, say, four teachers of courses in General Semantics meeting together find anything in a particular case which four teachers of sections in Administrative Practices might pass over, which would add a worth-while dimension to an understanding of that case? Again we must await some doing.

Men were using the case method long before there was a course in General Semantics. But teachers in both of these areas of interest share a common goal—the development in men of skills which go beyond the specialisms to the widest possible application in human affairs whether in the home, office, playground, ship, or heavy bomber. The skills of listening, questioning, analyzing, differentiating, describing, planning, proposing, deciding have to do with the least and most important moments in a person's life. They are also the skills which are basic in understanding, working, and talking with people. And it makes a difference whether we use them aptly or ineptly.

A couple of generations ago it would have seemed rather novel for students in one department of a university to look to another for methods and procedures. But the pressure for achievement outside the physical sciences has become so great that the idea of academic provincialism is itself not readily defensible. To this writer, at least, the effort to remove the barriers that keep specialists in one area from learning about what happens in another is part of that larger effort to improve and establish communication between men wherever they are.

The Use of the Lecture in a Case-Method Course

FRANCES MULHEARN FULLER

An important aspect of the so-called "case method" of instruction is to encourage students to do the talking. Frequently, instructors using this method are asked by other instructors, "Don't you *ever* lecture? Aren't there times when a lecture would be helpful?" In the early days of a case-discussion course students press for the instructor's opinion. They beg to be told. The instructor himself may often feel a compulsion to pull case discussions together, to indicate aspects missed by the students, or to point out to the class concepts that could have been effectively used in discussion. Especially to the new instructor, however, yielding to these external and internal pressures to "lecture" may seem at first thought a serious violation of the basic purpose of case teaching.

That there is a real place in such teaching for occasional short lectures and summary lectures has been demonstrated on a number of occasions. In order to make such lectures effective in terms of the purpose of a case-method course, the instructor must practice toward his class the same kind of situational approach he is trying to get them to practice in their discussions of case material. This implies that the instructor will (1) view the class as a social system and (2) recognize that this social system involves a number of different kinds of relations—between teacher and student, student and student, and student and the material of the course (cases, reading references, and so on). Of these relations, the first concern of the instructor is the relation between himself and the students. If this relation develops effectively, the development of other relations in the class will be greatly facilitated. The instructor's lectures, when properly conceived, can do much to promote effective relations and to enhance student understanding of the course's purpose. A lecture delivered without due attention to the particular purposes of a case-discussion course not only may vitiate many of the gains from class discussion, but also may lead to student protests that the instructor doesn't practice what he preaches.

Neither the timing of lectures nor their content can be determined apart from the individual class. The general rule of thumb, however, might be roughly stated as "put nothing into the lecture that hasn't come out of the class." Or (to paraphrase L. J. Henderson [1]), the lecture should reflect what has been said in class discussion, what has been implied but not specifically stated in class discussion, and what the students have not been able to say without help. The instructor's help should *not* take the form of giving a definite answer to each case or a specific statement of the concepts useful in each instance.

The help, however, may take many other forms. Two possible approaches are illustrated in the two summary lectures that follow. Each of these lectures was directed toward the special needs of the particular class involved, but together they may be useful in suggesting the sort of thing instructors may want to watch for and comment upon. The instructor may feel it most useful to dwell on the class's approach to the case material, summarizing the areas that were discussed and raising questions about areas that were not discussed. The summary lecture of May 24, 1949 is an attempt of this sort given at the final session of a full course.

On the other hand, the instructor may prefer to build his lecture around concepts and ideas that the students have been using implicitly or explicitly in their discussions. He may wish to expand or illustrate these concepts by cases, outside reading, occurrences in class, or personal experience. This was attempted in the summary lecture for the Summer School Session, August 19, 1949.

Another approach has been found effective as a summary device. A case may be used as the basis for the lecture. The students are asked to read the case before coming to class so that they will be able to follow the instructor's diagnosis and discussion. In his lecture the instructor can then relate his diagnosis of this particular case to earlier case discussion, to concepts, and to readings assigned in the course.

No matter what approach he takes, the instructor will do well to indicate that his remarks are only one man's way of putting together what seemed important to him in the class development. He will offer his lecture as a sample of the kind of thinking he has been trying to stimulate in class and he will encourage the students to make their own efforts to apply this thinking not only to the course work but to other facets of their lives. In this way the instructor satisfies a twofold need. First, he gives the students some leads about how to put together a variety of fac-

[1] L. J. Henderson, *Sociology 23, Introductory Lectures.* Lecture I, p. 14 (mimeographed; 2nd ed., rev. October 1938).

tors that have emerged in a specific situation (the course); he is illustrating *situational thinking*. Secondly, he is satisfying a very real need of his own. As a member of the social system that is the class, the instructor has certain purposes and feelings. If his relation with his students has been properly developed, he can reveal these purposes and express these feelings from time to time without being considered authoritarian and without taking from the students the initiative they must exercise to make this kind of course a success.

SUMMARY LECTURE, MAY 24, 1949 [2]

Today for a change I am going to do a lot of talking. Most of what I say, however, comes from my recollections of our discussions here in class during the past three months. I want to combine in this discussion three things: first, a review of our approaches to the case material and how these approaches changed and developed in the course of our discussion; second, some comments on the content of the cases and of the reading as it relates to our discussions; third, some general observations on where all this leaves us. I will give you an opportunity to ask questions after developing the first two points, and if anyone feels strongly moved to break in earlier, go right ahead.

I am going to begin with our approaches because, after all, that was our action problem as a class. We were faced at each meeting with a given set of circumstances set forth in a case, and we had to ask ourselves, "How shall we approach this situation in order to understand *what* we are dealing with and *how* it might be dealt with most effectively?" Some of you have been bothered from time to time about the relation between diagnosis and action, and some of you have felt that not enough attention was paid specifically to the latter. Perhaps if we look at the kinds of approaches we brought to the case material, we will see some of the things that got in our way in trying to relate our analyses to effective action and, on the other hand, see some of the approaches that facilitated this process.

We might first say a word about where these approaches came from. You all took the course with some expectations. These expectations were probably closely related to your experience with other courses. In many instances, you came expecting to find an answer. This is the sort of thing we learn to expect of education. With these expectations in mind, we began to ask certain questions of the cases. Later we reëxamined these questions, asking whether or not they were effective ways of approaching human situations.

What were some of our favorite questions?

1. One was the approach that I called the "whodunit" approach to the case material. In this we tried to find the evidence, locate the guilty party, and mete out just punishment. Our main difficulty when we took this approach was the lack of law to govern in these situations. We rapidly discovered that human relations lacked an over-all, specific code. Those of you who have read the suggested references in Judge Bok's book, *I Too, Nicodemus,* have his word for the fact that the able judge is up against the same problem in his courtroom every day. Bok says, speaking through the character of Judge Ulen, that the Judge's motto for the courtroom was:

> "Use as little law as possible." There is more in people's minds, when they go to law, than the hope that a set of rules will produce the result they desire. If that were true, it would be possible to write a code capable of providing for every contingency.[3]

In spite of the fact that we early discovered the lack of a governing code, we persisted in the idea that if we could just decide that some one person or one factor was responsible, we could deal with that and everything else would automatically fall into place. In short, we were indulging in simple cause-and-effect thinking. For example, in the discussion of Delman Forge,* some felt that Peter, the foreman, was to blame and that getting rid of him was the answer. We raised the question of what this would mean to the other workers, who had considered Peter "the boss" for so long, and what it would mean in a group whose code put heavy emphasis on seniority and length of service. In combatting this kind of oversimplification in our analysis, we invoked Henderson's idea of the interdependence of variables. In the portion of his lectures assigned, Henderson writes as follows:

> In a social system, and, as a rule, elsewhere, an action initiated in a certain thing leads to modifications everywhere in the system, and these modifications to further modifications which involve the very thing in which the process originated. So it is both "cause" and "effect" . . . Thus, reasoning from cause to effect in the study of concrete phenomena is often even more misleading than more general reasoning of the same kind. This is particularly true of interactions between men . . .
>
> We may fix these ideas by glancing at a case of a more familiar kind. A student who has just had three or four cocktails is shaving when his roommate slams a door. He drops his razor and cuts his toe, carelessly ties up the wound, and goes to the theater. His toe becomes inflamed, and he finally dies. What is the cause of his death?

[3] Curtis Bok, *I Too, Nicodemus* (New York: Knopf, 1946), p. 324.

The following causes, among others, may be assigned by various persons: general septicemia, by the doctor; a streptococcus infection, by the bacteriologist; there was no one to take proper care of him, by the mother; the doctor's incompetency, by the father; the slamming of the door, by the roommate; lack of discipline in the boy's upbringing, by an uncle; the boy's neglect of the wound, by a timid and also by a methodical friend; the cocktails, by a prohibitionist.[4]

Henderson goes on to say that unless you look at this case with the interdependence of all the factors in mind, the question becomes meaningless. The nearest approach you can get to a logical statement is that the death was due to bad luck. Henderson further points out that this kind of thinking about a single factor as the cause of the given situation carries over into thinking about the social system. He says:

When you notice a particular "evil" in a social system, say chronic alcoholism, you may be tempted to think that a single change in the system, for example, a prohibition amendment, will remedy the evil and produce no other important result. Experience shows, however, that, in general, this is not the case, but that on the contrary, while the desired result may or may not be realized, many other results will certainly ensue, most of which are unpredictable. The explanation of this is roughly as follows: Every factor of the social system is directly dependent for its continued existence upon many other factors, and these in turn upon it; that is to say, they are mutually dependent and interactive . . . A change in one factor is, therefore, accompanied and followed by a long series of changes involving all the factors of the system. Therefore, if you would preserve a certain factor of the system you must be willing to put up with the other factors.[5]

Closely related to our search for a single cause in the early discussions of cases was the "What is the problem?" approach. You may remember that in our discussions of the Marshall Company * and of Freedom Products,** we didn't "readily" see a problem, and we were inclined to dismiss the cases with comparatively little attention. We said in the case of Freedom Products that this company had handled a working force larger than its current one earlier in its history. Why was Nash having trouble now? Notice the words, *problem, trouble*. We were thinking in terms of crises, of very obvious breakdowns in an organization that demanded action with a capital A. As we persisted in our discussions, we began to see, however, that in human situations things do not come up to us (to quote Mr. Roethlisberger) all nicely labeled *problems*. Human situations come up to us in somewhat messy little bits, which we try to piece together slowly and painstakingly. This is the sort of thing we did in our class discussions in terms of the individuals in the cases, of their relations to one another, and of the relation of the particular situation to the background

[4] Henderson, *Sociology 23, Introductory Lectures*, Lecture I.
[5] *Ibid.*, pp. 55, 56.

against which it occurred. Remember the Brettwood ** case and our diagram of the concentric circles, the inner circles of the work group, the bigger work group, the factory, the community, and, finally, the world?

In addition to modifying the "whodunit" approach and the "What's the problem?" approach, we had an opportunity to reconsider a third negative approach to the case situations, that is, "We don't have enough information to do anything about this, though we recognize the area in which we would like to do something." This tendency to operate on the information that we do not have rather than that which we have led to speculation rather than to analysis. For example, in your reports on *Guard of Honor,*[6] while it was perfectly appropriate to devote a few sentences to what would happen to Colonel Mowbray if General Beal were replaced as the commanding officer, a paper which devoted the lion's share of its attention to this kind of speculation missed the point of the report entirely. The *fact* was that General Beal was *not* replaced.

A fourth approach which needed reëxamining was the "Is it true?" approach. For example, in the case of *Ida Geneva* † it was said that all we know of Ida is what she tells us. Is what she says true? In the Livingston Company * case, the question was raised, "Is Margaret Bickers getting the real story?" Gradually we shifted these questions until we were asking not "Is it true?" but "Why are these things important to Ida Geneva? Why does she say them?" Likewise, does Margaret Bickers care whether she has the "real story" or is she more interested in what the various people concerned *believe* the story to be and how their beliefs are influencing their behavior?

A fifth approach to the cases was somewhat more positive but equally limiting for effective handling of human situations. It was the habit of recognizing intellectually the complexity of the situation with which we were faced but, nevertheless, relying on a single answer to these complexities. This I call the "favorite-thesis approach." It was usually signaled in discussion by the generous use of the word "should." For example, in Youth Village,† it was said that Mr. Schneider should realize that his uneven handling of boys like this was bad. The question that we learned to ask of this kind of statement was, "*should*, from whose point of view?" We learned to recognize the fact that in making this kind of statement we were, perhaps unwittingly, using a value system which we brought to the case from other experience and which we never had made explicit.

As we began to reëxamine all five of these approaches, we came to recognize the validity of the idea that we all tend to look at the world through our own particular pair of glasses. We might think of these, for convenience's sake, as bifocals, one lens labeled "attitude" and the other

[6] By James Gould Cozzens (New York: Harcourt, Brace, 1948).

"assumptions." The material from which these lenses are ground is, of course, our experience, education, personal history, and so on. Whether the glasses aid or inhibit our way of looking at the world, however, depends on how we have assimilated these things.

How did our attitudes betray themselves in discussion? First, by the abundance of labels and stereotypes. For example, as far back as the first case in the year, the case of Ralph Stetson,** some students, upon finding out from the case that the wife was a 19-year old Southern girl, immediately interpreted this factor in terms of their own stereotype. She was "sweet-talking," "socially ambitious," "clinging vine," and a number of other evaluating phrases from which the general deduction was that she was the cause of Ralph's predicament.

We were not alone in this kind of thinking. We saw in the case material that Mr. Goodwin in the Marshall Company * had a definite stereotype of a "good worker." Danny Keefe in the Mu Nu Fraternity † case had one of a "commoner," while the girls in the Brettwood Company ** had a stereotype of someone who was "stuck-up." The reading, too, abounded in examples. In *Management and the Worker*,[7] the preconceptions of what constitutes a "fair day's work" or the "bogey" were of this order. In the literature of other cultures—the Oriental, the Irish, and the American Indian—we saw numerous examples of the special meanings certain words had for these people. As we considered each of the labels or stereotypes, we were not concerned with whether they were right or wrong. We admitted that they were all "possibilities," but we began to ask how useful they were, how much it profited us to call a person a "brat," a "neurotic," or a "hayseed," how much it explained or how it aided our understanding. We began to try to spell out these labels. In Hayakawa's terms, we began to extensionalize our thinking, to move from an intentional orientation where we were guided by "words alone" to one where we were guided by the facts, both logical and nonlogical. We began to try to avoid what Hayakawa describes as

such indiscriminate lumping together of sense and nonsense that "maps" pile up independent of "territory," and in the course of a lifetime we may pile up an entire system of meaningless noises that bear no relationship to reality whatever.[8]

Remember Hayakawa's story of the difficulty a person got into if he had a fixed idea of what, for example, was meant by a churchgoer, when he encountered a man who was, in fact, a churchgoer but who had none of the virtues generally attributed to one. You recall that the man who

[7] Roethlisberger and Dickson, *Management and the Worker*, pp. 412–416.
[8] Hayakawa, *Language in Action*, p. 219.

had the preconception concerning churchgoers was forced to one of three conclusions which Hayakawa described as equally absurd. The first was, "I don't care, he is the exception; churchgoers are nice people; I still believe that." Or, "He couldn't be that bad. He simply couldn't be. He's a churchgoer." Or, "I'm completely disillusioned. I can't have any more faith in anything."

Lest you think the restricting effects of this kind of thinking are limited to individuals and their relations to one another, look at Oliver's description in *The Endless Adventure* of the uproar in England when Walpole attempted to revive the idea of an excise tax. The English people made no attempt to distinguish between the economic situation of Walpole's time and that of a hundred years earlier, even though the two situations were in fact quite different. Even the merchant class, who would have been money in pocket had Walpole's scheme gone through, opposed it violently. Oliver says that you cannot understand this out of its context. The English people hated a word, "excise." [9]

In our own day there is an interesting example in a story which I heard recently of a discussion that a group of students at another university had on the problems of the Human Rights Commission of the United Nations. A United States member of the Commission present at the discussion told the students that an attempt was made to use as a departure point for a charter on human rights a clause so familiar to all of us that we scarcely think about it when we hear it: "All men are created equal." This clause provoked discussions that lasted for three weeks. In the first place, the word "men" was not a generic term including women in the languages of all the countries involved. The word "created" implied a Supreme Being, an idea that was not acceptable to all the members; and you can imagine the dispute over the word "equal." At the end of three weeks, all that could be agreed upon was, "All people are born." This is an illustration of what we have called "using language to disguise rather than to explain differences."

Out of such attitudes and assumptions as those just reviewed, there tends to develop a whole system of basic beliefs, in terms of which we act and expect others to act. When others fail to comply with our picture of the world, we label them "stupid" or "stubborn." We regard them a little as the Duchess regarded the sneezing baby in *Alice in Wonderland* when she said to Alice,

> "Speak roughly to your little boy,
>   And beat him when he sneezes;
> He only does it to annoy,
>   Because he knows it teases."

[9] F. S. Oliver, *The Endless Adventure* (Boston, 1931), pp. 245 ff.

We allow ourselves to be quite put out and often render ourselves ineffective as a result of such dependence on our own basic beliefs.

Underlying our discussion here there have been a number of such basic beliefs. For example, there have been a number concerning women, which I might sum up as follows: "Women are more emotional than men. They are much more easily upset by unimportant things. They are harder to boss on the job. But they like people who get tough with them." Do you remember Mr. Roethlisberger's effort to break down the general category, "workers," into "worker 1, worker 2," and so on? If you do, you will see its application in this instance. You will, of course, in your experience, find some women who are more upset by unimportant things than some men, and conversely, you will find some men who are upset much more easily by such detail than some women. Who, for example, in most popular sagas of American domestic life, has a fit if the top is left off the toothpaste? You will save yourself a certain number of headaches if you put no faith in such basic beliefs without first checking them against the actual situation with which you are dealing.

Some of the most interesting and important beliefs that have been implied in our discussions refer to the matter of authority. In four years of experience with this course, the staff has been interested to observe that the "personal experience reports" we have asked each class to write have been largely concerned with "authority" in some form or other. One kind of authority that preoccupies a number of students every year is a burdensome kind, such as that of parents who object to the student's choice of a prospective mate or that of a boss whom one considered inept or inefficient in his job. The underlying feeling seemed frequently to be that a civilized, educated person should get rid of these yokes of authority, that the kind of discipline and responsibility they forced upon the individual was primitive. Those of you who have read Eric Fromm's *Escape from Freedom* [10] will be reminded of the interesting distinction he makes between "freedom from" all the old ties and loyalties and "freedom to," that is, the use of one's "freedom from" to make a real contribution. You will remember also that he regarded as the principal tragedy of our world that "freedom from" the old restrictive ties had not become "freedom to" do anything vital or satisfying. The result in many instances was the "neurotic personality of our time." [11]

A second kind of authority problem pervading the personal experience reports concerned the exercise of authority. Many of these reports were based upon experiences in the service or in clubs or student organizations,

[10] New York: Rinehart, 1941, pp. 35 ff.
[11] This reference is to optional reading in Dr. Karen Horney's book, *The Neurotic Personality of Our Time* (New York: Norton, 1937).

where the student was suddenly raised above his fellows and placed in a position of having to get them to do things that they did not necessarily want to do. In our discussions in class, we have had much the same preoccupations. We have discussed friendship and authority and asked whether they mix. We said in our discussion of the Marshall Company that Alice was probably right when she said that she couldn't report her friends and she couldn't be an inspector. We had a lively discussion over the Youth Village case and what was expected of the leader of a gang. We brought in Whyte's *Street Corner Society* [12] and talked about whether, in fact, there could be any honor among thieves. In other cases we commented on the difficulties of a new foreman, how he missed his old gang and how he could not relate himself in the same way to his new crew and still be an effective supervisor.

The leading reference that you have had on the subject of authority is Chester Barnard's *The Functions of the Executive*. I am sure that some of you have at times found the vocabulary confusing. But what are some of the things that Barnard is saying that have been inherent in our discussions throughout this course? First, what is he saying about the individuals who go to make up any organization? If you look at page 71 of his book, you will see an interesting example, which he takes at random, from a man in the same organization as that with which he was identified until very recently. You will notice that he lists the organizations or groups to which this man belonged at one and the same time, consciously or unconsciously. First, he is "a citizen of the United States, the State of New Jersey, the County of Essex, and the City of Newark—four organizations to which he has many inescapable obligations. Second, he is a member of (2) the Catholic Church; (3) the Knights of Columbus; (4) the American Legion; (5) the Outanaway Golf Club; (6) the Democratic Party; (7) the Princeton Club of Newark; (8) he is a stockholder in three corporations; (9) he is head of his own family (wife and three children); (10) he is a member of his father's family; (11) he is a member of his wife's family; (12) to judge from his behavior he belongs to other less formal organizations . . . which affect what he wears, how he talks, what he eats, what he likes to do, and how he thinks about many things; and (13) finally, he gives evidence of belonging to himself alone occasionally."

Those of you who remember your reading in Figgis's *Churches in the Modern State* will recall that he says something very similar, part of which is:

Membership in a social union means a direction of personality, which interpenetrates it, and, according to your predilection, you may call either an extension or a narrowing . . . You cannot be a member of any society and

[12] Chicago: University of Chicago Press, 1945.

be the same as if you were not a member. It affects your rights and duties, at once limits and increases your opportunities, and makes you a different being, although in many different degrees, according to the nature of the society and the individual member. You are not merely John Doe or Richard Roe, but as John, may probably be a member of the Christian Church by baptism, a Doe by family, an Englishman by race . . . In addition to this you are a member of a school, an alumnus of a college, a sharer in this club, a president of that, and so forth. All these groups and unions have their effect, and limit and develop your life, make you do, or refrain from doing, what otherwise you would not . . . More than that, they penetrate your imagination and your thought and alter not only what you do but what you want to do. Between all these groups there will be relations.[13]

You will see that Barnard, with Figgis, recognizes the importance of the interplay between the formal and informal groups to which any given individual may belong. Much of our discussion has turned around the formal and informal relations of the persons in our cases. Barnard goes on in his discussion of organization to indicate that individuals make certain demands of the organizations to which they belong. Limiting himself to formal organizations for purposes of examination of the functions of the executive, he describes the two types of conditions which any organization must fulfill in order to endure. He calls them "effectiveness," by which he means simply the fulfillment of the purpose for which the organization was formed, and "efficiency," by which he means the fulfillment of the desires of the individuals contributing to that purpose. He says that to be enduring any given organization must meet both kinds of test.

The third thing Barnard discusses is what these first two points mean for the executive. He sums up the functions of the executive, to his way of thinking, as follows:

The first executive function is to develop and maintain a system of communication. This involves jointly a scheme of organization and an executive personnel. The processes by which the latter is accomplished include chiefly the selection of men and the offering of incentives; techniques of control permitting effectiveness in promoting, demoting, and dismissing men; and finally, the securing of an informal organization in which the essential property is compatibility of personnel. The chief functions of this informal organization are expansion of the means of communication with reduction in the necessity for formal decisions, the minimizing of undesirable influences, and the promotion of desirable influences concordant with the scheme of formal responsibilities.[14]

(Break for questions)

Where does all this leave us? What have we been trying to do in our discussions? First, we have been constantly calling attention to the multiplicity of factors in any situation, to the "six honest serving-men" whose

[13] J. N. Figgis, *Churches in the Modern State* (London, 1913), pp. 88–89.
[14] Barnard, *Functions of the Executive*, pp. 226–227.

names were "What and Why and When and How and Where and Who," and the need to look at their relations one to another, to look, in Mary Parker Follett's terms, "not merely at the totalness of the situation but the nature of the totalness." We have seen that there is no simple answer or easy solution to human-relations situations. Secondly, we have practiced a few simple skills of observing and listening in human situations, not only for what a person says and does but also for what he does not say or do and for what he cannot say or do without help. We have looked at the methods used by a number of people. In the Livingston Company case we built up the somewhat corny, but convenient, memory tag, "EARS" for "Explore, Accept, Reassure, and Structure." We tried to develop some useful ways of looking at things and of thinking about them. Thirdly, implicit in all our discussions has been the idea of process: *action* as a process, preceded by diagnosis of the situation out of which it grows; *administration* as a process, not as a series of separate, discrete table-poundings by a high-powered executive in the Hollywood tradition but as a continuous process of routine activities through which, in Barnard's terms, the administrator wins his authority of leadership day by day; *education* as a process, not what Alfred North Whitehead called "the fatal disconnection of subjects" but rather what he described as "the seamless coat of learning which you may not divide"; and finally, *life* itself as a process. Life as a process is generally disguised by the disjointed way in which we customarily describe the life of any given individual. We say he was born in a given year, he lived in such and such a place, he graduated from such and such a school, he took a given job, and he married so and so. Are any of these things important in themselves? The interesting parts of the man's life are completely left out—the process by which he went from one stage to another, the chain on which to string the beads.

Finally, we have been concerned to develop a certain awareness on our own parts of what we are bringing to any situation in which we are participating. We have been concerned to break down the idea of objectivity in human situations in the unreal sense of being the "little man who wasn't there." We have been interested in recognizing our attitudes, our assumptions, our basic beliefs, and seeing how they influence our thinking and behavior. We have been interested in recognizing them in others also. We have observed differences between our attitudes and those of others. That is appropriate. The problem is not to get rid of the differences but to handle them, to keep those of our own that we like and to make them work for us, not against us. In this connection, we have tried to point out the dangers of *overthinking* and *overworrying* human situations. We have made a variation of the plea that Bok makes in his book regarding the law. He describes the law historically as a kind of promise, and he says that the danger in the law today is that the promise will be taken out of it, that it will be nothing but a bludgeon. He says, "There is no plea to be made except to keep the law personal." [15] We might modify that to say that we have no plea except to keep the law in matters of human relations "situational" and to act rather according to the spirit than to the letter thereof.

SUMMARY LECTURE, AUGUST 19, 1949

As you may remember, on the opening day of this course I suggested to you that if we had time I should like to spend a few days discovering what you expected of the course—what your demands were. As the course has gone on, I think most of you have been aware that these demands varied greatly. At one extreme were those who were looking for an over-all theory of human relations. At the other extreme were those looking for practice that would immediately improve their skills in dealing with other people. Neither group, in all probability, feels that its demands have been met. For this I make no apology. Seven weeks is a very short time and nothing less than individual treatment over a long period could reasonably be expected to satisfy individual demands.

Today, however, I am going to review some of the concepts we have been trying to assimilate during the course and also to give you my impression of the meaning these concepts might have for you in your own theory and practice of human relations. This is one person's interpretation. I suggest you take it only for what it is worth to you.

In the matter of concepts, I should like to remind you that we are talking about them in Hendersonian terms. That is, we have been dealing with simple concepts, or as Henderson says in his first lecture,

Not a philosophical theory, nor a grand effort of the imagination, nor a quasi-religious dogma, but a modest pedestrian affair or . . . a useful walking stick to help on the way.[16]

The first concept with which we came in contact in the reading was the highly controversial idea of equilibrium. For convenience's sake I have put on the board an adaptation of a diagram (Fig. 1) from Roethlisberger and Dickson, *Management and the Worker*. I have adapted the diagram to include more than a work situation. I have attempted to indicate something of the time-space thinking about which we have talked by indicating the situation under study at any given time as the situation of "the moment." You will observe that the diagram is a representation of many interdependent forces at work at any given moment in the life of an indi-

---

[15] Bok, *I Too, Nicodemus,* p. 327.
[16] Henderson, *Sociology 23, Introductory Lectures,* Lecture I, p. 6.

vidual. Note that I said "forces at work"—not static, fixed, or rigid, but changing, growing, evolving, alive. In all our cases we saw examples of what a change in any one of these forces could do to the others and to the organism as a whole. We saw also that even the force which we regarded as initiating a change was itself affected by the change, so that simple "cause-and-effect" thinking was no longer very useful to us. Thus the idea of interdependence and multiple cause began to intrude itself in our discussions.

Take for example Danny Keith in the Mu Nu Fraternity case, our very first prepared discussion case. Where did we meet Danny? At the point in his career where he has just been turned down by the fraternity. Where did our discussion take us? We soon found that we could not talk about Danny without bringing in his family or what had happened to Danny in his early life and what had *not* happened. We began to connect these factors with the sense of values that Danny showed in his remarks and with Danny's way of thinking. In the latter we had our first illustration of the tendency to "obsessive thinking" that is, what Elton Mayo defined as "the overelaboration of an oversimplification" in any given situation. We saw this sort of thing repeated in a number of cases, of which perhaps Corelli * is the most outstanding example.

From the beginning of our discussions we were implicitly talking about "groups"—the groups to which people did or did not belong. We were discovering with Barnard, Figgis, and the anthropologists that "in truth, the notion of an isolated individual is the shadow of a dream"—that the individual's association with others has far-reaching effects [indicating the diagram on the board]. As we studied these associations in our case material, the idea of social systems began to emerge. We saw that wherever two or more people are gathered together for any purpose and interact to accomplish it, we had a social system—we had two or more of the intricate individual organisms each with its past and its hope for the future, related to one another in a variety of ways. The relation might be formal, that of the superior and subordinate as, for example, the relation between Mr. Avery and Corelli; it might be that of a team such as the slate splitters in the huts of the Superior Slate Quarry Company.* It might be that of a family such as the Michaelsons † or a doctor-patient relation such as that between Mrs. Stanislaus and Dr. Ware (Osler Memorial Hospital C).† It might be the teacher-student or the interviewer-interviewee relation. As soon as we began to try to describe the relations of these people one to another, we began to raise questions concerning such basic ideas as purpose, authority, leadership, and communication. I should like now to look at each of these in turn.

Concerning purpose, we found that there were at least two kinds, that of the individual and that of the group. This was discussed in Chester Barnard's book in terms of the effectiveness and efficiency of a given organization. It is put perhaps more simply in your reading notes as follows:

Group activities, if they are to be enduring, must fulfill *two* conditions: the reasons for the group's existence must be sufficiently secured and the individuals who contribute their services to the group's effort must secure sufficient satisfactions to make them want to continue their association. It should be clear that the attainment of one or the other of these aspects of a group's activity is not enough, if the group is to continue its existence.[17]

In the reading concerning other cultures, we saw that the practice of the primitives and certain cultures older than our own was to get the social organization straight first, and the economic organization followed. We saw that we have reversed the process in our own time and that frequently the two kinds of purpose—individual and group—are far removed from one another. This results in a growing sense of "aloneness," an idea that was particularly stressed in your reading, notably in Mayo and Eric Fromm. In the case material we discussed this idea particularly in relation to William Fay,† but also found evidences of this feeling in Joe Longman,* Riley Hall,† and many other cases. These cases raised for us the independence-dependence dichotomy and we began to wonder what we meant by being independent.

As individuals in the cases became more and more dissatisfied in their search for individual satisfactions, we saw them direct their dissatisfactions frequently against their superiors—for example, in the Brookmay Machinery Company * and in the case of Nora.** Around these cases we discussed the ideas of what constitutes a good superior. What is authority? We spent one whole class hour covering the board with our ideas about the qualities inherent in leadership, seeing for ourselves that what Barnard calls the authority of *leadership* and the authority of *position* were not always identical.

Douglas McGregor discusses the way in which people in authority bring about a change in a group in terms which he calls "augmentation" and "reduction." [18] He says that the individual in authority may make those below him see the possibilities of increasing their satisfactions by any given changes, or he may so behave that these changes threaten to reduce the satisfactions. In order to be in a position to augment satisfac-

[17] G. F. F. Lombard, *Notes on the Reading Assignments* for Social Sciences 12a and 12b, Human Relations, Harvard College 1948–1949. Distributed by Division of Research, Graduate School of Business Administration, Harvard University, Boston. Assignment II, page 22.

[18] Douglas McGregor, "The Staff Function in Human Relations," *Journal of Social Issues*, IV, No. 3 (Summer 1948), pp. 11–12.

tions, the person in authority needs to be sufficiently familiar with his group so that he knows what these satisfactions are. He needs to refrain from assuming that people want what he feels they should want.

I have quoted to you before from Professor Roethlisberger's article, "A New Look for Management," [19] where he talks about the unwarranted assumptions that people in authority frequently make concerning the nature of the individuals in the organization they are administering. You will remember that he comments on how very common is the "school of thought that assumes a clear order is automatically obeyed; that the logical and lucid exposition of an aim is sufficient for people to accept it; that any change is cheerfully accepted when the need for it is understood as logical." He says that this school feels that all problems requiring people's understanding are solved by the "tell-'em, sell-'em, explain-it-to-'em" technique. This is an example of explaining things in terms of the speaker's viewpoint rather than in terms of the viewpoints of those to whom the communication is addressed. We saw many examples of the ineffectiveness of this sort of communication. We recognized that the effectiveness of any authority has something to do with the relation between the person in the position of authority and those under him. To quote Mr. Roethlisberger's article again:

Without the coöperative attitudes of subordinates, the voice of authority can speak but the big booming noises it makes do not register upon people who refuse to accept it as authoritative.

From this Mr. Roethlisberger develops the point that the executive's job is to administer a social system with a variety of points of view, not to represent only one part of the system. The executive, in his terms, must not only be willing to recognize and accept this viewpoint, but he must acquire skill in the exercise of it.

As we discussed these ideas we began to ask how anyone finds out the things he needs to know about other people's points of view in any given situation. We discovered the importance of listening not only for what was said but for what the speaker cannot say without help or what he does not say. In short, we began to distinguish between "manifest" and "latent content," to recognize intensional use of language. We learned also the importance of accurate observation into the codes of any given group. For example, we saw how useful it would have been to the executives in Brettwood to know what a "party" meant to the "war contract" department. Even with such knowledge an executive may feel he has to violate certain group codes but he does it *consciously*. Thus he is presumably prepared for the reverberations of the violation and tries to prepare the other per-

[19] *Worker Morale and Productivity*, General Management Series Number 141, American Management Association, pp. 11–22.

sons involved in the change. The executive's job, we found, is to administer change. Does he have to do it all by himself? There is nothing that says he cannot use everything at his command. In fact, he will be wise to refrain from playing God. He needs to be very much aware of the distinction between the two kinds of knowledge that you saw discussed in Mayo's *Social Problems*.[20] He needs to be aware of the differences between words and reality. He does not send out blurbs saying "We must all coöperate" with no knowledge of the actualities of coöperation in the particular situation.

We saw that listening and observing of this kind was useful not only in the superior-subordinate relation, but in all relations between people. This leads me to the second thing I want to talk about this morning: how can we use what we have learned in class to develop our own skills in human relations?

Factors in Personal Equilibrium   Manifestations of Equilibrium (Communications, Responses)

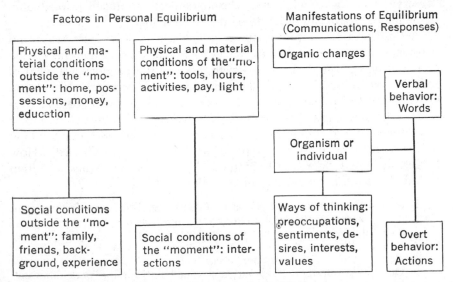

Fig. 1. The state of equilibrium.

We might begin with our relations to ourselves. We have to begin by accepting ourselves. Note I did *not* say by "approving" ourselves or by saying "what a good boy am I." I said by accepting ourselves—by accepting the fact that we are a complicated organism of the sort illustrated in part by this diagram (Fig. 1). We bring to any situation of which we are a part all the factors represented there. If we begin to think in these

[20] Mayo, *The Social Problems of an Industrial Civilization*, p. 16. The distinction is that between "knowledge of acquaintance" (from direct experience) and "knowledge about" (from abstract thinking).

terms, we may see how we are blocking our own progress in human relations. We may find that we do not have to look outside for the difficulties. Alfred North Whitehead says in his essay on "The Aims of Education," "You cannot postpone its [the mind's] life until you have sharpened it." Neither can we stop living a moment while we make up our minds what to do next. By applying some of these ideas to our own behavior we can begin to develop that kind of self-awareness that is the cornerstone of effective human relations.

A second area for reëxamination might well be our relations with others. If we begin to think of them also as complicated organisms, each bringing his own particular "mix" of factors to any situation in which we encounter him; we may begin to get clues as to how to establish effective relations with him. We may see that the assumptions and attitudes we have held concerning an individual do not, in fact, coincide with what we "observe" and "hear" when we take a "clinical" approach toward him. Remember Hayakawa's example of the "churchgoer"? [21]

A third area for review is our relations with words, with books and newspaper accounts and articles. We cease to take them at their face value or at a value we would like to assign to them. In this connection I want to read you two things that have come across my desk during the last couple of weeks in the ordinary course of events. I think you will see that they represent two entirely different kinds of thinking and I think you will have little difficulty in distinguishing the one that is in line with our thinking in this course. The first is a newspaper item dated August 16, 1949, "How to Get Along with Your Boss Explained," by Dr. Lester F. Miles. The item included five *musts* for getting along with your boss.

1. Accept the situation that you are an employee. Your superiors expect of you what you expect of the people under your supervision.
2. Avoid direct challenges. Let your superior see that you respect his position and accept his authority.
3. Don't expect praise from your boss.
4. Don't be a reformer. Find out how your boss likes the work done and try to fit into his way of doing things.
5. Play the game. The back-alley politician cannot command the respect of a good superior.

The second is a review by Crane Brinton, the Harvard historian, of a new book, *The Pilgrimage of Western Man*, by Stringfellow Barr. After speaking very highly of Mr. Barr's analysis, Mr. Brinton discusses what happens when the historian "begins to invade the realm of the prophet."

The historian knows that though human relations are subject to dramatic, even melodramatic changes, they are also governed by certain well-known uni-

[21] Hayakawa, *Language in Action*, p. 219.

formities. Political or social change is as real as change in the weather, and also as unpredictable—but likewise as basically regular. One of the uniformities is that going concerns like nation-states do not change basically overnight, or even in a generation.

It took in Western society somewhere between three to five centuries to outgrow the feudal state—social, economic, and intellectual "necessity" working hard all the time. Even granted the speed-up of modern times, "necessity" will still probably need a century or two to develop a world-state out of the several nation-states.

Meanwhile, of course, the job of the prophet is to help us poor human beings recognize necessity, and to push the inevitable along. Yet one rather regrets that the race cannot handle its great abstract problems with a little more practical resignation—that it has to be confronted so unrealistically with the dilemma of "either . . . or." Either world-government or world-ruin. It is a good slogan, but poor history.

Think over some of the famous formulas of that type: for example, "Fifty-Four Forty or Fight." We got forty-nine and we didn't fight. Do not say this is trivial and world-order is vital. If the trivial cannot throw light on the vital, there is no use in history—or in science.[22]

In concluding, I can only echo Dr. Brinton. "If the trivial cannot throw light on the vital," there is certainly no use in the study of human relations.

[22] *New York Times Book Review*, August 14, 1949.

Final Lecture, Advanced Management Program

RALPH M. HOWER

In the past I have consciously avoided lecturing and have always sought to have you do the talking. As you know, the main purpose of this approach was to develop your thinking and not my own (though my own developed, too, in the process). The case discussions have left us with a lot of pieces which should be put into patterns. It would be better to let you do the work of putting those pieces together. Because of the shortness of time, however, I shall try to do it in my own way. Today, then, I want to point up what seem to me to be the principal ideas which are worth consideration in your work as administrators. You will still have to decide on the full meaning of the material we have covered and the way in which you can put it to use.

I think I am, for the most part, summarizing what has been said by many people in our discussions. Of course, any attempt to pull pieces together inevitably will reflect the personal views of the man who summarizes. Unfortunately, too, this effort puts me in the position of an "authority" who is, in appearance, setting forth "answers" as if there could be general conclusions valid for all situations at all times in all circumstances. As you know, my position is to question such conclusions. I shall sound much more dogmatic than I have any right to be. This effort today I undertake reluctantly at your request, and I urge you not to accept any part of it without a critical examination.

THE PROBLEM OF COMMUNICATION

I wonder if you are aware of the significance to you as administrators of this simple fact: that it has taken a relatively long time for us to reach a common basis of understanding. Here is an important principle of administrative practices at the outset—that effective communication involves much more than mere words, even for intelligent, educated, and experienced people like yourselves; that it is much more than the exchange of logical ideas by means of verbal symbols. This process of understanding, in so far as we have achieved it, has involved a great deal of talking and listening, to be sure, but it also has depended upon our getting well acquainted personally, seeing one another day by day, eating together, drinking together, interchanging ideas both frivolous and serious, and much struggling and sweating through problems of common interest. It has been a long and complicated process, to achieve a small degree of common experience. Remember that long process when you are tempted to formulate a policy or to explain to someone else what you expect of him.

If you are now well aware of the inherent difficulty of obtaining genuine understanding among people, you have come a long way. You will realize that you communicate a great deal by your actions as well as by your words; indeed, that you may communicate a really shattering message by saying or doing nothing at all. That is a disturbing thought, but it is true, and anyone who ignores it will pay for his neglect. Remember Benson and Carlow in the Daycomb case! [1]

Now you understand why I have tried to avoid stating principles which you could note down and take home. Principles are of little value so long as they are mere words. It is the meaning behind these principles that is important; and until that meaning becomes a living part of your thought and behavior, the principles themselves are useless. I avoided saying much in the early part of the course because you would have heard (in the true sense of that term) very little that I said. In the second place, had you heard, you would not have believed me.

You would not have believed me because you would have heard my words in terms of your own feelings and personal situation, and your interpretation of what I had to say would have been far different from what I meant. In a large measure, if you can understand now, it is only because we now have some feelings and experiences in common.

To a considerable extent your understanding of what I have to say today derives from the fact that I have from the outset tried to understand you. It is well to keep that fact in mind as a basic element in communication between people—that if you want others to understand you, you must try to understand them. As a general rule, executives try frantically to have employees understand management's point of view. American business desperately wants labor to love management, but it has neglected its own responsibility in this respect. Communication, under-

---

[1] All the cases referred to in this lecture may be found in the index to Glover and Hower, *The Administrator*.

standing, loyalty—these are two-way propositions. To achieve them you must listen as well as talk; you must encourage subordinates to talk as well as listen. You must try to understand them rather than insist that they understand you. You must be genuinely interested in them and loyal to them, even in trying circumstances, if you expect them to go along with you. At least this seems to follow from our discussions.

This process of understanding others is a difficult one and no one can help you much in achieving the frame of mind essential to its success. It will require hard and continuous efforts on your part. And those efforts will be wasted unless you maintain an open mind and are genuinely willing to consider the other fellow's point of view.

THE CLINICAL APPROACH TO ADMINISTRATIVE PROBLEMS

One of the first things we had to work out together was the extreme complexity of any administrative situation. As you have seen, one is never confronted with the simple relation of a man to a subordinate or a group of subordinates, but rather of a great many relations frequently joined in

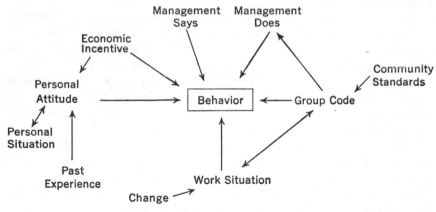

Fig. 2. Influences on behavior.

a network. In consequence we may say that behavior in organizations is the resultant of a great many determinants. To seize upon one or two of them as a basis for action and neglect the rest is to misunderstand the problem and do the wrong thing in its solution.

Let me refer to a diagram of the type I have often used in class discussions. It is somewhat generalized, but it may serve as a reminder of some of the complications encountered in specific situations (Fig. 2). Too often we act as if the only points that mattered were the orders from the top and the economic incentives, and yet it is clear from the cases we have discussed that these two elements are sometimes the least important. The good administrator will analyze each specific situation calmly, patiently, step by step, and not jump to conclusions. He understands that individual facts or actions cannot be interpreted except as parts of a larger picture.

This means looking at what management says and what management does. (Talk and action may be glaringly inconsistent.) It means looking at groups of people, their feelings and attitudes, and their codes of behavior. It means looking at the work situation itself to see, for example, whether people are working on individual operations or whether the work itself involves interactions between people, and so on. It means taking into account as much of the personal backgrounds as one can readily obtain. Each of us brings to any administrative situation his own personal way of looking at things, which in turn is resultant of present circumstances and past experience.

Change in any one of the elements involved is itself a critical item, and so is the way in which the change is introduced. When you view all the facts that you have in relation to the total situation, then—and only then— can you have any conception of their real significance. As I see it, you must always remember, too, that personal feelings are facts to be included in your analysis—both the feelings of the people you are concerned with and those that you yourself bring to the situation.

In passing, let me say again that nobody except a fool expects to get "all the facts." The important thing is to do some hard thinking about the facts at your disposal. The interpretation of facts will never be easy, although one does, of course, gain facility in this respect with continued experience. The point is to form the habit of giving these things explicit attention and not to take coöperation for granted.

You now know that you in this class, intelligent and experienced administrators, have frequently differed in your interpretation of a given set of facts. That difference, too, has meaning. Each of us views every situation in terms of his own past experience and present purposes, in the light of his own personal background and the preoccupations of the moment. Hence, each of us is bound to interpret any given set of facts somewhat differently from the way they are viewed by other people. If you will reflect for a moment, you will see that it is utterly impossible for any two people to view any object or any situation in precisely the same way. Sometimes the differences are of extreme degree. That realization ought to make you hesitate before taking hasty action. That fact ought to shake any cocksure judgments on your part.

Each of us responds not to the "facts" but rather to *his own perception* of those facts. The *perception* is the individual, personal element which varies so widely. That is why it is so vitally important that you obtain, and give careful consideration to, other points of view. That is why it is stupid, softheaded, unrealistic, and often disastrous to act upon your own individual judgment, unsupported by other evaluations.

THE IMPORTANCE OF THE ADMINISTRATOR'S OWN ATTITUDE

Is it not now clear that your own attitude is of primary importance in any administrative situation? It is a basic element not only because your attitude and your own preoccupations are bound to influence your interpretation of events and your thinking about them, but also because these aspects of your own behavior influence people's reactions to you. You will recall how Bryce in the Colebrook Box Company, by regarding the individual workers and their jobs as of no importance, materially increased high turnover and absenteeism; how Mr. Lincoln by his frank honesty and willingness to entertain other points of view has improved the cooperation and sense of responsibility of his subordinates; how Hicks in the Sussex Oil Company spread discontent through all his organization; and how Shannon in the Haig Chemical Company (B) alienated expert and experienced administrators by acting as if he knew the answers and possessed the authority to make decisions.

In short, *you* as an administrator are a very important determinant of the behavior of your organization. What you say, what you do, or what you do not say or do not do—these have an effect which is often far-reaching.

Our discussions indicate, I am convinced, that many administrative actions will be interpreted by various people differently according to the context. In a disturbed organization almost anything that management does (even "good" acts) will be viewed with distrust or worse. In the Postal Retail Company (B), for example, almost any action on the part of Cromwell would be interpreted wrongly until he had achieved a better working relation with his subordinates and until they were convinced of his sincerity. You seldom stabilize an upset organization by introducing new changes. Had Arthur Coleman spent a lot of time in the branch store, as was proposed in class, the staff there might have felt that he was giving them moral support; but they might also have regarded his actions as spying or interference. The moral seems to be that you had better consider carefully the kind of reaction which is likely to follow any moves on your part. It follows that you must be in constant touch with your people and know them well.

While on this subject of the administrator's attitude, let me remind you that the good administrator sizes up his own situation in the organization and gets acquainted with his colleagues before doing much in the way of specific action. He does not assume that they want to have him around or that they will welcome his help. Particularly when one takes a new position, there is a strong temptation to get busy and do something in order to create a good impression. Taking action in the wrong direction is usually worse than no action at all. The wise man quietly finds out first where his help is needed, what others think he might do to fit in. He finds out what the pattern of organizational behavior is before doing much, even though his ultimate purpose and need may be to change that pattern in radical ways. Especially in a new situation he keeps in mind the principle of *less action and more interaction* as a basis for dealing with people.

BASIC ASSUMPTIONS IN ANALYZING SITUATIONS

It is important not only to keep in mind your own personal preoccupations but also to be conscious of the assumptions on which you are operating. The administrator is obliged to act on assumptions in his daily work; there is no escape from this necessity. The trouble is that we are not always conscious of the assumptions on which we are operating; and, when we are conscious of them, too often we do not trouble to ask ourselves whether they are well founded. Obviously, this subject is too big to be dealt with effectively in this lecture. I mention it merely to remind you of its importance and to point out that certain assumptions are concerned with not only what is true or false but also your fundamental philosophy of administration.

Let me set forth one body of assumptions which many administrators have been making consciously or unconsciously for more than a century: [2]

1. That the administrator knows best what should be done and the subordinates do not. It follows that the administrator must make all decisions.

2. That subordinates will do what the purposes and circumstances of the organization require only under persuasion, compulsion, and logical incentives. From this it follows that the administrator, in one way or another, must be constantly driving his subordinates.

3. That the behavior of people in organizations is governed by a single or at any rate a few simple determinants. Consequently, the "cause" of any administrative problem is easy to ascertain and no careful analysis of the total situation is required.

4. That the behavior of people in organizations is governed by explicit logical thinking. Hence, if their behavior is wrong, all one needs to do is to straighten out their logic; you simply tell them clearly what to do.

[2] In what follows I have drawn heavily on some ideas first formulated by my colleague, Professor J. D. Glover.

5. That people usually do not have nonlogical feelings, sentiments, and beliefs. If they do, these nonlogical factors can be ignored, or people can be persuaded by logical reasoning to abandon them.

6. That the only relations that matter between people in organizations are those that are defined by organization charts and manuals.

Time does not permit me to deal with these assumptions in any detail. I want simply to point out that our discussions have cast serious doubts upon them. The limited amount of research that has been done in this area does not support the assumption that people are primarily motivated by economic interest and are logical in their pursuit of that interest. As Mayo points out, on the contrary, "The desire to stand well with one's fellows, the so-called human instinct of association, easily outweighs the merely individual interest and the logical reasoning upon which so many spurious principles of management are based." [3]

This view, of course, is sheer heresy in terms of most of the economic theory that has been developed since the time of Adam Smith. Further, some of you know people who seem to be governed by economic incentives. Indeed the constant striving for wealth has assumed such proportions in the past 200 years that some writers have talked about our present difficulties as the "sickness of an acquisitive society." I think Elton Mayo was closer to the truth when he stated that the real problem was "the acquisitiveness of a sick society." [4] As he goes on to point out, such reliable evidence as we have indicates "that the proportion normally actuated by motives of self-interest logically elaborated is exceedingly small. They have relapsed upon self-interest when social association has failed them." [5] Let me remind you in this connection of the situation in the Lincoln Electric Company. We found there that in probing beneath the surface one could discern a good deal more than mere "intelligent selfishness," that there were motivations which were essentially noneconomic.

Let me state another series of assumptions for your consideration:

1. That the administrator does not necessarily know what should be done. His subordinates may have better ideas. It follows that he should enlist the aid of his subordinates.

2. People, unless discouraged from doing so, will do their best to achieve what the purposes and the circumstances of the organization require. Consequently, they need to be informed about the situation but do not require driving to meet it.

3. Unless they are discouraged from doing so, people will regard their jobs as ends in themselves and as part of their daily lives. It follows that if

[3] Mayo, *The Social Problems of an Industrial Civilization*, p. 43.
[4] Mayo, *The Human Problems of an Industrial Civilization*, p. 153
[5] Mayo, *The Social Problems of an Industrial Civilization*, p. 43.

the jobs are reasonably interesting and responsible, people will try to do them well.

4. That the behavior of people in organizations is related only slightly to logical thinking. Hence, to explain, reason, or argue is of little value by itself in changing their behavior.

5. That people tend to have many nonlogical feelings, sentiments, and beliefs which are of paramount importance to them and hence to the administrator. In consequence, the administrator must be aware of these nonlogical elements and must have some means of coping with them other than logical argumentation.

6. People in organizations tend to draw together into informal groups and subgroups regardless of the formal organizational divisions; in these groups they develop many sentiments, codes of behavior, and social values which they regard as important. It follows that the administrator must be aware of these informal or nonformal structures within the organization and the values which develop around them.

Now these assumptions, too, need verification. When you find that they are in error in any particular case, obviously, you will have to act accordingly. But our discussions have indicated that this second set of assumptions has a good deal of validity. I do not think I need to underline the differences in the two philosophies which are implied in the two sets of assumptions.

Let me say again that the assumptions of the administrator are important not only for their accuracy, but also for their effect on the people involved. Many of you have noted that people behave in about the way that their administrators expect them to behave. The assumptions themselves influence the result. If you follow the first set of assumptions given above, you are likely to get one kind of behavior, and it will probably not be satisfactory. If you follow the second set of assumptions, you are likely to get a different kind of response and one which I think you will find much more desirable. This, of course, gets back to the subject of the attitude of the administrator which I have already touched upon.

GROUP MEMBERSHIP AS AN INGREDIENT OF COÖPERATION

As Mayo and Roethlisberger have so effectively pointed out in their writings, every organization must secure for its members:

1. The satisfaction of their material and economic needs.

2. The maintenance of spontaneous coöperation throughout the organization.

In the subject of Administrative Practices, we have been concerned largely with the latter objective. We have seen that it cannot be left to chance and that it is a complicated and difficult matter—so important that it is probably the chief concern of the good administrator. We have seen that it is effected by work interactions (Stubton, Superior Slate Quarry, Haig Chemical Company A). We have seen that it is influenced by the attitudes and behavior of the administrator (Colebrook Box Company, Gordon, Sussex Oil). We have also observed that lack of communication and the way in which decisions are made have a bearing on it (Calhoun, Lincoln Electric Company, Merson, Daycomb).

Suffice it to say that people get two kinds of satisfactions from their work—economic and noneconomic; that the noneconomic factors are of the utmost importance and that among them are two which stand out: (a) social or human associations on the job, and (b) the nature of the job itself.

As Aristotle pointed out more than 2,000 years ago, man is by nature a social animal. He is born into a situation which involves other people—not only the members of his immediate family but also the community around them. For this reason his relations with other people and his attitude toward them acquire a great deal of importance. The better he can relate himself effectively to those with whom he comes in contact, the more effective he himself will be in his daily life and in general the happier he will be. If for any reason he finds relations with others difficult or is prevented by circumstances from having satisfactory relations with his fellows, he inevitably turns in other directions for satisfaction, either to his own preoccupations or to material objectives. In either case the situation is abnormal, and he is usually unhappy and less effective than he would be otherwise.

Normally all of us seek to be members of some sort of group. As a general rule we find ourselves members of a number of groups, some of which overlap. It is a rare person who can stand isolation. We want to belong, to be accepted by others. Naturally, we tend to belong to groups of people with whom we are associated in some way, either on the job or in outside activities. That is to say, we usually find ourselves members of groups of one sort or another because of associations brought about by the activity itself. For that reason every business organization tends to be composed of an aggregation of social groups, to consist of an informal structure based on personal relationships rather than on the formal organizational setup. This informal structure may be in harmony with the formal structure or it may work against it, and we may be members of the formal organization without belonging to the informal organization. We gain admission to the informal groups and retain our membership in them by conforming to the codes of behavior of those groups—the routines and sentiments which develop within them.

The effective administrator understands that these informal groupings will inevitably take place and are normal and useful, provided he takes them into account. It is only by membership in such groups that the individual can in any real sense belong to the organization. Such entities as "the company" or "the management" are intangible abstractions, and one can only be said to belong to them in so far as he is satisfactorily related to the people behind those abstractions. It is also true, I think, that one can have no sense of belonging in a group which numbers 500 or more people. He can be a member of the organization in the true sense of the word only in so far as he belongs to a small group within the larger structure. The size of that group has never been accurately determined and undoubtedly varies with the situation, but it is of the order of 5 to 20 rather than 50 to 500.

In our case discussion we have seen a number of instances in which group activities and sentiments were a large factor in achieving or failing to achieve the objectives of an organization. In Stubton you saw groupings based on the work situation which management ignored, and you saw how Kay, being a member of two groups, got caught in the conflict of interest between them. In Superior Slate Quarry you saw how the groupings were based on work interactions and how management unwittingly broke them up, isolating the workers on the job and making them miserable as a consequence. In Lincoln Electric you saw how management, perhaps unconsciously, had developed a set of formal and informal groupings and relations which were an important factor in the success of the company and how management instinctively felt the need to protect relations in those groups when a question of disciplinary action came up. As a result the workers themselves handled the disciplinary problems. In the Colebrook Box Company you saw how management organized the daily work in such a way that it constantly disrupted the groups which were tending to form and hence prevented them from achieving any stability. In Peale Manufacturing Company, again, you saw management condemning the one way in which people in the organization were attempting to achieve associations, through drinking coffee together, which they could not enjoy on the job itself.

You yourselves, high up in management, form the sort of groupings to which I have referred. You value them. Such associations undoubtedly are one of the motivations which keep you working hard; and if they are lacking, about all you can do is to yammer for more dollars. You would resent deeply any move to destroy the groupings in which you are members. And rightly so, because we are all human beings with social instincts, not insensitive pawns. I suggest that you will find it wise to foster informal groups and enable them to conform, where possible, to the formal divisions, as Ryan did in Haig Chemical A. At the lower levels you will encourage situations which relate people instead of dividing them, or, if the isolation is inherent in a technical process, you will help the workers concerned to find ways of getting together from time to time within the company structure.

In striving for industrial efficiency, our modern technology has tended increasingly to specialize jobs and processes, to make people individual workers rather than members of teams, and we have generally assumed that there was no need to provide a substitute for the work interactions which have usually been eliminated. Along with this tendency, together with the growth in size of organizations which has accompanied it, there has been a tendency to diminish contacts between management and the workers, to eliminate the natural interchanges which inevitably take place in a small organization. And along with this, again, there has been a tendency to reduce the flow of information to the worker as to the organization's objectives and the reasons for such changes as were imposed upon its members. Thus we have come to regard individual men more and more as machines, to be moved about from place to place, or put together in different combinations at the slightest whim of management. It is really worse than that. We have regarded people as machines which do not require constant lubrication and maintenance.

It is true that we have increased production tremendously thereby (although it does not follow that this increase has come from ignoring human relations!). But we have achieved our industrial output at a terrific cost in terms of frustration, discontent, hostility, and obstruction, at a cost of human spirit which is now interfering with production itself. We have not yet finished paying the bill. I feel sure that a good deal of this cost has been unnecessary, that we could have preserved human values and relations to some extent had we been aware of their importance. When for technical reasons we could not preserve them, we could have provided alternative social interrelations, alternative means for getting people together on the job.

Further, we could, if we wanted to, take into account in our decisions the gradations in informal status that are so important to all of us, whether at management level or at the level of the unskilled worker. Remember the Calhoun case in this connection.

We cannot leave coöperation to chance. We have to give it explicit attention. In a world which changes as much as the one in which we live, teamwork is not likely to emerge unless we consciously and continuously foster conditions which permit it to grow. The cultivation of those conditions is one of your chief responsibilities as administrators. We must work at the fostering of a suitable climate.

DELEGATING RESPONSIBILITY

What I have said about the administrator's job makes it appear exceedingly complicated and difficult. You may well say that the administrator is already overloaded and that these additional burdens are more than he can handle. The answer, I think, lies in a reappraisal of your job as administrators—a reconsideration of the things which are your primary responsibilities and those which you can delegate.

The good administrator, as you all know, delegates unimportant work and handles the important jobs himself. For the most part he gets things done. He does not do them himself. He establishes the quality of thinking in the organization. He sets the pattern of behavior. He selects the main goals and leads his subordinates toward them. In a large organization it is quite impossible for him to consult everyone or to keep in personal touch with everyone; but if he handles himself properly in relation to his immediate subordinates, they in turn are likely to act right in dealing with their subordinates, and so on down through the organization.

I am suggesting that you have been doing the wrong things to a considerable extent and that you should transfer some of the load to others. At the same time I am suggesting that you take up some burdens which you may not have been handling but which cannot be delegated to subordinates.

Let me try to be a little bit more concrete. One of the really tough aspects of the administrator's job is to formulate policies and make decisions—or at least that is a widely held view about his function. I suggest that you should be sharing that load with your subordinates right on down the line, and that you should share this load for several reasons:

1. By getting the participation of subordinates, you are likely to get better answers. The people who have to execute your decisions and carry out your policies know better than you the modifications which are needed to make the decisions work. Indeed, they will know better than you many of the decisions which need to be made.

2. By obtaining the participation of subordinates, you will promote understanding in your organization. Subordinates will come to understand the problems with which you are contending and hence they will see why decisions and policies are necessary. And because they understand the problems and have a hand in formulating the answers, they will understand the answers themselves.

3. Because subordinates have participated in decisions and understand their necessity and purpose, they will accept the answers emotionally as well as logically. That emotional acceptance is essential for good results.

4. Through participation in the decision-making process, they will

develop a sense of belonging to management and a sense of responsibility for what goes on in the organization.

5. By this process of participation—and only by it—can industry develop a succession of administrators capable of managing our industrial organizations. The capacity to make decisions and to take responsibility is not one which is acquired overnight. It must be gained by experience. I am going to expand on this point in a moment.

6. By sharing the burdens of solving problems, making decisions, and formulating policies, you will ease your own load immeasurably, and also you can have more confidence in the results. At the same time you will be strengthening your subordinates.

There is more to all this than meets the eye. Let me read you a quotation from a famous English economist and philosopher:

> In a modern industrial society the fundamental antagonism is not between those who own capital and those who do not, important though that distinction may be, but is between those who take responsibility and manage and discipline, and those who are given no responsibility and are managed and disciplined, and no solution of industrial problems is possible unless that antagonism is removed.[6]

Management has steadily increased its own burden of responsibility and at the same time decreased or eliminated responsibility and thinking in the lower ranks. Is it any wonder that there is a serious shortage of men able and willing to assume managerial responsibility today? Is it any wonder that the people at the lower end of the scale do not understand what is going on and find their jobs uninteresting and frustrating?

That is not all. We tend increasingly in business to concentrate authority and responsibility at the top. Many of you are familiar with the statement of a famous English historian, Lord Acton, to the effect that power corrupts. He had in mind the effect of autocratic power upon the man who possesses it. Recently, we have seen that deterioration in Hitler and Mussolini and we have seen it in other places, in both military and business circles.

I would extend the idea further and point out that the corruption filters down through the organization, infecting subordinates. This kind of situation compels subordinates to curry favor and to resort to all sorts of strategems, devious or otherwise, to influence those in control. The people who make the decisions are many steps removed from the facts, and issues tend to be decided not on the basis of merit but on the basis of influence and personal whim.

Let us put this matter in a still larger context. We are pretty generally agreed that the overwhelming issue today is the struggle between the

[6] A. D. Lindsay, "Organisation of Labour in the Army During the War," *The Economic Journal*, XXXIV, No. 133 (March 1924), p. 77.

authoritarian and democratic ideologies, between a social system in which power and authority are concentrated in the top and one in which the ultimate control lies with the people. When most of us in this country say we believe in the democratic way of life, usually we are talking about government. Can we have democratic government and authoritarian business within the same framework? As I interpret history, business for more than a century has tended to move toward authoritarianism.

I think it is time to reverse the process. This is a serious question, and I am weighing my words carefully. I am aware that there are certain advantages in concentrating authority at the top of an organization. It simplifies matters—for a time. But eventually that system runs into trouble. Let us assume for the sake of argument that you can find an administrator of such infinite wisdom and skill that you can safely entrust authority and decision-making to him and get the best possible answers. That, of course, is an unlikely assumption, but let us assume it for the moment. Where do you get a successor capable of taking his place? It seems to me that you are gambling if you assume that somehow, somewhere, you can find the man with the right capabilities and fit him at once into your organization.

In my judgment, administrators are made, not born; you make them by selecting men carefully, training them, and giving them responsibility. Most of us recognize the validity of this process in the upper levels of management, but somehow we are reluctant to extend it further down in the organization. It is my view that you must extend participation in management right down the line in order to develop this thing we call a sense of responsibility.

In the last analysis a democratic way of life depends upon the ability of people at all levels to be self-reliant, and one gains that quality by experience. To the extent that business has been depriving people of a voice in the management of affairs it has been undermining them and making them dependent. To be sure, I am not proposing that the workers at the lowest levels be confronted with problems which emerge at the top-management level, but there are plenty of problems at the working level in the solution of which they themselves are capable of making a contribution if you will give them the right and responsibility to do so. Please bear in mind that I am talking in terms of both social philosophy and organizational efficiency. In general, good citizens make good workers. What I am trying to say is that business, by striving too narrowly for technical output, has been decreasing the over-all effectiveness of its employees, both as workers and as citizens.

In many of the cases we have discussed, you have seen changes introduced which decreased the skills required of the workers, which made their jobs less interesting (Kay in the Stubton case, the splitting teams in

Superior Slate Quarry, the molders in the Gordon company, the pressmen in the Beacon Publishing Company). We have also seen instances where responsibility for getting things done, especially for making decisions and formulating policy, was taken away from the lowel levels (Postal Retail, and at the executive level in Beaver Personal Finance Corporation).

Some of that process has been inevitable in a rapidly advancing technology, but not all of it. We have reduced the skills involved, taken away participation in planning work and making decisions, and made the individual jobs themselves much less interesting, less satisfying, and less important. Moreover, by a subtle process, we have been degrading the people concerned, depriving them of a sense of responsibility, weakening them in fundamental ways. We in business cannot ignore the impact of what we do to our employees upon their responsibilities as citizens. Indeed, they themselves will not permit us to ignore it. Herein lies much of the strength of the movement toward unionization.

SOME ESSENTIAL INGREDIENTS OF TEAMWORK

Sharing authority and responsibility with subordinates involves risks, to be sure. It seems to me, however, that the risks involved are less dangerous than those inherent in the authoritarian type of business organization. The latter stakes everything on one throw. The alternative way of administration means distributing risks. One is obliged, of course, to take risks in business—risks with people as well as risks with investments. That is inherent in administration.

The suggestions I have made will not eliminate risks or problems, but the administrative practices proposed seem to me to provide a way of dealing with problems effectively before they reach crisis proportions and to provide a means of living comfortably with the risks and problems which are inherent in business.

All this takes time. But does the alternative way of doing business, when you look at it in perspective, really save time? If you add up all the strikes and work restrictions that come from disgruntled people, all the misunderstandings which result from poor communication, all the delays and errors which result from poor decisions and mistaken policies, it seems to me that there is much to be said for taking the time which is necessary for good administrative practices.

We have seen that good communications provide a large part of the answer, good communications down through the organization and back up again, and laterally among people at the same level. In part this is a matter of attitude and behavior, as we have seen, but it is also a matter of free and easy discussion between people, not simply when matters reach a crisis but in everyday relations. By this means emotional pressures are released, problems are talked out before they become acute, and people achieve understanding in ways which will help avoid crises. Talk is a valuable solvent, and it is an important ingredient of teamwork. Coöperation is the result of many things, of many administrative acts which individually are of little importance but which add up to an easy interchange of opinions, ideas, and sentiments. Talking things over frequently is one of the many things which help.

In his last lecture here Elton Mayo lifted up and elaborated a conclusion of T. H. Greene (an important English philosopher of the late nineteenth century), to the effect that will, not force, is the basis of the state. That is also true of other organizations. I am talking now about "normal" situations, not crises. But if the administrator handles himself well in normal situations, he is less likely to get into trouble in times of crisis. You cannot buy loyalty and teamwork, as you well know. The best results come from spontaneous collaboration—from volunteer efforts—not forced contributions. It is the job of the administrator to elicit coöperation, to provide the atmosphere in which the will to do good work will thrive.

I hope our discussions have given you some notion of the many elements that go into the process of eliciting coöperation. Techniques and systems by themselves are virtually useless. Gadgets alone are not the solution. They may help, but behind them must be the right attitude and the right behavior on the part of the administrator. Nor are good intentions sufficient; good will must be backed up by intelligent efforts. You must invest your time and your interest in your subordinates. You must invest something of yourself.

I suppose it goes without saying that in all this there must be genuine sincerity and honesty on the part of the administrator. You can, of course, fool people if you want to. You can do all the things that we have talked about as means of getting to know people better in order to cheat them, to hoodwink them, or to compete better with them. This, of course, is an insidious form of exploitation. For a time it may work. Some men have made money at it. Eventually, I think, it will catch up with you. When people find out that you are exploiting them, you will be through. Quite apart from that possibility, you have to live with yourself; and I do not believe that an administrator can be comfortable with his own conscience and do a good job if he is being essentially dishonest.

No, I think we should get to know people better in order to understand them, to understand them for their own good and ours. In my opinion we have to deal with people on the basis that they are individuals of integrity, with lives of their own, with rights and responsibilities which belong to them and are entitled to respect, even though those elements are related to our own sphere of activities; that we want to understand people because they are worthy of our interest and because out of the process comes *mutual* growth and development.

To this end one must be open-minded but not soft-headed. Tact, diplomacy, and buttering-up people will not get us very far. Nor will we accomplish much by merely giving in to the demands of others. Indeed, some companies are guilty of doing too much for their employees. It is done with good intentions, with generous feelings, but the result is much the same as in the home where the parent gives his children everything they ask for. It may ease an immediate situation, but in the long run it piles up trouble. You might try giving subordinates a chance to plan and earn the things they want, encouraging them to be self-reliant without making life needlessly tough for them.

You must face the facts honestly. We tend to duck the unpleasant issues and the embarrassing problems of personal relations that come up in business, but nothing is solved by ignoring them. You must be willing to consider other points of view, to entertain other ideas, and at the same time to put forth your own. If your ideas are good, they will ultimately stand up. Sometimes if you cannot achieve agreement the best thing you can do is to wait and to talk matters over at greater length. Winning arguments does not guarantee coöperation.

THE PROBLEM IS YOU

In reviewing what I have said, it seems to me that it boils down largely to the question of your own behavior as an administrator. We tend to blame the conduct of others or to blame circumstances or bad luck—almost anything but ourselves. Yet the will and energy acquired to analyze administrative situations depend upon you yourself. The ability to discern pertinent facts and relations and the capacity to discover their meaning likewise depend upon you. As I have pointed out, what you perceive and how you interpret the factors you see depend upon your own past experience and your present purposes. Whether you understand others and communicate effectively with them involves your own social skills and your own willingness to understand others. All this requires patience, self-control, an interest in other people, and a desire to understand them.

And the ability to understand others depends in a large measure on the extent to which you understand yourself. I suspect that one of the things you have gained from the Advanced Management program and from our discussions in this subject has been a better understanding of yourself.

It takes hard work and intelligence to analyze the situations in which you work. It takes patience and determination to hear what others have to say and to fathom its inner meaning. Moreover, you must be willing to learn from others. It demands a genuine interest in your associates and subordinates. It requires a determination to do your own part in understanding them and in relating yourself effectively to them. If you fail, look to yourself first. In many instances the trouble will lie in your own attitudes, your own preconceptions, your own failure to handle yourself properly in relation to others. That is why I say that, in the final analysis, the problem is *you*.

As I think back over what I have been saying, much of it sounds obvious or platitudinous. And yet, as you have seen in many cases, it is the obvious which tends to get overlooked. And platitudes are "bad" mainly to the extent that they are empty—to the extent that there is no reality behind the words. Once we, individually, fill in the verbal symbols with real meaning, they become of value to us.

At best in our discussions we have only scraped the surface, and the end of the Advanced Management program, in a very real sense, is only the beginning for you. In attempting this lecture I have probably done an unwise and dangerous act—unwise, because I have attempted to cover so much ground and hence could only hit the high spots; dangerous, because the summation of these matters may tempt us all to stop thinking about them. I earnestly hope you will use this material, if you use it at all, as the rough framework that it is, and that you will continue to work on this subject and think about it.

No one expects you to do a perfect job, but, by being aware of the importance of little things like attitudes and relations and by giving attention to them, you can, I think, improve your batting average. Judging from my own experience, you will find that your awareness and skill will improve as you take an interest in people; that by giving more heed to administrative practices you will become more effective. Not only that, but your job will somehow become more interesting and more satisfying. You cannot control the circumstances in which you work, but you can do something about your own attitudes and your own behavior. Again, it is up to you.

Vandercook Chain Stores, Inc.
Case and Discussion

EDMUND P. LEARNED

This is the story of Stanley Kendrick, a recent graduate of the Business School. This problem came to me unexpectedly in connection with a research field trip. Names and places are disguised, but the facts are genuine and unchanged. This case was used in May 1949 in the final examination of the course in Administrative Practices. The comments quoted come from examinations written by Section A, which I read. These statements stimulate one's thinking about the case situation. I have ordered but not altered them.

I shall present the case and the students' suggestions for action, leaving to the reader the final decision.

The company involved was the Vandercook Chain Stores, Inc., a concern whose name may suggest both stability and reliability, but will not indicate what kind of chain it is, thereby protecting the organization.

Following the sudden retirement of the previous president for reasons of health, the board of directors of Vandercook Chain Stores, Inc., brought in Mr. John Thorp to assume the presidency of the company. Mr. Thorp was regarded as an "outsider" by many of the "old-timers" holding important positions in the company. Soon after taking over his new job, Thorp brought in Mr. Ernest Underwood to be controller. Underwood was also regarded as an "outsider" by the "old-timers."

Some time after Underwood joined the company, he was asked by Thorp to take charge of a study of the operation of the real estate department. The real estate department was headed by Francis Vincent, an "old-timer." Mr. Vincent, as head of the department, had held the title of vice president for the past ten years. The study of the operation of the real estate department was to be made by a "task force team," the members of which were to be drawn from both the controller's department and the real estate department. Vincent assigned Joseph Wilson to represent the real estate department on the "task force team." While Wilson was a younger man, he was generally thought of as being an "old-timer." A partial chart of the formal organization of the company is shown in Fig. 3.

We shall not hear much more about Mr. Thorp. All we know is that he is new, that he brought in the new controller, and that both are regarded as outsiders by the old-timers. When Thorp decided to order an investigation of the real estate department, he appointed Underwood to

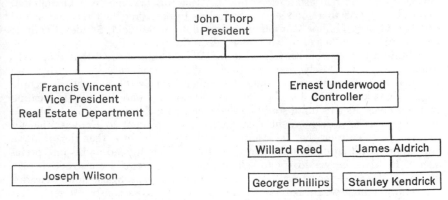

Fig. 3. Partial organization chart, Vandercook Chain Stores, Inc.

take charge of the study. Vincent, the old-time head of that department, might have inferred that he was on the spot, or that he could not be trusted with a presentation of his operations to the new management. In any event, the situation could have been a delicate one.

Ernest Underwood delegated responsibility for direct leadership of the "task force team" to James Aldrich, one of his key subordinates. Aldrich was a rather quiet man, and both Thorp and Underwood had high opinions of his ability. In addition, Underwood asked Aldrich and Willard Reed, another of his key subordinates, each to assign one man from their respective sections to the team. According to office "scuttlebut" in the controller's department, Reed was disappointed that he had not been selected for the leadership of the team. Aldrich assigned Stanley Kendrick, a recent graduate of the Harvard Business School, to the "task force team"; Reed assigned George Phillips. Stanley Kendrick and George Phillips, along with Joseph Wilson, were thus chosen to be the working members of the "task force team" constituted for the study of the operations of the real estate department. The study was to be reviewed by Ernest Underwood and Francis Vincent before being submitted to Mr. Thorp.

Note that the balance of membership of the task force team favored the controller's department. However, Joseph Wilson, representing the real estate department, was an old-timer in his department. Real estate was further "protected" by the provision for a joint review of the recommendations by Ernest Underwood and Francis Vincent prior to submission to the president.

Aldrich met with the three men who were to make the study. The four of them talked over the situation freely and divided up the work of preparing the necessary data. They agreed, among other things, that the data in the controller's department which related to the real estate department were scanty, and that most of the data which would be used were on records kept rather informally by the real estate department. After this first meeting, all felt that the study was "off to a good start." According to the agreement reached in this meeting, George Phillips soon left to gather data in the field. Stanley Kendrick and Joseph Wilson began to work together in the home office.

Within a few days, both Kendrick and Wilson came to feel that they were working together closely and effectively. Wilson was very coöperative and obtained facts from the real estate department which the controller's people did not even know existed and which they would have had difficulty in locating by themselves. As a result of studying these data with Kendrick, Wilson obtained some ideas as to a proposal he thought he might present to Francis Vincent. Wilson told Kendrick that he wanted Kendrick's assurance that the proposal was sound, and that he thought that if the two of them agreed on his interpretation of his data he would try to sell his ideas, as part of a constructive plan for the real estate department, to Francis Vincent. Wilson also told Kendrick that he thought it would help Vincent to come up with a constructive plan for his department.

As we shall see later, the simple, important facts in the immediately preceding paragraph have been subject to considerable differences of interpretation by people who have read the case. Kendrick and Wilson were apparently getting along well, exchanging ideas freely, and probably exhibiting mutual respect. Wilson showed his loyalty to the task force team by coöperatively uncovering facts which the controller's department did not know existed. As a result of studying these data with Kendrick, Wilson began to conceive ideas for a proposal he thought he might present to Francis Vincent.

The reader may wish to decide for himself at this point whether he thinks Kendrick should have encouraged Wilson to go ahead with his plan to present a plan to his superior affecting the operations of the real estate department. Numerous students felt that this action on Wilson's part vitiated a strong, coöperative task force attempt at a solution, and some of them criticized Kendrick for joining with Wilson in the study of such a program. Other students have suggested that Wilson owed an obligation to keep his boss informed and if possible to induce the task force group to accept the program sponsored by his boss. In other words, protection of an old-timer in a group dominated by newcomers was a requirement of his position. Some argued, in addition, that the best way for a new management to reassure the old-timers of their proper place in the organization was to give the latter full credit for any proposals which they made.

The next two paragraphs of the case describe the crisis.

Wilson left his data and a draft of his program with Kendrick for study. While studying the data and the proposal in his own office the next morning, Kendrick was called to the telephone. At this point Phillips came in, picked up the data, and looked at the three points in Wilson's proposal. As soon as the call was over, Kendrick explained to Phillips that these data and program points were loaned confidentially by Wilson for study purposes only. Kendrick told Phillips that Wilson wanted to discuss his ideas with his vice president before placing them formally before the "task force team." Kendrick asked Phillips to forget that he had seen Wilson's paper and to respect Wilson's request. Kendrick also told Phillips that he was sure Wilson would bring the matter up with the team at the right time. Phillips presumably heard, though he made no formal reply.

Late that same afternoon Kendrick went into Phillips' office to confer with him. While Kendrick was there, Phillips' boss, Willard Reed, came in to talk to George Phillips about the "three points" Phillips had mentioned that morning. These points were the three points of Wilson's proposal. Reed said he wanted additional data because Underwood, the controller, planned to talk with Vincent, the vice president of the real estate department, about the points before going home that night.

These two paragraphs led to considerable speculation by students writing upon this problem.

The case finishes as follows:

Kendrick was much irritated by what he observed. He knew that both Phillips and Reed had reputations in the office of being "eager beavers." The die, it appeared to Kendrick, was apparently cast because Underwood had an appointment with Vincent. It seemed to Kendrick that he had to decide at once what action, if any, he should take.

It should be recognized that Kendrick had to decide either to do nothing or to take some sort of action, and probably within fifteen minutes to half an hour.

The majority of the men agreed that Kendrick had a right to resent some of the interpretations which Phillips and Reed apparently had placed upon the actions of Wilson and Kendrick. The view of many men is well summarized in this quotation:

"Needless to say, my first reaction is one of immediate indignation; placing myself in Kendrick's position, I'm quite sure the question would be immediately discussed.

"Immediately I feel Mr. Kendrick should inform both Phillips and Reed that the paper was simply a confidential draft written for study purposes. How much he can say or how much good it will do to talk at length with the two men is a question that can't be answered; however, it is doubtful if they would be prone to listen. His first action, nevertheless, is to emphasize emphatically, but as coolly as possible, that the proposals were prepared by Wilson for Mr. Vincent and were given to Kendrick merely for study and comment. This behavior that I am recommending to Kendrick is necessarily prejudiced by my own reactions to such an incident. A betrayal of confidence such as has occurred justified an immediate expression of disapproval. Perhaps this wouldn't be the smoothest way to deal with the occurrence, but a forthright expression of opinion is necessary when dealing with such an incident."

Other men thought that "eager beavers" were likely to be irritants. Several pointed out in contrast, however, that the very fact that Kendrick felt that Phillips and Reed were eager beavers may have been an indication of what he himself was; in other words, he was describing other people in terms of his own conduct.

Numerous students made interesting recommendations for immediate reflection by Kendrick. "Kendrick," one man said, "should take a walk around the block to give his emotions a chance to calm down from their present boiling temperature. He should check his facts to be sure he doesn't blow a slight misunderstanding into a major crisis." Another student put the matter in a slightly different way: "Kendrick should sit back, review the situation, see if he has any preconceptions or has made any snap judgments which are clouding his mind and giving him a biased line of thought." This same gentleman suggested that "Kendrick should do nothing in action to widen the gap between old-timers and newcomers, and that whatever action he did take should be to bring the parties together." Another man recommended that "Kendrick slow down and not jump to the conclusion that Phillips had stolen the information and is not a man of any integrity. It is quite possible that he had asked Wilson for permission to display the program to Reed, and the least Kendrick had better do is to ask Phillips whether he had received such permission from Wilson."

Other comments were: "Kendrick might do well to sit down after talking with Phillips, Wilson, and Aldrich to watch events as they occur. He has a lot to learn and can best keep his eyes and ears open and his mouth closed." "He should realize that he was relatively new in his own department and that his coöperation with Wilson might be regarded as pro real estate and anti controller's group." "And since he is in the controller's department with both Phillips and Reed, he must not do anything which will incur their ill will, thus damaging future relationships and creating a bad situation for everyone. Bad feelings might easily spread to other departments, and the whole organization would be in an uproar. Such things do happen, often, and over just such trivial things as this."

There was a wide range of proposals for action. Few men recommended doing nothing. They realized that Kendrick might take the view that his or others' reputations and relations with co-workers had been damaged, but that efforts at complicated repair might make the situation worse. They understood that he could refuse to coöperate with Phillips and Reed, thus permitting them to "stew in their own juice." Phillips was in a strategic hole of his own making and might only get out of it with the help of Wilson, to whom it would be necessary to confess. This course, however, could damage the relationship and mutual respect of Wilson and Kendrick.

As one man said, "Kendrick is in a pretty tight spot, one which would make him right cross. He has just witnessed Phillips and Reed trying to 'steal thunder'—to get the three points to Underwood first, so that they will receive the credit in Underwood's and Thorp's eyes for the work of the task force team. Such a move on their part will also alienate Wilson, the one who has made the biggest contribution of all to the team.

"Wilson, I believe, was a good administrator in this situation. After thinking up the recommendations (and, after all, he should have thought them up, because he was the most familiar of the three with the operations of the real estate department), he wanted to present them to his boss alone, thus to make Vincent aware of the fact that the proposals had come from within the department, and had not been suggested from without by the newcomers. Wilson, I think, had enough common sense to see that this was the easiest and most practical way of getting the proposals adopted—in fact, the only way of getting them adopted without *hard feelings.*"

Another person said: "Wilson's action is commendable and shows complete loyalty to his boss. His attitude was most coöperative and constructive and I admire his actions in not playing his cards close to his chest even when his office was involved. He was honest in his motives and actions.

"The actions of Reed and Phillips now, by throwing the proposals at Vincent from the controller's department rather than telling him they came up through his own department via Wilson, threaten to wreck the acceptance of the entire scheme. Perhaps Reed's pique is his reason for taking the attitude he does."

It is possible to group the suggestions for action around the following: (1) Should Kendrick talk to Wilson? (2) Should Kendrick get Wilson and Phillips together? (3) Should Kendrick go to Aldrich? (4) Should Kendrick speak to Phillips? The list does not exhaust the possible solutions.

A large number of students thought Kendrick should go to Wilson to confess his dereliction in revealing confidential material. Others excused him for it because of the phone call at the time Wilson picked the information up and the warning given Phillips which Kendrick presumed he heard. Nevertheless, they thought "Kendrick should explain what happened so Wilson may contact his boss, Vincent, before the latter's conference with Underwood. This would protect Vincent's enthusiasm for the departmental plan."

Views on why Kendrick should talk to Wilson varied widely. Some strategists believed the incident provided the opportunity to find out "whether Wilson intended his plan to be his own or *the* task force plan. They thought Kendrick could do little more than ask, since he was new and Wilson was senior to him." "If it was to be a team plan, now was the time to throw it into discussion with Phillips and probably Aldrich." Such a move, moreover, might give Phillips a chance to suggest a delay in the Vincent-Underwood conference.

A few men doubted Wilson's good faith and thought "he might have been trying to cover for the real estate department by a red-herring plan."

Two men stated their objectives for the conference with Wilson. One said: "Kendrick's purpose in talking to Wilson is to prevent the incident from damaging coöperation which is needed. The talk may help to minimize friction between Vincent and Underwood and the two departments." The other thought: "Kendrick should not incite Wilson against Reed and Phillips," and Kendrick "should not play the role of informer."

Whether Kendrick should start the conference by asking Wilson if he had briefed Phillips, and possibly Vincent too, or should start by confessing the "theft" of the confidential ideas represented the extremes of student suggestions. Some hoped that Wilson would advise Kendrick about desirable future steps for him within the controller's group.

One student thought Kendrick should forget any idea of getting Wilson and Phillips together. He said: "Kendrick cannot work out the situation by himself. His action in splitting the task force was one of the major causes of the friction, and further attempts at leadership from below would only compound the trouble. Kendrick has made the mistake of failing to recognize the feelings and attitudes of his fellow workers and has attempted to take much of the 'task force' responsibility upon his own shoulders."

Another man said: "Kendrick and Wilson have excluded Phillips from the task force and have not analyzed the data he may have collected. The proposal is not the decision of the whole team and Aldrich has been left out of the picture." He did not explain how Phillips could have worked with the team while he was on the road collecting facts or how they could analyze his facts while he was gone. The point of the man seems to be that team members have to be treated as such at the earliest and at *every* opportunity. They must share information quickly and unreservedly with each other and argue out conclusions. "This was a task force in name only." Another student said: "Kendrick faces the problem of two members of the team who are still working for their old superiors rather than for the team." However, as one man put it: "They will be reporting to their superiors long after the task force is dissolved."

The conflicting views which the men expressed regarding the task force reveal that Kendrick's problem is not too simple. One student said, "Phillips reacted as any man would. He left the office having faith and confidence after the conference with Aldrich because he believed they were all working toward a common goal. Then when he returned to the office, he finds the other two members of the group have been planning a report to the exclusion of himself. Up to this point he was all right—in that he was perturbed at seeing what had gone on in his absence. He should *not*, however, have told Reed about the three points. He should have gone to Wilson and inquired as to how the 'operation' task force was progressing. Then perhaps this entire misunderstanding could have been avoided."

One man suggested that "sending Phillips to the field alone and having a team behind may have meant 'shoving him out of the team.'"

Another fellow stated the break-up of teamwork this way: "Kendrick must realize his and Wilson's error—that they have violated the purpose of the team and have acted selfishly. He must *now* admit to Reed and Phillips that they (Kendrick and Wilson) have not *coöperated* with Phillips. He must tell that Aldrich and Vincent know nothing of the three points and that the points are merely an idea which has not been talked over by the working part of the 'task force.' With this admission, he must then ask Reed for a day (or the necessary time) to discuss the plan with Phillips and Wilson."

We can close the discussion of Kendrick and the task force by one final quotation: Kendrick "seems to be working with two men who have very little moral obligation to their fellow workers. It is an 'all-for-me' attitude."

There have been so many references indicating that Kendrick had taken too much responsibility for informal leadership of the task force upon himself, that we should consider whether the current incident is the one to use to reëstablish the leadership of Aldrich.

The principal reason given for seeing Aldrich is to keep him informed. It might be embarrassing to him (albeit to Reed as well) to have Underwood ask him why Reed was reporting on matters assigned to Aldrich for study. Conferring with Aldrich, Kendrick could obtain advice regarding any next steps he should take, or Aldrich might determine to take the matter out of Kendrick's hand entirely.

Students differed regarding what to ask of Aldrich. One said: "Aldrich is responsible for the operation of the team and it is his duty to get Wilson, Phillips, and Kendrick together to suggest a unanimous plan. Kendrick should suggest to Aldrich that an immediate meeting of the team be held. The suggested procedure at the meeting is to accentuate a team decision as opposed to individual opinions. Phillips should be mollified to the extent of insuring that Kendrick and Wilson include the consideration of his data. It is true that Wilson may still regard Phillips's action with disfavor, but it is considered better to air grievances at a meeting on this comparatively low level at once, rather than have the matter go through department heads and thereby increase the feeling between subordinates."

Two other principal approaches of Kendrick to Aldrich were proposed. The first was to ask him to go to Reed suggesting that he have the meeting canceled. Aldrich would make no comment on the "eager beavers," would not inform the boss about their indiscretion or misunderstanding; he would make it easy for them to "get out of the hole." He would rely on their "sense of guilt" to furnish any remorse that the situation calls for. He would let them teach themselves whatever lessons there were to be learned from the events. As one man said, "He lays a foundation stone for better relations in the future."

The second suggestion of the men was to have Aldrich arrange a meeting of Vincent, Underwood, Reed, Phillips, Wilson, Kendrick, and Aldrich. Other men thought such a meeting would be premature. A variation of this proposal was to induce Aldrich to give Underwood enough information to make it possible for him to decide to call off the meeting; or having called it, divert it into a general discussion of progress of the group without attention to specific proposals for action. If Vincent and Wilson wanted to bring the three points into the meeting, the opportunity was provided and the choice was theirs.

Many reasons for Kendrick to talk to Phillips have already been given. One student summarized this point of view as follows: "While to Kendrick there may seem to be only one answer, double cross, I can think of several possibilities and am sure that there are others which, when explained, are perfectly logical but which I would never have thought of. Depending on the actual facts, Kendrick might take any of a dozen programs of action . . . The simplest, least complicated way for all concerned would be to go to Phillips and, without emotion or appearance of prejudging or passing judgment during the conference, view the events to date. If Phillips has jumped to the wrong interpretations of events, he will have a chance to see it and to initiate action which will forestall further misunderstanding. If he originally acted in a malicious manner and his 'sense of guilt' is at work, he may wish *now* to make moves to straighten the situation out . . . This would be good for him and make for better relations between Wilson, Reed, Aldrich, and Phillips. Even Kendrick might assume that Phillips was well intentioned and had made a mistake through a misunderstanding of events." Another man argued that "this method gives Phillips the opportunity to do the right thing, that is, give Reed better facts on the current status of task force activities. Reed, alone, or working with Aldrich, could endeavor to induce Underwood either to cancel the conference or make it a general survey of progress because the task force had not completed its deliberations. Reed would merely explain that a decisive type of discussion was premature. This method would keep friction, ill feeling, and possible prejudice at a minimum."

In the background, however, lurks the large number of men who believe that a scoundrel should be "told off" and shown up. Thus, if Phillips failed to respond to the opportunity presented above they would have Kendrick go next to Reed, and, if necessary, over him to Underwood. The majority of men, however, felt that Wilson should have a chance to react before the matter got to Underwood and they agreed that Kendrick should go to Underwood only through his superior, Aldrich.

I close with one final student quotation. "How should Mr. Kendrick approach his particular problem? It seems to me he must pattern his decision taking into consideration three major questions. How will my action affect people within my department? How will my action affect other departments? How will my action help alleviate the present over-all strained relationships with the new management and benefit the company as a whole?"

What Is an Unsatisfactory Examination Paper?

STEPHEN H. FULLER

Once examinations have been given and course grades recorded, there begins that procession of students to professors' offices to voice mixed feelings of shock and surprise summed up in the statement, "I don't see how I could possibly have failed." For the student who has received a failing grade, probably no response by the instructor will be entirely satisfactory. Indeed, the instructor often cannot point to any one thing and say it caused him to write "Unsatisfactory" [1] across a student's blue-book. While he can show the student a sentence here or there which merited different treatment, or suggest factors which should have been considered but were not, it is usually difficult for him to distill out the ingredients which gave the paper the tone of an unsatisfactory performance. As a subjective activity, grading cannot be justified in objective terms.

In courses employing the case method of instruction, the examination itself is a case, or a series of cases, typically accompanied by two such general questions as: "What is your analysis of the situation described in this case? What action, if any, would you recommend?" Even these questions are considered by some instructors as being unnecessary after students have been exposed to the case system for a time. The final examination in the first-year course at the Harvard Business School called Administrative Practices has, on occasion, consisted of the examination cases without any questions whatsoever. Since every student in the case type of examination has the same material with which to work, and the questions, if any, give him almost unlimited scope, whether his examination is considered to be of passing or failing quality is largely dependent on how the student perceives and then handles the case material.

[1] The term applied to student work at the Harvard Business School which is not considered worth a passing grade.

What does constitute unsatisfactory handling of such case material on an examination? In the hope of throwing some light on this question, I have reviewed a set of final examinations of students who had recently completed one year of Administrative Practices. I gave special attention to those papers which received failing marks.

The particular examination I studied consisted of three separate cases, the first of which was made available to students a day in advance. The other two cases were distributed during the examination period. The first case was distributed early because the instructors wished to see what a student could do when he was required to record the understanding of a case which he had been able to develop after discussing it with other students and considering it overnight. The instructors wished to see what a man could do with the second case when he was required to work independently on a case with ample but not unlimited time (two hours) for analysis and reflective thought. The instructors wished to see what a student could do with the third case when time limitations (one hour) required that his response be largely determined by his habitual way of thinking rather than by the kind of analysis and reflective thought made possible by an extended period of time. The examination was "open-book," that is, the student was permitted to bring and use any material he desired. A written announcement about the examination, including a statement by the instructors concerning their purposes in designing the examination was issued to each student about two weeks in advance. Student questions arising from this announcement were discussed as raised in the remaining regular class meetings.

The examination papers were graded by the instructors who had taught the course. The identity of the student was unknown to the instructor. The three answers of any one student were not graded consecutively. Instead, instructors read a number of answers to the first case before considering the second case. One of the reasons for this procedure was to prevent any possible carry-over of impressions formed on reading the first answer from coloring the evaluation of subsequent answers.

A careful review of examinations receiving failing grades has led me to form two conclusions concerning such papers: (1) there were striking similarities among the answers in *all* the failing examinations; (2) with very few exceptions, there were no observable differences in the quality of the three answers *within any individual book* which received a failing grade. I shall attempt in the remainder of this paper to set forth the observations that led to these conclusions.

THE APPROACH TO THE MATERIAL

Students whose work was graded "unsatisfactory" tended to approach the case material in one of three ways. Most of them gave a literal and unqualified acceptance to all statements in the case. For example, no discrimination was made between the relative significance of two such case statements as, "The president asked the sales manager to determine if better forecasts of sales could be made available," and, "In the opinion of the planning and procedures manager, the divisional sales managers had been employing 'delaying tactics.'" The latter statement was not considered by the student to be indicative of an *opinion* by the planning and procedures manager—a "fact" to him, but not necessarily "true." Instead, poor papers *assumed* that the opinion was a fact, "true," "concrete," "real," observable by all. And on this assumption (which was never stated as such) students proceeded to blast the divisional sales managers because they *had* been using delaying tactics.

Accepting as facts all opinions expressed in the case regardless of how much they differed, the student who thus failed to discriminate soon found himself trying to add apples and pears. The result was that while he tried to evaluate first one opinion and then another, he found that he was unable to "make any sense out of this messed-up situation." The pieces of the jigsaw puzzle would not fit together. Written page piled on written page as the student resorted finally to a "rehash" of the case itself— almost entirely devoid of analysis or evaluation except for occasional futile speculation.

A smaller group of students, while recognizing opinions expressed by people in the case to be just that and nothing more, summarily rejected all such opinions as being of no value for analytical purposes. Students who followed this course, in contrast to those who gave wholehearted acceptance to all case statements, were generally explicit about their rejection of all opinions expressed in the case. "This is, however, only a statement in his own words and, therefore, should be *fully* discounted." "There is no such thing as impartial evidence away from the line of authority." "These are just opinions—an *objective* picture which I can deal with is not given in this case." [2]

Whether the students treated opinions as facts or dismissed them entirely, in neither case did they see the possibility of using these opinions together with other information in the case to throw light on the behavior of the individuals concerned in the situation.

[2] These three sentences and all subsequent quoted material were taken in substance from the failing examination books studied, except where otherwise stated.

The third approach to the case material characteristic of failing work will be no surprise to those who have taught by the case method. "Not enough information is given in this case to be able to do anything with it" was one way in which a student begged the question of attempting an analysis at all. Instructors recognize the right of students to raise questions concerning the lack of facts which they believe to be significant.[3] However, better students did not stop with a mere plea for more facts. They indicated specifically what further information they desired, why it was significant to the problem, and how they would have gone about obtaining it.

Whichever of the three inadequate approaches to the case material the failing student used, he demonstrated that he could not read in a discriminating and meaningful way.

THE LANGUAGE AND THOUGHT OF THE FAILING STUDENT

In addition to showing in his answers that he could not read, the failing student betrayed the fact that he could not write, that is, select and use words with discrimination and meaning. Throughout his entire examination book, the student's use of language was clumsy and ineffective.[4] Time after time the student resorted to the use of words which he had heard in class discussion or had seen in outside reading, but which gave no real meaning to the situation at hand. The supply of examples was almost inexhaustible: "The problem is a lack of communication"; "The problem is one of coördination"; "Insecurity is the problem"; "There is no concept in this company of the context"; "Bilateral communication is lacking"; "This must be accomplished tactfully," or "diplomatically," or "informally," or "indirectly," or "gradually"; "They have no social feelings"; "They need to consider the human aspects"; "A high level of morale is essential to an organization that depends on coöperation among groups—this is the key point"; "I recommend that they arrive at meaningful understandings"; "The conditions for good communication must be established"; "This company should achieve efficiency."

While there is nothing necessarily wrong with these phrases *per se*, standing alone as a statement of a problem or as an answer to one, they have no meaning. Better papers recognized this fact. If the phrases were used at all, they were explained by the way in which they were related to

---

[3] That students will raise such questions seems to me inherent in the case method, for the case writer attempts to present no more of a situation than was evident to the people in it at the time. One of the lessons of the case system is that decisions often have to be made even in the absence of all the facts.

[4] The failing student's general difficulties of expression were often intensified by poor mechanics which interfered with the intelligibility of the answers.

the specific facts of the cases. In the best papers these words, as such, did not appear at all.

A related, and perhaps more serious, weakness in the language selection of the failing student was his constant reiteration of expressions which revealed a stereotyped way of *thinking* about human situations. Among the expressions that occurred most frequently were: "This foreman is the egotistical type," or "the perfectionist type," or "an unfortunate personality," or "a psychopathic case," or "a problem child," or "a big 'I.' " This worker "has a persecution complex," "is a self-integrated personality," "is not the type who can head a group," "has a case of ego-consciousness," "is a maladjusted personality," "has the kind of difficult temperament that is hard to get along with." One student, apparently hoping to give his answer an authoritative ring, described an executive as being "the exact kind of man whom Professor Fritz Roethlisberger would classify as an 'obsessive-thinking type.' " (Another example of inability to read?)

Presumably the student who uses the language of stereotypes to describe his thinking believes that by so doing he is explaining something or someone in the case situation. Actually, he is doing nothing more than labeling or classifying the material in a way that has significance only to him, or to others who would assign their own meanings to the stereotypes of the student. At best, such labeling describes the case in generalities and ignores the individual differences which make the situation unique. Since the emphasis of Administrative Practices is on considering each case as an individual situation before making generalizations, students whose answers consist only of categorizing problems have missed the chief point of the course.

It has been my experience that the majority of students substitute such labels for analysis in the classroom at the beginning of the course. Phrases such as "the average worker" and "the typical company" early identify themselves as being among the most used tools of the beginning student. However, after but a few hours of class discussion, some students begin to raise the questions which eventually spotlight the faulty thinking underlying the labels themselves. "In what way is Joe an average worker?" "From whose point of view is this a typical company?" "What do you mean when you say, 'He isn't the *type* for that kind of job?' " These are difficult questions to answer for one who has thought for most of his life in terms of his own preconceptions. Before many weeks, stereotyped expressions absent themselves from the class discussion. Even those students who resorted to them most often at the beginning are quick to challenge the labeling technique when it is used by one of their classmates. But the kind of thinking lying behind the label seems to remain even though verbal expressions of it disappear. For under the pressure of the examination, some students revert to the same patterns of language and thought which they followed the first time they participated in a class discussion.

Still another observation that can be made of the failing student is that he characteristically thinks in terms of limited alternatives. In both his analysis of a case and his recommendations for action, he is generally explicit that it is "either/or." For example: "The case gives no indication of the girl's problem. It is a case of sexual misbehavior or drinking." To this student, "the girl's problem" could not possibly have been both—or any one or all of a hundred other possibilities. "This case raises an age-old problem: whether company efficiency or worker happiness will be achieved." Company efficiency and worker happiness are apparently incompatible. "If the defect lies in her home life, tell her to forget it and to profit by the experience. If the defect lies within the worker, the *only* recourse is to dismiss her." Here the student not only limits himself to one of two possible analyses, but still further limits himself to one course of action in each case! Again by the very nature of his "either/or" thinking, he implies that there could be no relation between "the defect within the worker" and "her home life." Thus most failing students do not see case situations as being complex or multifactored. Instead they follow simple cause-and-effect analyses which almost invariably are oversimplified. "The solution is simple: either fire him or make him establish positive relationships."

Combining his "either/or" thinking with his inclination to label, the failing student almost always discussed action taken by the principals in the case as being "good" or "bad," or "she is clearly *to blame* for the situation" and "he is *not at fault.*" The failing examination is one of blacks and whites with very little gray in between.

If the student feels compelled to assign such definitive plus's or minus's to individuals and to events described in the case, must he not have a standard of values by which he judges human situations? What are the components of this standard which underlies his thinking? At first reading, this standard is often not clear to the reader. Possibly the student assumes that his reasoning will be self-evident, perhaps that such reasoning is even unnecessary. More probably, however, the student is not even aware of the values which he himself holds to be true and which he applies in evaluating the actions of others. If the instructor could but more clearly understand the student's implied standard for judging administrative action, he might be much closer to understanding the student himself. Is this understanding to be denied the teacher? Not if the student's paper is read carefully for the purpose of determining by what standard the student is judging a human situation. For the student generally sets forth quite explicitly and forcefully what I have chosen to call his "principles" of administrative action.

THE FAILING STUDENT'S PRINCIPLES OF ADMINISTRATIVE ACTION

The following principles have been taken directly from examination answers of failing students. They were set forth by the student as accepted, universal truths. The only changes that I have made in restating them were to substitute occasionally the word "administrator" for the various executive titles—"the president," "the sales manager," "the personnel supervisor,"—which the student used. I am particularly interested in this list of principles, since in no way were they related to, or apparently influenced by, a year in the Administrative Practices course.

Principles Concerning the Role of an Administrator:

1. "An administrator who lacks power and authority is inefficient."
2. "A good administrator should exercise the authority of his position."
3. "A good administrator should act informally."
4. "A poor administrator is generally guilty of a lack of supervision over those working for him."
5. "A good administrator does not just let his subordinates do what they want to; he should give them his recommendations and then check up to see if they are being followed."
6. "An administrator specifically outlines the tactics and procedures to be followed."
7. "An administrator should always keep a check on the progress of his team."
8. "A good leader is one who takes the initiative himself."
9. "An administrator should give his subordinates a specific program of action as well as a deadline."
10. "An administrator should 'take over and see to it . . .'"
11. "An administrator is not paid to be a mere spectator; he should take action."
12. "A good administrator keeps close tab on all workers under him."
13. "An administrator must control his department and maintain respect."
14. "An administrator should not allow family problems in the office—definitely."

Principles Concerning Superior-Subordinate Relations:

1. "An administrator will not incur the criticism of his subordinates, regardless of what he does, as long as he stays within the formal channels of the organization, but he will definitely incur their criticism, no matter what he does, if he departs from formal channels."
2. "When a subordinate criticizes a superior it is always embarrassing."
3. "Giving approval to a subordinate's suggestion constitutes a threat to a superior's position."
4. "Only equals or superiors can make executives listen."
5. "Leaders resent subordinates making suggestions."
6. "No supervisor should take time from regular duties to talk to subordinates."
7. "It is bad taste for anyone to interrupt his boss."

8. "No one can admit a mistake to either subordinates or superiors without weakening his authority."

Principles Concerning Line-Staff Relations:

1. "Line and staff people are two different types of people."
2. "People who don't get along well as line officers should be made staff experts."

Principles Concerning the Nature of Coöperation:

1. "When people refuse to coöperate, they should be put in their place by taking a stiff attitude toward them; this will convince them of the futility of their own absurd stand."
2. "The supervisor should have notified the people in his department to coöperate."
3. "Normally, if a person gets a good explanation of the need for something, he should be willing to coöperate."
4. "A foreman refuses to coöperate and seizes authority away from other foremen only when the others are incompetent."
5. "A supervisor develops coöperative relationships by being a friendly pal; but he also must be the top dog so he can influence the relationship."

Principle Concerning "Communication":

"When orders and directives are put in writing, they will be understood and carried out."

Principles Concerning Status:

1. "By resisting changes, men in a company will be able to preserve their status."
2. "When a formal leader is appointed he has status; an informal leader has no status."
3. "Any administrator will fear any temporary loss of status for it will become permanent."
4. "Supervising women has far less prestige than supervising men."

Principles Concerning Age and Seniority:

1. "Old bosses—in age or seniority—are naturally opposed to new concepts."
2. "If by any chance the supervisor's behavior is changeable, and this is practically impossible since he has been with the company for 24 years . . ."
3. "He cannot change his attitude. At age 44, reëducating him would be impossible."
4. "Older people and younger ones often cannot get along because they are so different."

Principles Concerning Promotion and Criteria for Promotion:

1. "After a 'certain time' in any job, one should be promoted."
2. "A company does not promote anyone unless he is qualified."
3. "If a man cannot delegate responsibility, give him a job that is so big that he has to."

4. "If a man considers only a few factors in making decisions and thereby creates unrest, advance him to a position where he is responsible for all factors; he will then consider them all."

Principles Concerning the Emotions of People in a Work Situation:

1. "Since this foreman is technically competent, naturally all other foremen resent it."
2. "She doesn't really want what she says she wants because no individual would want more monotonous work, less status, and less money."

Principles Concerning Women:

1. "Women are always inquisitive."
2. "Unmarried women are emotionally unsettled."
3. "There is a natural resentment by men as providers of a household against women workers."

Principles Concerning Time as a Factor in a Situation:

1. "Two hours is too long to listen to any complaints. All objections should have been overruled short of two hours."
2. "Five men have worked two months on the report; therefore, it must be good." (Could this reflect the student's feeling about his own work? "But I spent hours studying for this exam!")

In my opinion, most of these "principles" of administrative action represent a fairly consistent point of view, one with another, and with the either/or thinking and labeling tendencies of these students. This is particularly true, I believe, of the principles dealing with the role of the administrator. They also represent to me a philosophy of authoritarianism, centralization, and bureaucratic control which is diametrically opposed to the philosophy of the Administrative Practices course. And yet these principles represent the thinking of a number of different students. Thus, they stand as striking testimony to the prevalence of such principles and to the tenacity with which they are held.

Failing students were so concerned with enunciating their own principles that they often used the cases only as an incidental means by which to illustrate those principles. And many of the same principles were made to apply in all three cases on the examination. (They stood the test of consistency.) Better students, on the other hand, examined the material carefully to determine on what basis administrative action was being predicated in the particular case under consideration and to evaluate that action in terms of their analysis of the case.

The Failing Student's Concept of Action. More sharply than in any other respect, the failing students' recommendations for action differentiated their examinations from those of the better students. In almost every case, they felt there was an urgent need for immediate action to be taken. "It is imperative that something must be done, and at once." This is, of course, consistent with the principle that "an administrator should give . . . a specific program of action *as well as a deadline.*" Usually the students' recommended action was directed at overcoming the opposition of an individual or of a group to a change. In each case, the failing student *assumed* (1) that the proposed change was "good"; (2) that the opposition was not justified.

In almost all cases, failing students went on record as believing that there were only a limited number of definite, definable alternatives for action which could be pursued. They usually selected one of these courses of action and gave it decisive and unqualified endorsement. Such support was not lessened even when the action they proposed was inconsistent—at least to this reader—with their own previous analysis.

Student's analysis: "The general sales manager has by-passed his divisional sales managers; this has created an impasse." The same student's recommendation for action: "The president should tell the general sales manager that he by-passed the divisional sales managers; *the president* should then apologize to the divisional sales managers for the mistake of the general sales manager." (Thereby by-passing the general sales manager?)

Student's analysis: "This girl doesn't feel a part of the work group, or of any group. She is even willing to take a cut in pay to get away from the group." The same student's recommendation for action: "The manager should tell this girl that a productive day's work is expected for the pay she is receiving. He should cite her responsibility to her group of fellow workers." (When the girl wants to get away from the group?)

Student's analysis: "He doesn't delegate enough responsibility." The same student's recommendation for action: "As his boss, I would tell him he has to delegate more responsibility to his subordinates." (Thereby remedying one error by making a similar one at a higher level of organization?)

In those cases where the failing student did not give unqualified support to *one* course of action, he went to the other extreme by qualifying everything he wrote to the point where it was meaningless to the reader. Occasionally such a student graded his own paper by concluding that "I doubt if any of these suggestions would do much good. Probably not."

The *point of view assumed* by failing students in taking action was of interest to me. Almost invariably they identified themselves with the individual described in the case who had the highest position in the company. This was true in each of the three cases about which they wrote. In several instances, students ran entirely off the organization chart in assuming the identity of the *superior* of the highest person (organizationally) described in the case. One student who did this gave his reason: "Only by being someone out of the picture can I be objective." Another student stated his choice as being predicated on the following basis: "I am assuming I am the president because he has done nothing I would not do."

One student who had originally identified himself as the president of the company interposed a personal point of view as he wrote:

I realize that business is not a psychopathic clinic, but I have been in the situation where some sympathetic help would have done wonders for me . . . If a fellow human being can be helped and I have the *position and power* [5] to do so, it is my duty, and all people's duty, to do so. I have taken a personal role in this case since it touches the heart, not the head.

But in his recommendation for action this student shed the personal role and, unaware that he was revealing his own ambivalence, declared: "If rough treatment is needed, the president should fire her, but never look back."

Does the student who wishes to avoid personal involvement find an escape in identifying himself with the top administrator in each case—an administrator whom he feels to be protected by "position and power"? By such identification, does the student fulfill his own definition of the administrator's role as being one in which the administrator should "take over and see to it," "take the initiative himself," "control his department," "exercise the authority of his position"?

Another general comment can be made with reference to the action proposed by the failing student: he spelled out in great *detail* what should be done. A part of one answer illustrative of such detail may be of interest to teachers on another count—its striking resemblance to the traditional idea of a classroom discussion:

What [the division manager] should do . . . is to list all the objections . . . on a blackboard. When all of the objections have been listed they should be examined point by point. Any [valid objection] . . . should be referred back to the working group with instructions to modify the plan in some way to get around these objections. Any objections which do not appear to be valid should be discussed in such a way as to show the [objectors] that it is not a good objection . . . The meeting should then break up with instructions to the working group to work out any valid objections . . . [If the lesson is not learned in class, a homework assignment is in order.] Another conference can be held and perhaps the [objectors] will be more reasonable this time.

The various *forms of action* suggested by failing students were, like their administrative principles, not peculiar to only a few answers, but permeated a number of different examinations.

[5] Professor Fuller's italics.—Ed.

Action One: Operate on Individuals—Transfer, Promote, or Discharge

(1) "Replace or transfer this supervisor, or replace or transfer the other people."
(2) "Diplomatically and tactfully transfer him."
(3) "Move him into an office by himself."
(4) "Promote him to a technical job where he will have no administrative problems."
(5) "Promote him to a staff position in the main office; he cannot handle a line position because of his inability to deal with people."
(6) "If they continue to object, fire them all."

Action Two: Operate on the "Paper" Organization

(1) "Revise the organization chart."
(2) "The organization chart is not followed in the modes of operation. The latter must be made to follow the former."
(3) "Put in writing his *exact* duties and responsibilities; do the same for his department and for the company as a whole."
(4) "Set up a formal job of 'assistant supervisor.' "
(5) "Expand the personnel department."
(6) "Post special rules for employee conduct."
(7) "This company should adopt a policy of putting all notices to supervisors and workers in writing."
(8) "The company should keep a strict record of all infractions of rules to have evidence to prove employees guilty when they want to dismiss them."

Action Three: "Tell 'Em, Sell 'Em, Explain It to Them"

(1) "The recalcitrants must be told to accept the changes and to coöperate."
(2) "Get them to respect the ideas of their subordinates."
(3) "The only hope of changing their attitudes is to use facts and figures. The argument must be rational."
(4) "This supervisor should be made to understand that he must get his ideas accepted."
(5) "The president should explain the setup to the worker. Then he should repair the relationship between the worker and her supervisor by telling the supervisor that the worker now understands what we are all working toward."
(6) "The superintendent should explain why the company uses women."
(7) "The president should insist on bilateral communication."
(8) "The president should see to it that his division managers contribute ideas."
(9) "Sell the plan to them since the company's efficiency depends on their attitude."

Action Four: Exercise Line Authority

Many students recommended that the case problem could be resolved through the "use of line authority." This term was used in an almost mystical sense. While no student described exactly what he meant by the term, each seemed to have great faith in it as a cure-all. What the student had in mind when he used the term becomes clearer, however, in light of other statements such as: "Moral support from the president (line) should help the manager *suppress* any objections and *impress* [6] upon the group the futility of its opposition."

Action Five: "Dear Hearts and Gentle People"

Lip service was given to what the student *believed to be* the philosophy of the Administrative Practices course in the form of:

(1) "Sympathy requires that she be given another chance though it's really not desirable to do so."
(2) "Humane ways and kindly efforts should always be tried before cracking down."
(3) "If the plant were nonunionized, I would fire her. However, since the union is in control,[7] I would transfer her to keep the union steward happy." [8]

Action Six: The Interview

The failing student often employed "an understanding, nondirective interview" in the hope of achieving the results he desired. In so doing, he indicated an alarming misconception of the listening orientation, for his "interview" was neither "understanding" nor "nondirective." It was always interviewer-oriented with the interviewer holding the reins at all times for his *own* purposes. Either (1) he talked, explained, advised, or clarified for the person in difficulty and thus "changed" the latter's attitude and behavior, or (2) he listened to a point where he had enough "information" or enough of the person's confidence, or both to do (1). More than once it was emphasized that "just listening" was neither a form of action nor a form of participation. Innumerable quotations from student papers could be given. A few will suffice:

(1) "The interview would be used to get the people resisting change to clarify their arguments; once clarified, the arguments could be disposed of one by one."
(2) "I would let him talk to me until I have his confidence. Then I would gradually try to get across to him the problems of the company by getting his advice on my day-to-day problems. This will inculcate in him a better understanding of how to handle people."
(3) "We should listen to her in order to get her attention. When her attention is gotten, the manager should recommend: (1) that she see a psychiatrist; (2) that she move away from her family; (3) that she realize that her supervisor has been kind and good to her."
(4) "In an interview, the manager can reorient her to what he knows is best."
(5) "Let her talk. If she doesn't want to talk, I would tell her that any more actions will be grounds for her dismissal."

[6] Professor Fuller's italics.—Ed.

[7] This was not a fact. The only fact given in the case was that a union represented the employees in bargaining with the employer.

[8] This statement betrays the student's belief in expediency as a guide for action. Other examples could be cited.

Action Seven: The Conference

The conference as a method of resolving differences also received the especial comment of students. One of the examination cases described a conference among company officials during which differences over the adoption of a proposed plan for forecasting sales and inventory requirements had been enunciated. These differences had not been resolved after two hours of discussion. In reading the analysis of one student, I was impressed with the applicability of his views concerning the conference to a class discussion in Administrative Practices.

I'm not inclined to think that two hours [9] of apparently fruitless discussion is a good investment of time. I think this speaks badly for the leader of the discussion [the teacher?], who *apparently* is Mr. X because he started the meeting by asking who was going to report. [The student appears to be somewhat reluctant to ascribe leadership position to Mr. X simply because he initiated the discussion. Many instructors in Administrative Practices begin their classes by asking, "Who would like to open our discussion today?" In student-centered case discussions the responsibility for the continuation of the class rests primarily upon the students, not the instructor.] The leader [the teacher?] should have recognized that an impasse was being reached . . . and narrowed the talk down to some manageable segment. Perhaps it would be possible to reach agreement on part of the recommendations, and then negotiate the others, with Mr. X [the teacher?] being both moderator and final judge on each little point. [The teacher should tell the students which answer is "right" and which is "wrong"?]

The discussion was heated, and when it is heated and emotional, it is difficult—for me, anyway—to think rationally. [I could not think in the cross fire of a class discussion?]

A formal leader [a *real* teacher?] would have kept enough respect so that the meeting would not have developed into the discussion it did. [The teacher should control what is said in class?]

I think that the leader [the teacher?] should discuss the report entirely. [The teacher should lecture?] I do not think that personal observations should be allowed to enter. [Feelings are not valid; stick to the "facts"?]

What can be done? (1) If an impasse has been reached . . . call in the president and let him give a decision. [If the teacher won't give the answer, the dean of the school should?] (2) Mr. X can duck and tell another manager to decide. [Get the answer from some other teacher?] (3) Mr. X can really step into the thing and make a decision. [The teacher could give the answer if he would?]

If I were Mr. X [the teacher?] and liked the participants [the students?] pretty well, I would omit plan 3—and at least keep my friendships secure. [Students would resent the teacher's "stepping into the thing"? The teacher or student who gives his "answer" will lose the friendship of students who do not agree with him?]

After two hours of discussion, I might be inclined to side with Mr. X [the teacher?] but not to the extent of actually forcing a decision. [The student should try to side with the teacher, try to anticipate what the teacher wants—but beyond that the student should avoid making a decision?]

[9] Administrative Practices classes are scheduled as two-hour meetings.

I think I would then go over the points to reach some agreements and leave the other points for someone else to decide. [Let someone else think through the case?]

It is always dangerous to impute to someone else's words, expressed in one context, meanings in another context. Therefore, my interpretations of this student's comments may be grossly unfair. However, to the extent that his views were expressed as being applicable to any conference, and not exclusively to the conference described in the examination case, they may be applied to a classroom conference on a case. Given this student's views of the responsibility of a conference leader and given his personal difficulty in "thinking rationally" when a discussion is "heated and emotional," is it any wonder that his examination indicated little, if any, growth from a year of education by the case method?

Action Eight: "Ad Prac" the Situation

Sometime after the first six weeks of classes each year, students begin to make an interesting distinction between the meanings which they assign to the words "Administrative Practices" and the bastardization, "Ad Prac." These expressions are used to characterize two different kinds of behavior in the handling of human situations. The first signifies to most students mature and responsible action based on an understanding of the relations involved. The second is the term they give to any suggested action that smacks of "soft-soaping," "apple-polishing," "flattery," or generally insincere behavior directed toward getting another individual to do something that the latter does not want to do. Despite the fact that "ad prac-ing" is challenged whenever it occurs in class discussion, examples of it are to be found throughout the failing examinations.

(1) "X should give all the credit to Y for developing the plan in order to get Y's support, *even though* X knows that he, and he alone, thought it all up."
(2) "This motivation should be handled very carefully so that they [those opposing the change] will believe they thought of it themselves."
(3) "I will *induce* [10] in the three managers a desire to do what is wanted."
(4) "I will tell him how well he is doing [when, in fact, he was not doing well], give him hope of a promotion, but won't let him be aware of the trick setup."
(5) "I will praise him to win his confidence."

While most of these students apparently make such statements in good faith and out of true ignorance of what we are trying to teach, a few are frankly aware of the implications of their suggestions. For example, one student, referring throughout his examination to his plan of action as a "scheme," concluded: "The scheme will show whether they can be 'brought round' or not; *it does not solve their efficiency as administrators. Here is the essential point . . . he who understands the techniques is in control*[10] [of the behavior of others] . . . these managers I want to have every chance to learn [what I believe they should learn?]—if not, I must recommend their retirement." Such statements as this are clearly the result of something more than any one course. To determine their origins would entail more study of the "whole student" (e.g., his background, experience, ethical values, etc.) than the classroom situation permits.

SUMMARY

A review of all of these inadequate forms of action reveals that they have two things in common. First, they treat a small and limited area of the case which the student chooses to call "the problem," but never show an awareness of the need to consider the administrative process which is set in motion by this problem. For each of these limited problems is an occasion for the exercise of administrative behavior. It is the nature of this administrative behavior—*the process by which is determined* (1) *what is to be done, and* (2) *how it is to be done*—which is of particular interest to Administrative Practices. Failing students usually discussed what they thought should be done in fairly forceful terms. But their action was directed toward resolving "the problem" and *not toward improving the administrative process* by which the problem and the innumerable ones to follow it could be more effectively resolved. They miss not only the part that the administrative process plays in the solution of problems, but also the part a faulty one may play in the creation of them.

Second, the failing students' forms of action rested primarily on authoritarian solutions which violate the entire spirit of the course.

CONCLUSION

This review of failing examinations has pointed up to me the complexity of the teaching problem in this area of human relations. The student's habitual ways of thinking, feeling, and acting as well as his mode of expression all present problems to the instructor. And the way the student thinks, the way he feels, the way he acts—all are deeply imbedded in his pattern of behavior long before he enters the classroom. Under the pressure of an examination, the poor student relies upon them practically entirely and to the exclusion of what he may have appeared in class discussions to have learned.

In his personal affairs as in his business life the student will have to make many decisions "under pressure." To the extent that an examination warns both the student and the teacher of the likelihood of the student's reverting under pressure to rigid ways of thinking, preconceived ways of feeling, and authoritarian ways of acting, the examination can serve as a useful educational tool.

[10] Professor Fuller's italics.—Ed.

A Group Discussion of the Dashman Company Case

JOHN D. GLOVER

About Christmastime 1951, a second-year student at the Harvard Business School told an instructor engaged in the first-year course, Administrative Practices, that he and about a dozen other second-year students, whom the instructor had had in class the previous year, would like to meet regularly with the instructor to discuss cases in the area of Administrative Practices. This student pointed out that there were, for example, a number of cases in the case book they had used in the first year [1] which had never been taken up in class. He said that the men for whom he was speaking would like to discuss some of those cases and perhaps others which had been prepared recently at the School. The instructor expressed a lively interest in working with such a volunteer group of second-year students. But he questioned whether second-year students really had the time to spend on such a project in view of the work load of second-year courses. The instructor went on to offer the advice that, before undertaking this venture, each of the men concerned should thoroughly appraise his own situation to see if he really could take the additional time for this "outside" activity. In particular, the instructor advised that each man should not only assure himself that he was "on top of his job" as a second-year student, but that this additional activity would not interfere with his getting the most out of the work for which he had a formal responsibility. The spokesman said he would relay the advice back to the other men.

In February 1952, shortly after the beginning of the second term, this same spokesman and another student each informed the instructor that the group of students were now ready to proceed with some case discussions if the instructor were still willing. Accordingly, a group of about a

[1] Glover and Hower, *The Administrator*.

dozen men and the instructor set a time which seemed to suit all concerned. The discussions usually ran for more than an hour and a half, and sometimes for more than two hours.

In anticipation of a conference on Human Relations to be held at the Harvard Business School, April 3–5, 1952, the group was asked whether they would be willing to have one of their discussions transcribed. They agreed. By further agreement, they selected the Dashman Company case from among several short cases for the purpose.

The discussion was recorded by an engineer of the Lowell Institute of Boston on magnetic-tape recorders loaned by the Institute for the purpose. The discussion began promptly at the hour agreed and ran for about two hours and ten minutes. In the following pages are reproduced the first fifteen minutes of the discussion, fifteen minutes taken from somewhat less than half-way through the discussion, and the last half-hour.

THE CASE [2]

The Dashman Company was a large concern making many types of equipment for the armed forces of the United States. It had over 20 plants, located in the central part of the country, whose purchasing procedures had never been completely coördinated. In fact, the head office of the company had encouraged each of the plant managers to operate with their staffs as separate independent units in most matters. Late in 1940, when it began to appear that the company would face increasing difficulty in securing certain essential raw materials, Mr. Manson, the company's president, appointed an experienced purchasing executive, Mr. Post, as vice president in charge of purchasing, a position especially created for him. Mr. Manson gave Mr. Post wide latitude in organizing his job, and he assigned Mr. Larson as Mr. Post's assistant. Mr. Larson had served the company in a variety of capacities for many years, and knew most of the plant executives personally.

One of Mr. Post's first decisions was to begin immediately to centralize the company's purchasing procedure. As a first step he decided that he would require each of the executives who handled purchasing in the individual plants to clear all purchase contracts which they made in excess of $10,000 with the head office. He felt that if the head office was to do any coördinating in a way that would be helpful to each plant and to the company as a whole, he must be notified that the contracts were being prepared at least a week before they were to be signed. He talked his proposal over with Mr. Manson, who presented it to his board of directors. They approved the plan.

[2] Reprinted from Glover and Hower, *The Administrator*, pp. 653–654.

Although the company made purchases throughout the year, the beginning of its peak buying season was only three weeks away at the time this new plan was adopted. Mr. Post prepared a letter to be sent to the twenty purchasing executives of the company. The letter follows.

Dear————:

The board of directors of our company has recently authorized a change in our purchasing procedures. Hereafter, each of the purchasing executives in the several plants of the company will notify the vice president in charge of purchasing of all contracts in excess of $10,000 which they are negotiating at least a week in advance of the date on which they are to be signed.

I am sure that you will understand and that this step is necessary to coordinate the purchasing requirements of the company in these times when we are facing increasing difficulty in securing essential supplies. This procedure should give us in the central office the information we need to see that each plant secures the optimum supply of materials. In this way the interests of each plant and of the company as a whole will best be served.

Yours very truly,

Mr. Post showed the letter to Mr. Larson and invited his comments. Mr. Larson thought the letter an excellent one, but suggested that since Mr. Post had not met more than a few of the purchasing executives, he might like to visit all of them and take the matter up with each of them personally. Mr. Post dismissed the idea at once because, as he said, he had so many things to do at the head office that he could not get away for a trip. Consequently he had the letters sent out over his signature.

During the two following weeks replies came in from all except a few plants. Although a few executives wrote at greater length, the following reply was typical:

Dear Mr. Post:

Your recent communication in regard to notifying the head office a week in advance of our intention to sign contracts has been received. This suggestion seems a most practical one. We want to assure you that you can count on our coöperation.

Yours very truly,

During the next six weeks the head office received no notices from any plant that contracts were being negotiated. Executives in other departments who made frequent trips to the plants reported that the plants were busy, and the usual routines for that time of year were being followed.

DISCUSSION: [3] THE FIRST FIFTEEN MINUTES

Instructor: Well, who would like to start our discussion today—or maybe I should say, who would be willing—who would be willing to start our discussion?

[3] This discussion of the Dashman Company case was recorded on tape on March 21, 1952. The names of the participants have been disguised.

Student S: There are a few aspects I found somewhat interesting in this case. I'm not too sure at the very beginning of the case, as outlined in the first paragraph, that there is a clearly evident problem. I'm not too sure that the man they brought here—uh—Mr. Manson—uh, Mr. Manson—is president—Mr. Post, is clearly aware of what this problem is and what the magnitude is. But just assuming for purposes of discussion that there is some problem, I looked at Mr. Post in a situation in which he had several factors to deal with. Let's say that there is a scarcity of some of the items that he is going to be purchasing and procuring for the company as one of the factors in this situation that he is faced with. He also is faced with meeting the aims and objectives of this company and also with working through the personnel—uh—that are presently responsible in this work. And I find in that last area of working with the personnel that he—uh—did not consider the effects of his actions upon them at all. He went up to Mr. Manson—uh—with his original idea, and it was O.K.'d by him, and it was O.K.'d by the board of directors, but he didn't go down and consider what the effects of this action would be upon the individual purchasing agents who had originally had quite a bit of autonomy in their operation. And I think that in many ways he may have somewhat destroyed—uh—the concept these individual purchasing agents might have had of themselves. He was destructive of their self-concept. And in that way he might not get the coöperation that would be needed—uh—in a program, if there was a clearly evident need. And I just wonder as to what regard Mr. Post has for the individual in this situation by not considering what his needs are or what their reactions would be to any action he might take.

Student C: Do you figure their reaction was bad? As shown by what was done here?

Student M: Was there any reaction?

(*Several voices.*)

Student M: How about the last paragraph, "Executives in other departments who made frequent trips to the field . . ." saw that nothing was happening—that everything was going on as it was before.

Student A: The thing that bothers me is how do you know that they aren't going along with this because maybe there has been no contract for more than $10,000 negotiated?

Student S: Well, the thing that bothers me about this is the fact that Post was in a position of having to work with people and that by sitting aloof from them and never going down and meeting them, never discussing with them, never finding out their problems, never even testing one or two to see how they might react to any of his administrative decrees, he went ahead and acted. Well, to me this appeared acting without regard to these individual needs of the people with whom he was going to be working and without too much regard for the individuals themselves. He seemed to be more preoccupied with a problem, in quotes, which I am not even too sure existed and certainly wasn't very clearly outlined here.

Student B: Nothing is hurt here by this letter, because they wrote back a lovely reply saying that "we're doing just exactly what you told us to and we think it's a good idea." The company is going along just fine. Nothing is being changed.

Instructor: "This suggestion seems a most practical one. We want to assure you that you can count on our coöperation."

Student H: I think that is a significant word: suggestion. It shows that —uh—there is a distinct difference between the letter Post sent out and the letters he got back—the typical letter he got back. He is asking for something. I think he is asking for two things. Look especially at the second paragraph, saying, "I am sure you will understand." Now he wants one thing—"I'm sure you will understand." I don't know quite what he wants us to understand. And then he has an "and."

"I also want you to"—"I'm also telling you about the fact that I'm going to coördinate purchasing."—uh—Then he gets back a letter saying—"Your suggestion"—apparently about purchasing—"seems to be a good one."

Instructor: You're picking up the word "suggestion" here?

Student H: Pardon?

Instructor: You're picking up the word "suggestion" rather than, for example, "your order."

Student H: Yes.

Student B: Well, it is in fact an order. It says "will" up here in the letter.

Student H: That's why I picked up the word "and"—see that word "and"?

Student A: I think it's a misprint. If you take it out, it reads better. (*Laughter.*)

Student J: Don't you feel the word "suggestion" is merely a diplomatic way of replying to a superior?

Instructor: Does it seem diplomatic to refer back to an order of a superior as a "suggestion"? (*Laughter.*)

Student J: Remember this is a civilian organization.

Unidentified Student: This is what?

Student J: A civilian organization—in a civilian organization sometimes you get away with those things. (*Laughter.*)

Student A: In the Service you can be more defiant? (*Laughter.*)

Student J: That is a very interesting point to me in the fact that this new appointee refers his proposition to the president and to the board.

And the president and the board were not sufficiently acquainted with the way their company was operating and with the feelings of their various purchasing agents to discover what seems—I believe each one of us sees as an obvious error in the way in which this man has handled his—uh—human relations problem with his subordinates.

Student H: Wouldn't you say he is making decisions in a vacuum?

Unidentified Student: Yeah.

Student J: It might be, but I would think if the board of directors and the president were on top of their job they would have seen right through it in a second.

Instructor: If they understood their own organization—and what this thing meant—they might not have approved it?

Student J: That's it.

Unidentified Student: Oh—

Instructor: They might have suggested something else instead?

Student J: Well, they would have seen what feelings would be generated.

Student B: Oh, I think . . .

Student J: I think for one man to sit back for a week or two as is indicated, is a short time to me and to go ahead, and then put out a bold order requiring—taking away some of the autonomy from the individual purchasing officers in these various plants.

Student E: Are you suggesting, then, that what he should have done is go out and take a trip around to these 20 plants and—uh—build relationships with—uh—20 purchasing agents and then thereafter get all their acquiescence with this program and then come back and—and consolidate—

Student J: Whether he had a trip or whether they had a conference or whether he asked for recommendations, or however he did it, I think that there should have been some buildup to such an order, or at least some evidence of consideration of their problems so that there was a feeling of working together between the plant purchasing officer and the vice president for purchasing. There is no evidence here of their working together outside of this rather—uh—"diplomatic" communication we have at the end of the case, which is as much as saying, "Well, O.K., but don't count on it."

Student H: Are you suggesting, that Post's efforts are not so much misdirected, as not well managed, I mean . . . and that he doesn't communicate well?

Student J: Shall we say that the whole venture was poorly launched.

Student H: He started off on the wrong foot?

Student J: I believe so, yes.

Instructor: In what way was it poorly launched? Obviously we're making some judgments here. What is it that we're judging? What is the nature of our judgments?

Student J: I think he has been most directive in his approach to his subordinates who don't know him from Adam, don't know why he was put there, don't know anything at all about him except this one letter which they all of a sudden received saying, "Here's the story. I want you to—from now on you fellows are going to report to me."

Student C: Does he say that, J? He just says—this $10,000—is a pretty big thing, I think—

Student J: Well, from now on—well, let's say, that "From now on any *important* decisions will be reported to me before you make them."

Student C: Yes. My point was— is it even important? In other words what this might be—I don't know anything about purchasing, which obviously you do, but $10,000 seems like a lot to delegate to anybody to me—a company with 20 different offices, 20 different plants, to let a man purchase things—uh—$10,000—that doesn't seem to be a sharp cut-off. Ten thousand dollars may not be very much; maybe they have a lot of orders that much. But to me—maybe he's just sending that out—is not putting a hard control over the man or anything, but just saying, "Well, when we get one of these big orders why don't we talk it over"; and maybe the language of his letter doesn't indicate that. But to me this isn't a severe step, or sharp crackdown—"now that I've taken over we're going to do things this way from the central office." It's just saying something that maybe should have been there all along, "when you have a contract for $10,000—for something this big—why don't we just talk it—over here in the—"

Student J: I see no disagreement there—that maybe it should have been there all along. Maybe that's absolutely right. But the way that he approached them, to put this plan of his over is not in my mind conducive to getting their support.

Student B: Larson had a suggestion to make. He knew all these executives. He suggested that— I think this relation between Larson and Post is quite interesting, because Larson suggested that Post see these guys before he mailed the letter out.

Instructor: What do you think he had in mind?

Student B: Well, I would rather suspect Larson thought maybe the letter wouldn't do any good just going out unless the purchasing agents had some idea of the purposes or were at least in sympathy with the idea.

Student J: You think that Larson agreed with my opinion then?

Student B: Well—I don't know—uh—Larson certainly agreed that the idea was good, or the indication is that he agreed the $10,000 limit was probably necessary and worth while. At least he didn't complain about that. What he complained about—not actually—was Post sending out the letter, never having seen the executive before.

Student J: It was the way he presented it!

Student B: Yes. But executives that Larson knew. (*Pause*)—uh—

Student H: I just wonder. Take a look at that sentence—"Mr. Larson thought the letter an excellent one." Is that what Mr. Larson's saying? I mean—If you talk to a person and he says, "I think it's an excellent idea, *but*—" Does that mean to you he thought the idea *was* an excellent one? Or does it mean to you that he *said* that he thought the idea was an excellent one?

Student P: Sure, I think you're right. That—instead of saying, "This is a lousy letter, do this," he wanted to be more encouraging and—

Student H: Well, should he?—Well, I—one of the things I asked about this case was, "What are Larson's responsibilities?"

(*Several voices.*)

Student P: He's a subordinate—

Student H: Should he have told Post, "I'm not going to stand for this kind of treatment—"

(*Several voices.*)

Student P: His role, his position is subordinate, so—uh—

Student H: He becomes evasive. He doesn't tell—

Unidentified Student: I disagree.

Student A: Is he really evasive?

Student H: Saying the letter is excellent?

Student P: Saying this idea is "all right"—why—would that be better?

Student G: Well, if he did disagree with the idea—if he thinks it's a bad idea, maybe one way to get Post to realize it is a bad idea is to suggest that he go out around visit the plants. I mean, uh—If he got out around there and saw that these purchasing agents were really cracker-jack men, perhaps—

Student H: What if Post doesn't accept this? What do you do? Do you just sit back and watch them go to hell, like Larson?

Student G: No, maybe that was the first step he had in mind—Larson might have had in mind—in telling Post to go out around the plants— (*Pause.*)

Instructor: Are you suggesting here, H, that Larson should have said, "I think this letter is a miserable one *and*," instead of "but"—"*and* I suggest that since you haven't met . . ."

Student H: No, I'm not making any judgments about Larson as presented here, I'm just asking—is—perhaps Larson doesn't think actually the letter is an excellent one.

Student A: Well, I agree with what you said, that I think that, what is what he should—his objective was—uh—in other words Larson's objective was to discourage him from doing it in this manner and his objective was to say that this is a miserable letter and I suggest that you go out and talk to these fellows before you do anything. I don't think he could have gotten compliance and any agreement.

Student P: I think he was just a very tactful person.

Student H: Yes!

Student A: What I'm saying is that—I just saying—this is what he hoped to accomplish.

Student B: Maybe this was just a very honest response. (*Several voices.*) Maybe he thought this was a very good idea, but he thought he would have much more chance of success if Post would go out and see these guys. Why do we have to complicate it with all these motives?

THE LAST FIFTEEN MINUTES OF THE FIRST HOUR

Student J: How do you think Post feels about his job?

Student B: I think he feels that he is going to jump in and do a technically competent job and everything else will take care of itself. This is just sort of a "gut" feeling.

Unidentified Student: He's done it before.

Student B: Sure. He's an experienced purchasing executive.

Student P: It seems to me that there's a problem that you can put your fingers on—finger on it—to enlist—to enlist the aid—uh—of these individual purchasing agents and—and—enlist their coöperation. It seems to me he goes—the way Post goes about it is to—uh—I mean, I think what McGregor calls it regressive.[4] First he appeals to the authority in the letter. He sits down, cites the authority of the board of directors. Then there is the other instance where he "dismissed the idea"—Well, that may not be conclusive. But it seems to me his way of administering is not the best way.

(*Several voices.*)

Student P: He makes, he makes, he writes the letter before really he makes a complete appraisal of the situation. He hasn't been out and observed the situation yet.

Student E: Our assumption then is that his most important job in coming in, rather than doing these things that keep him busy at the office is to first go out and establish relationships, either face to face, or by letter or some other way? Mainly, we seem to be pointing the finger at him for that reason. That he shouldn't be so busy with the other things, that he should take time off first.

[4] The reference is to "The Staff Function in Human Relations," *The Journal of Social Issues*, IV, No. 3 (Summer 1948), pp. 5–22.

Instructor: What's he so busy doing?

(*Several voices.*)

Unidentified Student: What are the other things that he has to do?

Student M: What is he so busy at that he can't do his main job?

Unidentified Student: Forecasting?

Student J: What's his main job?

Student P: To be captain of the team of 20 people is my theory—and he hasn't even met the team yet. He's—(*Laughter. Several voices.*)

Student B: I think that he's placing reliance on the board of directors.

(*Several voices.*)

Student B: Post talked the proposal over with Mr. Manson and then gets approval of the board of directors. That's quite interesting. It hasn't been my experience that board approval for a job like that—uh—is always —uh—well, ever happens. And then, boy, he's got the authority line in this letter—by order of.

Student A: Yeah.

(*Several voices.*)

Student A: In other words, P, your point was that if he had really worked this situation out, this—whatever action he would have taken would have naturally followed—out of his establishing relationships, and so forth, and his reference to the board of directors would have been completely unnecessary and irrelevant.

Student P: He operates, "By order of the commanding general."

Student J: He was afraid that unless he put that there, why, he wouldn't get any recognition from them.

Student A: Isn't that the way they do it in the Services, as I recall it. (*Laughter.*) "You are hereby ordered to—" (*Several voices.*) That's been my experience. (*Laughter.*)

Instructor: P was in the process of putting a pattern together here a little while ago. Would you want to try some more, or go over that stretch of track again? In what Post is doing, there is some kind of a pattern?

Student P: Yeah. Well—I'm not sure I can get all the evidence to make it conclusive, but I—I—have the feeling that he's regressive—by that I mean, to use McGregor's word, he does things to stifle coöperation rather than to get it, to enlist it, and I think that the letter is definitely one of them. The fact that he—uh—did not—well, that's not too conclusive—but— that he doesn't even meet with the people that he's leading . . . or—

Student J: His position is one of the staff organization, isn't it?

Student P: Well, that's a good point. What is his position?

Student A: His position is of wide latitude and he has interpreted it, to be well—

Student J: If he—(*Pause.*)

Student E: You think the action of Larson fits into a pattern—the authoritarian—almost not paying any attention to it?

Student P: Stifling coöperation, you might say. That's sort of an abstraction.

Student H: He seems to be working with certain assumptions—about the need for expressing his authority, and maintaining his opinion, for showing Larson how right he is, for dealing with technical aspects. But I found it an interesting point in what you said. You said he hadn't met—he's a coach, who hasn't met the team. That's a very nice way of putting it, but is it always necessary for the captain to meet the team? For instance, a commanding general taking over an army—is it necessary for him to meet every private soldier before the person is in a position—

Student P: Of course, I didn't mean—physically. But isn't it good to put a—some sort of a communication in front of the people—uh—well—I'm not sure that you'll like the wording of it, but "I've been elected, or I've been appointed to do this, and I'm going to do this—and—so, and I hope that I can—I'd like very much for you to coöperate with me"—some sort of verbal communication, written communication, something to tell these people down here that for reasons beyond their control—there is nothing wrong with the way they're doing their job—outward conditions have forced some sort of a change. Explain to them the new rules—or the new situation.

Instructor: But he's not explaining. He says, "I am sure that you will understand."

Student P: Yeah. Well—(*Pause.*)

Student F: ". . . that this step is necessary to coördinate."

Student B: Think of all the paper he saves that way.

Student W: Well, P, you're trying to see something like—along the line of perhaps if he had the time—it's this matter of expediency here—but if he had the time—maybe he should take the time—to find out what their problems are, what their suggestions are. Or put the problems the company faces before them and say, now, "Here is our problem. What are we going to do about it?" And—uh—see what these men have to say. Maybe all of them will say, "Centralize purchasing." Maybe all of them will say something else which may be even better, I don't know. In any case, out of that, then perhaps he would be able to proceed.

Student F: The problem of expediency comes back in there, perhaps, I think. Perhaps Mr. Post assumes that Mr. Manson and the board want action—which will help to solve this possible problem by the time the peak buying season arrives.

Student W: Well, how good is that action, though?

Student F: Well, I don't know.

(*Several voices.*)

Student F: I agree with that, but this is just possibly a point of view Mr. Post is taking. He feels that he has to do something to justify his position.

(*Several voices.*)

Student H: Isn't he addressing himself to a technical problem?

(*Several voices.*)

Student F: Oh, I agree. I think we are all in pretty much agreement about that phase of it, aren't we? We feel that he has been abrupt, that he's tended to stifle any coöperation and he's not attempted to seek out any of these men—I don't think there is—I thought we're all pretty much in agreement with all that.

(*Several voices.*)

Instructor: . . . Well—we are in agreement. I think I stopped you, P, a few minutes ago. You were talking. I raised a question. I didn't mean to stop it. I was trying to see if you could put together some things I'm sure we all feel here. That Post is wrong—he is doing some things, and what is the pattern which fits together here? Why does it fit? What assumptions—you were raising the question a moment ago—what assumptions does he seem to be making about certain kinds of things which gives rise to a pattern here? Can you state more clearly what it is—what is the indictment against Post? We're all making an indictment, but what are the counts in the indictment?

Student P: H-m-m-m—

Student M: Well, first of all, does he assume these people can do the job as they were doing it before? Does he assume that he has to make edicts for them to follow? Or does he assume that they can get together and do it themselves?

Student P: I guess—I guess—

Student J: I guess he assumes he can do it better than they can.

Unidentified Student: . . . better than they can.

Unidentified Student: Yeah!

Student C: He assumes from his analysis thing that he has been doing this purchasing now, and "my analysis of the situation is that we do it the way I've been doing it instead of the way they've been doing it." When F was talking before about what analysis he made of the situation, I think his analysis was simply the way he would do, what his experience has been, rather than what the actual problem necessarily might have been in this particular plan or in this particular job. He read from his experience and his life into the job what *he* would do in the situation. And he may not have said, "There is a big problem, therefore we have to have central purchasing." He might just have said, "I always work better under central purchasing, I think this is a more efficient way to do it, and—uh—looking the situation over—I've got wide latitude of authority, I'll present my views to the board, if they go along, that's fine, I won't have to look at the problem, I won't have to waste time by writing a letter to each one of these 20 guys and getting their opinion. I've been hired to do this job. Now they must have looked around for some men, they had this problem here, they hired me. Well, what did they want? They wanted a man of my capabilities. Here's the way I would do it." He made his analysis from an egocentric point of view. "Here's what I would do in the situation I would face," rather than necessarily making his analysis from the point of view of the actual case in hand. I think that's the pattern that's causing a little trouble—and what we worry about these things. He doesn't even think how it's going to react to the other people because he's got it so solved in his mind. He can just feel the answer here, so he writes out this letter, "authority of the board of directors," "$10,000," "centralized purchasing," and "I know this will help." He just feels that's it, "Now I've solved the problem."

Instructor: I think he solved the problem without looking at this particular instance. In previous cases—from generalizations—from something that he has, "Now the problem is solved, now you people put it into effect. I don't look at the particular circumstance."

Student H: He's saying in effect, "I'm boss. I know what the problem is. I've got all the answers. All you have to do is follow me."

Student P: He's leading by pulling instead of getting everybody pulling together.

Student B: One of the assumptions that he makes is brought over from his old experience—is that—by the fact that he has authority. It may be a "Navy" authority. (*Laughter.*) He has the authority. He guarantees success. He gets Manson's approval. This is authority. Then he says in the letter "by authority of the board of directors"—by the very definition that he's got authority, this means that his program is going to be successful. Even in dealing with people, which is what he's doing. This is a real assumption that he's making.

Student F: I think another assumption which might go along with that, either he feels that authority in and of itself will prove successful or else he may be assuming that a good analysis which he has made will necessarily be successful, just by handing it down without any attempt to solicit coöperation or to sell the idea.

Instructor: "My authority and my good analysis . . ."

Student H: . . . technical analysis . . .

Instructor: " . . . add up to a program which will be accepted and put into effect"?

Student F: Yes.

Student A: Yes. I think we've done pretty well on indicting Post. I just wondered if we would be—if another issue would be more justified in indicting Manson.

Unidentified Student: He started it!

Student A: Yeah, he started it and I think we've really hit Post. Now as F brought out before, it may be Post was under some compunction to—uh—he was under pressure to eliminate this step of really digging out the facts of the situation because he was under pressure to Manson. That fact—that's my hypothesis, of course, that he was under pressure from Manson. Secondly, there is another point, which is a less—less hypothesis —is the fact that he talked it over with Mr. Manson and then he presented it to his board of directors and they approved the plan and—and—well, this is imputing something here, but I thought perhaps—uh—this might indicate they were willing to go along with this quick decision and also a quick decision which wasn't based on a great deal of reasoning as per our earlier indictment.

Student M: Yeah, that's it! What are the assumptions that Manson was under when he got Post in to do a job when something was going to get tough. Does he think you'd have to get in somebody to coördinate . . .

(*Several voices.*)

Unidentified Student: "Hire an expert!"

Unidentified Student: Management consultants!

(*Several voices.*)

Student M: . . . to take over when things get difficult. Our man can't do it, therefore get somebody else to do it.

Unidentified Student: Sure.

(*Several voices.*)

Student B: Maybe you can indict Larson, too, though, for not throwing himself on the spears, and telling Post, "You're all wrong—you'll never get anything done unless you go out and see these guys individually."

Student A: Throw Larson on the spears you say. (*Laughter.*)

(*Several voices.*)

Student B: It is Larson's responsibility, really, as assistant to this guy, he's sort of guiding him around his new job. Even though he is an assistant, it seems to me it's Larson's responsibility to make sure that Post does the best job possible.

(*Several voices.*)

Unidentified Student: How can he do this, B?

Student P: How can he fulfill that responsibility? It seems to me he tried—

Student B: You mean without getting fired?

Student P: Well, yeah.—So—"The man's not doing it the right way so I quit."

Student M: Well, he may have tried—

Student F: That assumes you know all the answers or that Larson knows all the answers. (*Several voices.*) We don't know if Larson knows all the answers and he probably himself does not necessarily think he has all the right answers. Now he has made a suggestion. He has suggested that Mr. Post do this and I think he has done his job in doing that.

Instructor: His responsibility does not extend to his insisting, and demanding, and making a great speech that he must do these things?

THE LAST HALF HOUR

Instructor: Now, coming back to F's proposition, with some of these ideas, and with the last one, too. "In this way the interests will best be served." What is he going to do when he goes to the field? What attitudes and what kind of ideas, does it now seem, and what analyses, should he take with him when he goes out to the field?

Student H: Doesn't this last sentence suggest to you a conflict of interest . . . between each plant and between plant and company?

Instructor: Some conflicts and what?

Student B: I think when he goes out to the field he's not going to succeed in F's suggestion.

Instructor: Why not?

Student B: Well, because I think he has a one, preconception that because he has the authority people are going to do what he says and *agree* with him and—well, I don't know specifically what we picked up from each one of these sentences, but they all add up to me to show that—uh—this—this guy has got some very strong ideas about his technical competence and about the value of this program and in the way he is—certainly in the way he has presented this letter, that, by golly, the best interests of the company will be served if everybody does this and "because I've got the authority everybody is going to do it."

Student W: We indict a man because of the letter or because of a certain action, but does this mean that he is always going to have this type of an attitude or—

Student B: And can he change?

Student F: Or does it mean that he will react the same way in entirely different situations where he is not writing a letter, where he is actually talking to people, to different people.

Student W: I don't think it is a hopeless situation by any means.

Instructor: When he is talking with someone face to face, these attitudes which are involved disappear and are replaced by some other attitudes?

Unidentified Student: I don't think so.

Student H: This is not true, but he may be able—to gradually improve. We are not looking for an instant conversion.

Student F: But, Mr. Instructor, aren't you saying that these few—that these indications which we have picked out of this letter are in fact the man?

Instructor: Well, I should think that's part of the question: Is this the man and, if so, what is the man? What is he now?—one thing. What may he be twenty years from now?—something else. What may he be next week if he goes out into the field? And, as against those questions, what, if anything, can Larson do to be helpful?

Student F: Is it possible that in a situation like this—I'm not sure myself—but is it possible that in a situation like this in which he is, say, writing a directive to people, he will couch things in terms which possibly are not reflections of his whole attitude?

Student B: There is too much evidence.

Student F: I'm not trying to propose that he's going to make a glorious success of going out into the field. On the other hand, I hate—I hate to damn him eternally, as H says, on the basis of the letter which he has written.

Instructor: Well, now is that the alternative we have? If we damn him now, we are at the same time also damning him eternally?

Student F: That was sort of mentioned before, I thought—We saw no hope of his going out into the field and making a success of it.

Student H: But that's not the only thing he can do. I mean, there are other things he can do.

Student F: True—

Student H: I think we've got to recognize that perhaps he's not beyond hope. Perhaps we can draw him into the organization somehow, perhaps he will pull himself into the organization. There's always a chance. What can we do to improve his chances?

Student F: As Mr. Larson?

Student H: As Mr. Larson.

Student P: It is conceivable to me that if he goes out into the field with these attitudes and outlooks, he may destroy the confidence of the individual purchasing agents. They may feel that "we have to look to the central office," and then, if he's not equipped to do the purchasing in the twenty plants, the purchasing may become a real problem.

Student H: That's why I suggested that Larson himself has got to look closely at Post to see what it is—I mean, I don't know—my analysis of

Post may be a little too trick. I think there is something that Post is really worried about. Afraid of something. And, I don't know, I said before, perhaps Larson should reassure him. Perhaps that's a stupid idea, perhaps that's a stupid suggestion. But, at least, what I am trying to do is to say Larson should find out, what are the things that Post is worried about? What are the things that are behind Post's idea? If Larson can find out some of the things that Post is worried about and some of the assumptions that are in Post's mind then perhaps Larson can, by understanding them, do something about them.

Student F: H, how do you go about this?

Student H: That is a theoretical question.

(*Several voices.*)

Student F: Can you go right in and say, "What is troubling you today?" Obviously not those words, but—(*Several voices.*)

Student B: A nondirective interview—(*Laughter and several voices.*)

Student P: A counseling relationship—(*Laughter and several voices.*)

Student P: Sure, it can be done on a subordinate level, I'm sure. But not—You're not sitting down in a therapeutic room or something. It seems to me he's going to be with him every day. It seems to me that he will be able to get Post's attitudes on things—that Post is going to talk all the time; he can play those back to him.

Student H: That's why I would like to return to this sentence about Mr. Larson "thought the letter was an excellent one but suggested," etc., etc. Because I don't know how sincere Larson is. If he—thought that Post should go out and meet the purchasing agents—is that what he is saying, or is he suggesting something else? Isn't he really suggesting that Post has left out something which is vital to the success of this plan?

Instructor: Is there a question here?

Student H: Should he have come out and said it?

Instructor: If this be insincerity, can a man who has established the relationship of insincerity now, subsequently, establish the counseling relationship that you were talking about a minute ago, P?

Student F: I don't think you can say this is insincere. I don't think you know. This may be—can't this just be on the level of a suggestion? Maybe Larson hasn't analyzed this thing so deeply as we have—or as we've attempted to here. Perhaps this is in effect just a suggestion. He thinks that the letter is all right, but he thinks it might be better to do it in this other way—and that's all. This is not a vital issue with him. This is not something he has analyzed completely. It is nothing that he is going to throw himself on the spears for.

Student H: I quite realize that when we approach a case which is written down, what we do—we approach it from our own attitudes and we each put certain biases into all these words, and what—I think this is only natural. He seems to me a person who talks—talks like this: "I think your ideas are excellent *but* . . ." and then goes on to say something else. Then he—there may be another kind of way to do it. There may be another way to tell Post that maybe it's not right to send this letter out.

Instructor: He might say, "Gee, I don't think this will ever work in the world. You will just raise a hornet's nest here and not get any coöperation."

Student H: He might say that. "I don't know if this is good"—But—it just depends on Larson. Now, if Larson says that kind of thing and Larson is sincere about it and—at least we know something about Larson. We know that Larson is playing a straight bat.

Student F: We not only don't know whether it is good, but we don't know whether Larson feels that way. He might not feel that way—

(*Several voices.*)

Student A: Even if he does feel that way—I am quite sure, even if he does feel that way, maybe he knows Post already. He knows him well enough to know darned well that—he stands there—he's just going to lose out completely. Post won't care, won't care for his suggestions and he has got to do it much more tactfully. He just can't tell him bluntly. That's all there is to it. He has got to tell him in rather, rather a roundabout way.

Student H: Does this—you're saying he can't tell him bluntly—does this add up to an indictment of Post, of Larson, or of both of them?

Student A: It might be either.

Instructor: Why can't he say: "Gee, I just don't think this will work. After all, these people have been operating for years. They have established relationships with their own plant managers, and they are responsible to their own plant managers. Now you want them to be responsible to you instead. You want them to take a company-wide point of view on negotiating contracts and allocating materials. And I don't think you can do this by writing a letter."

Student P: Because doing that just cuts—cuts off Post's bridge. I mean, he's left—he's left saying—"Well, I'm going to write—I've written a letter and I'm going to send it anyhow."

(*Several voices.*)

Student P: It does, doesn't it?

Student G: There are two reasons he couldn't say it if he really feels as though he can't say it. One, either he feels that Post doesn't have much respect for his judgment, or else he feels that Post is bullheaded and that he stands to lose much more by—than—if he goes about—

Student P· It leaves him just two alternatives: To state, "I'm going to send it anyhow," or, "That's no good."

Student B: Or, "By Jove, you might be right."

Student P: Now, there's no other alternative, is there?

Unidentified Student: Well—possibly.

(*Several voices.*)

Student P: All right: "I'll go consider it again."

Student B: I think Post's reaction to this—to such a statement as Mr. Instructor just made—is the key to it. I think that Post will not react favorably, although I don't feel so strongly on that point as I do on the point that he couldn't handle himself in the field. I think Post might conceivably listen to him and say, "By golly, you *are* right."

Student P: Maybe it was Larson's responsibility to say this.

(*Several voices.*)

Student B: Maybe Larson analyzed the situation after reading the letter —competent in "Ad Prac" and things like that—read the letter and decided that Post would react unfavorably if he was so direct.

Student H: Is this a useful way of handling the situation? Is it a useful way to handle the situation to be what we call tactful? Not to tell the truth because the truth will hurt?

Student H: Also is it a useful way of approaching it to antagonize people so that they don't do it anyhow?

Instructor: In this particular case, applying a kind of pragmatic sort of test here as to whether this was useful conduct or not, what can we say?

Student B: It wasn't useful.

Instructor: It wasn't useful.

Student B: Maybe it didn't hurt, but it certainly wasn't useful.

Student F: Well, that's assuming it hasn't worked.

(*Several voices.*)

Instructor: Something is going on here about which—at least we don't know what is going on, out in the field.

Student P: Are you suggesting that, when he said that it was an excellent letter, he was being guilty of bad faith or something like that? Or was he reassuring him where he shouldn't have? He wasn't being as responsible—

Instructor: I think he was "being tactful and diplomatic."

Student P: But implicit in that is that's not the way to be responsible.

Instructor: I don't think it was very useful in this case—at least—I don't want to generalize beyond there, but—

Student G: Does that mean it was no good because it didn't work?

Instructor: What's that?

Student G: It did no good because it didn't work? It might have worked.

Instructor: Well, I have some other feelings about that. (*Laughter.*) Just at the pragmatic level.

Student H: Well, I think that this goes beyond the pragmatic level—and just bullheadedness. If it *had* worked, if Mr. Post had actually taken up the suggestion—then has Larson got the kind of relationship with Post that he—he should have? Is not the relation between Larson and Post now one of—half-truth and diplomacy and juggling of figures and juggling of ideas?

Student A: Post could always come back to Larson and say, "Well, you said it was an excellent idea."

Student H: Yes, I know, but what kind of relationship is it—this half-truth thing that's established? I mean, even if it is successful, even if Post went out into the field, what's the relationship between Larson and Post?

(*Several voices.*)

Student A: Yeah, soft and dead.

Instructor: Having gotten off to a bad foot—if this is indeed a bad relationship—this lack of candor and free communication. If, indeed, we don't have a relationship like that, what do we do now? You were suggesting we ought to establish a counseling relationship?

Student H: Perhaps Larson ought to go back to Post and say, "You know, I'm sorry, I told you that letter was an excellent one and I told you that you should go out into the field, but that wasn't really what I meant to say."

Student A: Now he tells him! (*Laughter.*)

Student H: At least he is telling the truth.

Student F: Well, yes, O.K., well, now I think I'm back with my old theme here. 'Cause I'm not sure that he is being insincere here or not telling the truth.

Student P: He doesn't have the insight that we have.

Instructor: You're suggesting that we may be reading too much into the case here.

Student F: Into these individual words I think we are perhaps reading an awful lot. To take the extreme other end—uh—which I don't propose to take—just point it out. "Your letter is an excellent one but how about trying this." This might be just analogous to saying "Good morning" on a rainy day. It isn't a good morning at all. This is just something to introduce his sentence. He doesn't want to start out by saying, "No, you should follow this other suggestion." He says—"rephrase and use a different word." Perhaps, "Your letter looks very good but wouldn't this be a better approach?"

Student H: But it is not true that this letter looks good—This letter is stinking!

Student B: To you, H—

(*Several voices.*)

Student H: What I'm saying—if I were Larson—this—

Instructor: If you were Larson, you would say, "I think this letter stinks"?

Student H: No! (*Laughter.*)

(*Several voices.*)

Student H: I wonder—this is—the point we are all talking about now is, if we think it stinks, should we tell him it stinks?

Instructor: Yes. If we think literally, in our own mind, it stinks, do we say, "I think it stinks"?

Unidentified Student: Yes.

Student F: No.

Unidentified Student: Now wait a minute.

(*Several voices.*)

Student H: Are we criticizing the letter or the idea?—Well, Post could say, "What's this young whippersnapper telling me how to write letters," *or* he could say, "The ideas, Mr. Post, are not very good. I don't think they'll work in this organization."

Instructor: "I think this is a well-drafted letter, but I think the ideas behind it stink!" (*Laughter.*)

Student A: Yeah, that's good.

Student H: But that is in actual fact what he's saying, isn't it?

Instructor: "Given the point of view—Given an authoritarian kind of point of view, this is an excellent bit of draftsmanship, but I don't think very much of the point of view."

Student A: I don't think he would stay very long. (*Laughter.*)

Student H: Well, I don't know. He might.

Student B: No, he wouldn't. He'd see Manson the next morning and say, "Hey (*Laughter*), get Larson another job."

Instructor: Well, gentlemen, I see we've run for almost two full hours. Is there any last kind of speech that anyone would like to make? Here are some things that he would like to pull together?

Student H: Would you like to say something, sir?

Instructor: Not particularly. I think the points have been raised— I think one point which particularly did interest me was mentioned several times, was the responsibility of Manson and the board of directors in here, that they had an opportunity to see some thinking of Post here. And, did they see that his approach here was not going to be a useful one, and, if so, did they let him, as it were, get off on the wrong foot at that point? Did they see, in terms of the concrete relationships of people as established, and the ways of doing things, what this procedure was going to mean? In terms of the operations, that are now going to be different; directed differently; different sets of values; different criteria for making decisions—all these things being implicit in the new procedure? Did they fail to see that? That is an interesting question, if they did fail to see it. Then, if they saw something like this, why did they let poor old Post walk into the lion's cage?

Student B: Maybe they thought it would be a good way for him to get his feet on the ground.

Student F: At the expense of the entire organization.

Student H: Sometimes they have to do that—and let things slip—slop all over the floor—

Instructor: I guess there is one other thing. I guess—very bluntly—I don't think we did too good a job on it, although we did put some things together. What are the pieces in this authoritarian pattern?—"I am sure you understand."—The way in which decisions are arrived at. We do not arrive at decisions in terms of making a concrete analysis of a particular case. We draw from generalities. We draw from other experiences and do some other kinds of things—rather than—"Let us look at this concrete situation. Let us draw on the people who are in this concrete situation, this particular situation, to help cast up the plan. Not in terms of selling the plan, but casting up the plan, making the diagnosis, making the analysis in the first instance."—We don't do that. And then this blind—it seems to me—blind faith in authority—"you will do this." Not in a nasty sense, or overbearing sense, but just in a guileless expectation that they will indeed do it. This kind of fits in. And then this sentence here—again perhaps at the danger, the risk of reading too much in here: "He dismissed the idea," whether at once or otherwise, but anyway he doesn't do it. The reason he doesn't do it, which is to say, go into the field, is he's too busy doing other things in the head office. Now, this doing things in the head office, whatever that is, is more important than going out and working with people and getting this thing going along. The scale of priorities here, the scale of values, I think, is suggested. What are these other things in the office? They must be of the order of—what? Shuffling papers around, shuffling figures around, writing reports, reading these reports, reading newspapers, ideas at the intellectual level, activities at the intellectual level, abstract level. "This is so important, it is so important I can't possibly go out and meet the team I am now captain of—get the team organized." Somehow I think this fits into the pattern. Things of this sort are important. People, their ideas and relationships, are not important. Ideas are important.

Student M: Are you saying that we felt these things, Mr. Instructor, that we didn't express them very well?

Instructor: I think I was saying something like that. I think all the things I'm saying were kind of around, but somehow or other, I was hoping you would put this in a neat package, an authoritarian syndrome, you know. Something like that.

Student P: We got the ideas—I mean—we just didn't verbalize them as nicely as you just did. Isn't that how—haven't we thereby gained something from it? Of course, I am not saying that we all did, but—

Instructor: Oh, sure. In terms of practice, in terms of practice, it seems to me the kinds of things and the kinds of attitudes which are being reflected in the group are likely to be leading the group, as individuals, into the right pattern of behavior. Right, which is to say, Business School doctrine, "I think!" (*Laughter.*) But this—this intuitive ability, this intuitive capacity, this intuitive understanding. One of the great questions which I am sure this group which is coming here this first week in April are concerned with, how strong is it as against a logical barrage of reasons you shouldn't think this way? What good rationale do you have for thinking the way you do think, feeling the way you do feel? Do you have the logical superstructure to go along with the intuitive understanding, and will your intuitive understanding, and so on, be strengthened and stronger if you had the logical rationalization and—rationale—to go along with it. The Business School, the whole Human Relations group here, has often been criticized for not having a theory. This brings us into it. "You don't have a theory—you have a lot of individual pieces, but you do not have an elaborate, highly articulated systematic theory of things. We think you would be better off if you did have."

Student H: Do you think perhaps that having a highly articulate theory might destroy this—intuitive ability—to sense a situation?

Instructor: I think that is one of the questions we of the teaching group and of the research activity that is going along with it, I think, have got to come to: Does, in fact, a logical superstructure of theory reinforce intuitive understandings, or indeed, are they incompatible?

Student P: Well, look, to be very specific, if we were—I mean—one thing which we have sort of gotten out of this: it doesn't pay to administrate by authority—in this case. If you, in your superstructure, were to put this as a principle and we learned this, which I think probably has already been done some place, what good would that do us?

Student H: We could read it and we wouldn't know how to apply it to the case.

Student P: In fact, didn't Brown or somebody write something like that?

Instructor: There are all kinds of theories and pieces of theories which have been written. I suppose our position around here, when it comes right down to it, is that what we are more concerned with actually is turning men out who can actually do this, rather than theorize about it.

But the question still comes up, would they be able to do it better if they could also theorize systematically about it?

Student B: Take old Cox [5] in that case we had last year. Cox theorized beautifully, but he sure never got anything done.

Student H: Isn't the trouble perhaps that, if we were trained to recognize these theories logically, that we might be able to recognize situations ex post facto—when it is too late to have done anything. We have got to do things instantaneously.

Instructor: Instantaneously.

Student H: Instantaneously.

Instructor: Instantaneous adaptation.

Student P: Maybe we are expecting people, like—Professor Roethlisberger says that Elton Mayo was the man who could run up and down the abstraction ladder, see concrete situations, and to abstract, and come right back to reality again. Running up, as he said, running up and down the ladder. Well, I mean, of course—this is not Elton Mayo but—(*Laughter and several voices*) Elton Mayo didn't have—

Student M: But that was in a case, P, one particular case, he went up and down.

Student H: But how fast do you go up and down the ladder? Do you do it just like Sherlock Holmes? [6] Just in a split second?

Student P: Apparently Mayo did it—

Student H: Perhaps this was what was meant by posing a superstructure, a superstructure, of some kind of logical graft—to the facts of life.

Student P: You don't look at reality and run up to this, to some high abstraction. You make them up as you go along.

Student H: No, don't you—what I meant is, that if you were face to face with the situation—Sherlock Holmes runs—to a—his mind runs to a whole lot of things and then comes back instantly. If we, if we learn only part of that—in other words, if we learn only in a situation to run up the ladder but not down the ladder. Perhaps that's what getting a logical superstructure means. Perhaps this getting too much logical superstructure means we got to run so far up the ladder that we can't get down quick enough to make a reaction instantaneously.

[5] The reference is to Mr. Cox in the Flint Electric Company series (unpublished).

[6] The reference is to a passage from A. Conan Doyle, *A Study in Scarlet.* Holmes, speaking to Dr. Watson: "You appeared to be surprised when I told you, on our first meeting, that you had come from Afghanistan." Watson: "You were told, no doubt." Holmes: "Nothing of the sort. I *knew* you came from Afghanistan. From long habit the train of thoughts ran so swiftly through my mind that I arrived at the conclusion without being conscious of intermediate steps. There were such steps, however . . . The whole train of thought did not occupy a second."

Student P: It seems to me—(*Several voices.*)

Instructor: One of the questions that we have frequently raised about the Marshall Company cases—the people in there, in that company, by and large and on the whole, exhibited a pattern such that they could in fact work well with one another and solve problems. There were individual blocks, but they frequently, when they came up, they disappeared quickly. They got around them. They—their attitudes, their approaches, their instantaneous responses were of the order which led to coöperation rather than away from it, led to problem solving. Now none of these people there were very articulate as to what their theory of administration was. Perhaps many of them were entirely unaware and took these things for granted. The question has been raised in our own teaching group as we discuss these cases: would this be a stronger system if people were aware of what their system of values was and what their assumptions are. And things of that sort—so that if, let's say, they brought in a new vice president in charge of production who was a fellow like Post, that they could protect themselves against Post, and make it clear to Post why such an approach isn't useful in the Marshall Company? Or would they be rather tongue-tied and not able to explain to him why this isn't a useful approach here?

Student P: You will still be left in the air some place with things like "coöperation" and "attitudes" and that, wouldn't you? If people—say you were able to set down an excellent analysis of why the Marshall Company worked. It was due to, say—I have forgotten the man—their outlook and all this, you were able to spell this out for them and they knew about it. What good would that do them? Would they say, "Well, now I am engendering coöperation when I say—uh—what are you doing, John?" or something like that?

Instructor: Graham saying, "I operate with a permissive attitude."

Student P: What good would that do Graham?

(*Several voices.*)

Student M: And Post couldn't understand it if you'd tell him.

Student B: If they were very articulate, mightn't they find themselves—doing things in order to—that we have this policy—uh—Graham says, "I am permissive, so I must act this way." Might not that hamper the operations in the Marshall Company—if they did have this thing spelled out in detail?

Student P: I think it probably would.

Student F: That is the danger of looking at a set of rules and picking out what you think you should be and then applying it to a specific instance or situation, as opposed to not looking at a specific set of principles and picking out what you should be or what you should do, and looking at the situation first.

Student B: Maybe Brewster someday will think of firing someone.

Instructor: Oh, he has fired people, I'm sure.

Student B: Cold?

Instructor: Cold as a turkey.

Instructor: Well, gentlemen, I see we have run overtime even so, and I guess we have to call this to a halt sometime. Poor ——— (another instructor) has been waiting for me since 5:30. (*Laughter.*) Would you like to take a look at this ad [7] for next time, or would you like to go on with the "Stevenson Associates"? [8]

Several Students: Let's look at the ad.

Instructor: I think the ad might be quite useful.

---

[7] The reference is to a case entitled "An Advertisement from the New York *Times,* November 20, 1951."

[8] The reference is to the unpublished case, "Stevenson Associates."

Administrative Practices and Human Relations — For What?

ANDREW R. TOWL

ADMINISTRATION AND PURPOSE

By authority of long tradition and the Hippocratic Oath, doctors treat with equal care all men who come to them. Public Enemy No. 1, if wounded, is as eligible for medical attention as the President. Society is not concerned whether the doctor uses his skills in behalf of one who is destroying or one who is strengthening the structure of society.

Society is much concerned, however, with what the administrator uses his skills for: whether for self-aggrandizement or for building a better community, or in what proportions for both. Moreover, the situation is complicated, for the standards of judging the purposes of organizations are themselves in evolution. Distilleries and breweries are legitimate enterprises, but some of their managements have felt that the trends of public interest justified identifying their companies also with chemical and pharmaceutical contributions to society.

The role of the administrator in the determination of organization purposes cannot be ignored. Mr. Donham put the problem to those interested in administration in a succinct passage of *Education for Responsible Living.*

> When we have learned how to train men to better their understanding of human relations and correspondingly to accomplish things practically through better human relations, *this whole field of purpose still remains.* Policy depends on purpose. Judgments and action must be related to objectives.[1]

In a democracy we cannot and would not, as educators, impose our purposes for society upon students. At the same time, educational institutions have a peculiar responsibility for transmitting to succeeding generations the vital elements of our heritage. Let us consider more concretely

[1] Donham, *Education for Responsible Living,* p. 112. The italics are mine.

some of the problems involved for those of us who have a professional interest in administration and human relations.

In the Administrative Practices course at the Harvard Business School, the teaching group calls attention to the administrator's role of balancing the purpose of the organization with the needs of individuals in the organization. Professors in other subjects of the curriculum have been given the assignment of working with students in learning to make decisions in, for example, marketing policy, financial policy, production policy, and so on. The professors in Administrative Practices have been allocated the task of working with students on cases emphasizing not policy and purpose but human relations.

In most of the cases in the course, marketing policies, for instance, are not under question. The case evidence presents relationships and encourages the student to consider how the administrator should conduct himself. For several years the description of the course in the catalogue emphasized "getting things done through people," in contrast to emphasis in other subjects upon learning to make decisions. Perhaps it is not unnatural that, in spite of explanations to the contrary by professors, the term "Ad Prac" came often to be synonymous with persuasion, manipulation, and "Machiavellianism."

THE ADMINISTRATOR: RESPONSIVE AND DECISIVE

Much of the emphasis in our courses in Administrative Practices and Human Relations is upon the need for responding to the total situation, in contrast to acting by deduction from assumed premises. It is important, however, to observe that the emphasis upon *responsive* behavior does not obscure its popular contrast, *decisive* behavior, which is commonly seen in executives. How these two aspects of executive behavior merge has much to do, I believe, with the integration of purpose in a business organization with the ambitions of individuals.

A fruitful place to begin is in *a distinction between what might be called business decisions and administrative action.* Perhaps this distinction might also be labeled as the difference between the expert and the executive. In practice, one can never unscramble the egg and say that this is a business decision, and that is administrative action. Actual life mixes these things all together. It is useful to think of business situations as falling on a continuous scale.

SPECIALIZATION IN THE FORMATION OF POLICY

In a sole proprietorship one man makes decisions up and down the entire scale. It is he who decides, for instance, to buy 90 days' inventory of material—obviously a "business decision." It is also he who decides to fire the plant superintendent—obviously "an administrative action," and one likely to be followed by many more reactions throughout the organization.

In larger organizations specialization of function and awkwardness of communication make it even more difficult to integrate these two kinds of decisions. The marketing vice president, for instance, uses the pressure of salary increases and promotion on the sales manager to get sales and then finds he must add a market research executive to learn what needs to be sold. The manufacturing vice president puts pressure on superintendents and foremen to get production, and then finds he must add personnel staff experts to learn why workers are not productive.

A positive program for keeping both responsibilities in balance is illustrated in one large oil company. In this company the president has developed a management committee of key men under the chairmanship of the executive vice president. This management committee is responsible for coming up with a balanced recommendation that relates expenditures for exploration, production, refining, transportation, and marketing to the over-all development of the company. These management-committee meetings run on for hours with detailed debate about the dovetailing of operations in all departments. The president of this company has chosen to let these aspects of his job be thrashed out by subordinates. He has reserved time for himself to deal with each department. His door is open to executives running major functions who wish to discuss promising personnel, proposed changes in personnel, and questions about personal prospects that would be inappropriate in open meeting.

All too often it seems that companies have isolated outposts manned by experts highly endowed with "the instinct for new combinations." From these points of vantage impending changes in markets, technology, government regulation get put together as "policy." The management then must "ad prac" these changes through to acceptance. Such bifurcation of vision and action really is not the kind of administrative practice that efficiently produces constructive purpose.

For instance, the chief of a staff research and development department in a large eastern company fairly radiates new ideas—but they do not foster a sense of purpose within the organization. Even within his own department a mutual protective association has developed to accept and bury most of the boss's ideas so that a few sturdy ones can be nurtured to maturity. Need it be added that over the years the chief has become more and more frustrated? Only widespread personal affection for him appears to make the situation tolerable. The instinct for combination has showered down dreams but left the organization to sort out its own purpose. It may be worth while to note further in this instance the chief's relations with the operating head of the business to whom the research and development department reported. The operating head had been brought in because of his reputation for economical operation and persistence in hewing to an established line. He said of the research and development chief, "He makes me nervous. I'm frank to admit he thinks so fast I can't follow him, and by the time I catch up, he's off on another proposition."

TRAINING MEN FOR DECISION-MAKING SITUATIONS

Training men for making business decisions does not automatically train them for action through organization. Different methods are appropriate in training a salesman and in training a sales manager. There is a difference between training an investment analyst and training the manager of an investment department.

May we refer again to the experience at the Harvard Business School in trying to find effective subdivisions in education for business administration. The Faculty elected to set up units of instruction for Marketing, Production, Finance, Control, Public Relationships and Responsibilities, and Administrative Practices in the first year. In the second year Administrative Policy, Procurement, Sales Management, Government and Business, and other areas of policy determination are set up alongside the course in Human Relations. Under this particular functional subdivision the expectation is that in the Human Relations courses policy or purpose in an organization is considered relatively fixed while attention is directed to human relations and administrative practices within this framework.

Let us illustrate by the way cases might be written for courses in Foreign Trade and in Administrative Practices from the same situation. A certain company has an export division and also has several autonomous domestic divisions whose products can be purchased by exporters. The resulting competition abroad between independent exporters and the corporations' own export division brings up many considerations which are important to the student of foreign trade. For this particular purpose the case writer submerged some questions of administrative relationships. In the Administrative Practices course the case would have been written to highlight other facts. The manager of the export division recognized the problem of competition abroad, for example, and was unsuccessfully endeavoring to get the help of one particular domestic division on a more workable price schedule. The president of the company had newly taken office and was not disposed to get into this particular controversy.

A tabulation of some cases used in the Administrative Practices course might be of interest here. The following list indicates roughly: (1) how the administrative situation, "the problem," appeared to the administrator, (2) the changes he introduced, and (3) the results.

Dashman Company.[2] (1) "New purchasing policy and organization needed."

(2) New man brought in as vice president of purchasing who issues orders.

(3) Orders ignored by plant purchasing agents.

Starledo Company. (1) "New distribution needed."

(2) Assistant to president sent to investigate; takes an interest in distributors.

(3) Their coöperation leads to constructive changes unanticipated when "problem" first sensed.

Calhoun Company. (1) "Economy needed in stenographic services."

(2) Stenographic pool formed.

(3) Frictions arise—costs go up.

Gibbons Finance Company. (1) "New collection policy needed to get more bank loans."

(2) New man brought in from big company as collection manager. Ratios enforced.

(3) Salesmen confused and customers lost.

This list raises a question as to what extent the situations represent policy decisions made without reference to the people involved and without their participation. These cases may well illustrate a whole range of situations where the skills of human relations and administration are needed in order to *discover what the situation facing the company really is* and the kind of change which will lead to the growth of the organization.

For instance, in the Dashman Company the problem may well have been finding out what needed to be done instead of finding out how to get plant purchasing agents to do what the new vice president ordered.

Management has reciprocating functions of (1) *learning what needs to be done* and (2) *getting things done.* Specialization of function within the organization unfortunately often obscures this dual administrative responsibility.

USING "AD PRAC" IN DETERMINING PURPOSE

Exclusive emphasis upon either the economic or the human problems of a particular organization may be necessary and appropriate in teaching. In practice, however, the two kinds of decision often are inseparable. The skills in human relations and administrative practices which students now

[2] The Dashman and other cases referred to here may be found in Glover and Hower, *The Administrator.*

learn under our present division of curriculum *may appear* to be useful primarily after the purposes of the company have already been determined. *In practice, they are just as relevant to the problem of determining what the purposes of the company should be.* In both administrative action and business decision the skills of relating one's self to others are useful in learning what needs to be done.

The administrator needs social skills; he also needs to know his business. Quite possibly these social skills are his avenue to knowing his business. Look, for example, at the Livingston Company. Margaret Bickers exhibited the social skill of effective listening. She knew the business. And the combination of skill and knowledge led to a resolution of the war in the dress shop. Often the creative aspect of executive behavior consists of the executive's bringing into the situation in one group the values of another. Thus the values of both groups appear in the emerging common purpose.

PURPOSE EMERGES FROM THE RECONCILIATION OF MANY GROUPS

Now that public relations has become stylish, it is rare indeed for a corporation not to have a nicely worded statement of objectives. Yet in at least one company which has such a statement executives and workers still complain of lack of purpose: "They [the management] don't know what they're doing." Men in the staff units complain that economy drives have squeezed out the executive layers which might have interpreted one group to another to give common meaning to membership in the organization.

The emphasis on foremen as part of management also tends to block understanding—because they really need to be a part of management, surely; and *also* part of the work group. We need more executives at all levels who are accepted in two or more groups within the organization. Almost by definition, the executive must be a member of many groups, if he is to provide meaning, that is, a sense of purpose, to those looking to him for leadership.

The higher one goes in executive position, the more groups he must move in and out of, the better he must know his way around, and the more important it is that he interpret to one group the reasons why another group views a given situation differently.

FORESIGHT ESSENTIAL TO PARTICIPATION AND VICE VERSA

In order to have time for the participation needed in the creative kind of purpose-making we have been discussing, foresight is essential—and in a subtle way the kind of participation we have been describing seems almost essential to foresight. Those of us at the Harvard Business School who have been studying the role of directors in business management have repeatedly come across this phenomenon. For instance, one director of a well-known company characterized the president as follows:

Mr. Judson as president is always thinking at least three to four months in advance. Members of the board are located in such scattered cities that there is little opportunity for personal contacts during the intervals between board meetings. In advance of each meeting, however, we receive the agenda from Mr. Judson with comprehensive reports by the executives in charge of manufacturing, distribution, and finance. In addition to these reports, the president and each of those executives submit brief statements of their thinking about future developments. At the board meeting we quickly dispose of the legally required actions such as approving contracts and authorizing bank accounts. Most of the time is spent in thinking together about the problems that are likely to be coming up in the next three to six months. Mr. Judson throws up a lot of trial balloons. Many of them are punctured, but a few survive. We have learned by working together, however, that the directors' reactions to these problems will be considered carefully by the whole executive organization. In the next month or two modified proposals will appear, and eventually there will be a meeting of all the minds. Even then we do not make specific decisions, because that is an executive function to be performed at the time of action. The board of directors and executives consider that policy-making is based on thorough understanding. Mr. Judson contributes to this process by keeping the board thinking in advance instead of merely having it confirm what already has been done.

Foresight allows for gradual growth rather than disruptive arbitrary changes imposed as "policy decisions."

Most of us in modern society are generating changes which are taking the meaning out of life for others. And conversely, changes by others have their impact upon us. The response to changes in organization is not logical, but depends upon the meaning of the change to different people and groups in terms of routine relations. Therefore, we must ask in advance: What relations are involved? What is important to these groups? What will the change mean to them?

Let it be said that one does not get at the meaning of events for others by relaxing in one's arm chair. One gets at these data only by direct contact with people in continuous relation, where events and feelings about them can be dealt with in early stages. Getting new vision, seeing facts in new relations calls for participation rather than brass-knuckle management. Foresight, like insight, comes best in an atmosphere where one can drop defenses and look at the situation for what it is. And that attitude of management which creates this atmosphere is the last of the topics we shall deal with.

THE FORWARD-PASS FRAME OF MIND

Few experiences give such a lift as working on a tough situation in a group with a leader who has a forward-pass frame of mind. He meets even impossible proposals with, "Although we can't do it that way, let's see if there isn't some other way of accomplishing what you want."

Unfortunately, it is easier to illustrate the need for this forward-pass frame of mind than it is to describe it. But that does not mean one can easily detect the executives in an organization who are blocking the play instead of giving it a forward pass. According to the *Wall Street Journal's* report on August 28, 1951, Mr. W. S. Mielzinger, president of the Impact-O-Graph Corporation, says "General Electric engineers at Erie, Pennsylvania, puzzled over damage to refrigerators, clamped recorders on shelves inside the refrigerators as they left the assembly line and left them on until they arrived at the loading dock. They found that every box sustained a severe jolt just 3½ minutes after it left the line. A check disclosed the man stenciling addresses on the crates was letting them drop to the floor." Wouldn't it be simple if the Impact-O-Graph Corporation could produce a little black box to ship along with each idea that starts around through an executive organization?

I suspect that the Impact-O-Graph carried by most ideas would show a high proportion of lateral passes, a few spots where the idea is "dropped to the floor," and here and there all too few forward passes. Thought needs to be given to the detection and clarification of this forward-pass frame of mind. Some men may be born with it, but evidence indicates that good management, that is, good coaching, can do a lot to cultivate it. Also evidence indicates, for instance, that warped ideas of authority and position are among the common poisons which stunt the growth of this frame of mind.

The contrast between an executive's effectiveness while he sought participation and his failure when later he endeavored to impose his arbitrarily chosen objectives became tragically clear in the case of a $300,000,-000 corporation just before the last war. At that time the executive vice president was incapacitated. Nevertheless, he remained in office. One of the younger vice presidents stepped forward, largely on his own initiative, to keep business from being lost by default. On such occasions he would approach other executives directly responsible for the problem in question. He would discuss the situation as it appeared from his own department's point of view. After going over the situation, he would leave the other executive to do as he saw best. Time after time the company went forward as one department head after another put into action the ideas that grew out of such informal discussions. A year later the executive vice president finally resigned and the younger vice president was promoted to take his place. Thereupon his attitude and approach seemed to change. He had a staff department work out the ideal form of organization for company operations. At a formal meeting of all executives he announced the findings of this department and a timetable for making the necessary shifts. In place of the earlier coöperative action, resistance and inaction followed. The resistance was so widespread that, in a series of face-saving maneuvers, the new executive vice president was assigned a highly specialized mission, removed in effect from executive position.

Many students approach case situations asking, "How do you get people to do what you want them to do?" The forward passer, however, never has to consider so futile and ill conceived a question. His distinguishing feature is his search for a forward opening which anyone can see and welcome. He keeps asking in one way or another, "What's going on that leads people to resist or persist?" Feeling in this direction, he finds the breaks and charts a course which people follow with assent to purpose understood.

To the point of view just set forth many raise questions such as, "Isn't it management's job to determine direction?" In a sense it *is* management's function to determine direction. This function is not abdicated by participation; in fact, looking into the unknowable future, the role of the executive becomes more clear. Looking in that direction, the determination of purpose is a creative activity calling for all the skills the administrator can bring to the situation.

Somehow there has fallen to business administrators the opportunity to provide the materials for living. The administrator has the opportunity as well to give meaning and sanity to living. All our research keeps elaborating this major theme in one variation or another. Executives are always working with double exposures—their task is never simply a picture of machines, money, and market maps. Along with this picture is the web of human relations. In every transaction the executive is not only conducting his business; he is weaving or raveling out the fabric of our society.

PART TWO

TRAINING IN INDUSTRY

Training Supervisors in Human Relations [1]

F. J. ROETHLISBERGER

In the past decade heavy stress has been placed on the need for a better understanding of human relations on the part of supervisors—foremen, office managers, or others whose role it is to supervise men and women at work. As a result, training programs designed to teach supervisors how to deal with people at work have become increasingly popular. These programs have run the gamut from those that try to teach general principles of human behavior to those that are organized at the "how to do it" level, such as how to handle grievances or how to induct new workers.

In view of the increasing importance and popularity of these programs, it would seem timely to ask ourselves some questions. How successful have they been? On what assumptions are they based? How can they be improved? In this article I should like to try my hand at answering these questions. If I speak feelingly about some of these matters, let me remind the reader that it is because they are very important to me and because it is one good way of being "objective."

HOW SUCCESSFUL?

For some time now I have been impressed by how ineffective and unrealistic many of these programs are. They do not accomplish what they are designed to do, that is, to help supervisors with the human aspects of their jobs. Many of them raise "loaded" questions, give facile answers, indulge in platitudes, present principles that cannot be applied to concrete situations, and discuss unreal situations—situations that never have existed except in someone's imagination. In many of them the conference

[1] This article is based in part on a talk given at a conference of the Training Directors of America in Philadelphia, March 15–17, 1951.

leader is armed with the points that the trainees are supposed to make. He is allotted so much time to draw these points out, and, should the trainees fail to respond, he is instructed to make them himself.

In many of these programs supervisors are instructed in "why employees behave as employees." Very few have much to say as to "why supervisors behave as supervisors." Most of them *tell* the supervisor how he should behave. This *telling* may be done directly or indirectly, tactfully or not so tactfully, in terms of facts or principles or by sentimental appeals, persuasion, and "pep talks." But no matter how thin you slice it (just like baloney), it still remains *telling*.

What so often astonishes me is how docilely supervisors go through these verbal hoops and how readily they learn the proper verbal responses with which to please their conference leader. Every supervisor in the country knows by now that he should have "all the facts" before he acts, and that when all its said and done about these problems of human relations, their solution is just a simple matter of applying the golden rule.

What are we trying to do? Surely we must hope that what goes on in these training sessions will make some difference in the way the trainees will behave in the future, in the shop or office. But when the trainee goes back to the shop or office, he is under particular pressures, both internal and external, which determine his behavior there far more than anything that has gone on in the training meetings. Very little is done about these matters in our training sessions.

Rather, we apparently prefer to spin out our good intentions and beliefs, mostly erroneous, about an ideal supervisor—a little tin god on wheels that never existed at any place or any time; a man who is always "objective," who gets all the facts before he acts, who never loses his temper, who is always courteous and kind and, above all, fair, who treats people the way he would like to be treated, who can tell an introvert from an extrovert, who knows about the private lives of all his employees and just what is troubling them, who knows the four methods of resolving conflict, while of course at the same time he gets out the work and maintains cost and quality. What a guy!

BASED ON WHAT ASSUMPTION?

Because we do not know in a very clear way what we are after in our programs, we underestimate the difficulty of the job. We bring to our training sessions an odd assortment of beliefs and assumptions not only about what a supervisor should be and how he should behave but also about the way he learns, grows, and changes and the time it takes to accomplish these things. So long as these beliefs and assumptions persist, we cannot improve upon what we are doing. One of the most persistent of these assumptions is the belief that learning from experience is a simple process.

Learning from Experience. From childhood we have all heard that we learn from experience and that experience is the best teacher. All of us would agree that what a supervisor learns from his personal experience is likely to be more important to him than what he gets from any training meetings. Yet often we seem to be asking supervisors to apply to their problems rules and principles that ignore or deny their personal experiences.

Let us explore more carefully this idea of learning from experience. One of the interesting things about experience is how personalized it becomes, how important to each of us our own personal experience is, and how difficult it is to communicate this importance to others. What does this personal experience teach us? Astonishingly enough, personal experience seems to teach different people quite different lessons. It often teaches the wrong as well as the right lesson. The school of hard knocks makes criminals as well as businessmen.

In talking to supervisors I have found that personal experience has taught them a number of things, if we can take the beliefs that they express at their face value. For example, it has taught them that women are more easily upset by unimportant things than men, that you have to let employees know who the boss is to gain their respect, and that "it's not what you know but who you know" that counts in getting ahead in most organizations. Such statements and many others like them can be frequently heard.

These beliefs are not entirely unfounded. For the people who hold them, such beliefs reside in personal and social experiences they have had. Some of them can be traced to certain experiences that particular supervisors have had with particular employees, bosses, and organizations. Some of them have been picked up as part of the collective beliefs of certain social groups of which supervisors have been members. But these are not very adequate generalizations from experience; if applied too rigidly, they may get the supervisor into trouble, and, perhaps even more important, they may prevent him from learning any new lessons from experience. More often than not, instead of helping supervisors to do better jobs, the function of such beliefs is to allow supervisors to maintain their self-respect in the face of their inadequacies.

Once such beliefs have been built up, it is astonishing how they persist and how experience has a way of confirming them. For those of us who believe the world is essentially a hostile place, experience has a curious way of fulfilling our expectations. People with chips on their shoulders are more likely to find other people with chips on their shoulders. This is because we are constantly selecting from experience those aspects which prove our point and also because our attitudes toward other people are likely to determine their attitudes toward us. There are always enough instances of poor women drivers to reinforce our conviction that women drivers are always poorer than men. There are always a sufficient number of people talking about us to confirm our suspicions that we are being talked about, particularly if this belief that we are being talked about makes our behavior sufficiently peculiar to provoke comment. Just as attitudes of hostility and suspicion tend to provoke similar attitudes from others, so do attitudes of friendliness tend to provoke attitudes of friendliness in return.

If my analysis is correct, it would seem to follow that learning from experience is not the simple process we so often assume it to be. On the contrary, it is a rather difficult achievement to learn the valid and useful lessons experience can teach us. Our limited backgrounds, let me emphasize, often tend to produce inadequate generalizations, beliefs, and attitudes. Hell or high water, logic or evidence to the contrary, they tend to persist.

Assumptions versus Facts. It would also seem to follow from my brief analysis that, if we are to learn the useful lessons new experience can teach us, we have to question and reëxplore continuously the assumptions and attitudes we bring to it. And this for most of us is a difficult business. It is much more comforting to believe that women are peculiar beings than to face up to the uncomfortable feelings of inadequacy we have when trying to relate ourselves to them in a work situation. If this be so, the difficult task, then, which faces most training directors is not how to tell supervisors what they do not know about human behavior; it is how to get supervisors to "unlearn" what they believe about people that is not true. As someone has so aptly said, it is not people's ignorance but "what they know that ain't so" that gets them into trouble.

However, when trainers teach "what they know that ain't so" to supervisors who are equally convinced of "what they know that ain't so," the confusion is confounded and compounded. We have a veritable Tower of Babel. Take, for example, the precept that the supervisor should have all the facts before he acts. How often have I heard this said in one course or another? Why do we persist in telling supervisors to do what is not only difficult but impossible to do? No supervisor, or executive, for that matter, has ever acted or ever will act in terms of all the facts, let alone all the relevant facts, in a situation. All action is based on certain assumptions about the unknown and even the unknowable. By the kind of assumptions he makes about these matters the wise man is differentiated from the fool.

Moreover, in this precept we gloss over the difficulty of getting even some of the relevant facts in any human situation. We talk of "facts" as if they were crystal-clear, simple entities which any fool can observe and find and which will also be considered "facts" by all other observers. In the human-relations area, I find nothing more elusive and difficult to determine and to find than the "facts." Moreover, as has been said, "facts do not speak for themselves; they have to be interpreted for their meaning."

That we teach supervisors such untruths does not bother me so much. I realize there are some important and useful half-truths. What does bother me is that this kind of nonsense goes on in the name of common sense, realism, and practicality—and that the grim, earnest, and serious discussion of these silly little points is not even helpful. It takes all the adventure out of learning. It is the best way I know of losing not only your mind but also your sense of humor. And from what I hear, the supervisor does not enjoy it or learn much from it either.

Perhaps we need a more concrete example. Let me record for you an actual discussion that took place in a particular training session between a conference leader and his trainees.[2] The topic under discussion was "emotions." The conference leader was asking for comments on whether or not the various emotions listed in the training manual were good or bad. Included in the list was the word "loyalty." The discussion I shall record starts here.

1. *Conference Leader:* How about loyalty?
2. *Trainee:* Good, you have to have it.
3. *Conference Leader:* Is it ever bad?
4. *Trainee:* When the company gives you a raw deal, you can't be loyal.
5. *Conference Leader:* Well, then you'd quit.
6. *Trainee:* Well, I don't know.
7. *Conference Leader:* Here we have an emotion that is unequivocally good. To whom do we have to be loyal? First to the company—to all executives and to all workers.

With this pronouncement the discussion about loyalty ceased. Somewhat later the group discussed the emotion of "ambition." Let us listen in to the conversation as the conference leader is again speaking.

8. *Conference Leader:* Now take ambition. Is it important in a group like this? Damned right! We all want to give the impression of success to outsiders

[2] These selections have been taken from A. Zaleznik, *Foreman Training in a Growing Enterprise.*

as well as to our inner self. Suppose you were put in the vice president's office to copy the encyclopedia at a salary of $10,000 a year. How long would you be happy?

9. *Trainee:* All my life. [Laughs.]

10. *Conference Leader:* He doesn't want a cinch. He wants to do something. And $10,000 is not enough to keep you satisfied. What about fellows who don't have ambition, are they executive timber?

11. *Trainee:* No.

12. *Conference Leader:* You want to shoot for the boss's job. All right. But ambition has a twist. Can it have a bad effect?

13. *Trainee:* If a guy has a swell head.

14. *Another Trainee:* If you try to chop down smaller guys, that's bad.

15. *Conference Leader:* Ambition might drive a man to underhand tactics. That's completely undesirable. Ambition drives him. Ambition is like fire—it's essential, but when uncontrolled, it's dangerous.

16. *Trainee:* Is a man without ambition useless?

17. *Conference Leader:* If he is an executive, yes.

18. *Trainee:* Suppose a supervisor gets to be an assistant general manager, and he is satisfied and does a wonderful job?

19. *Conference Leader:* That's not good. He can't continue to do a wonderful job.

As I see it, many of our training programs fall short in the area of human relations because (1) they are oriented more to words and techniques than to the understanding of situations; (2) they ignore the feelings and attitudes which supervisors bring to these training sessions; (3) they misevaluate the complexity of the learning process; and hence (4) they substitute good intentions and wheezes for intelligent reflection about experience. As a result, it is not surprising that supervisors often leave these meetings little changed except perhaps for having acquired a slightly enlarged vocabulary and a few tricks.

HOW SECURE IMPROVEMENT?

This evaluation of our training efforts shows the need of more realistic objectives. For our aims I feel we should choose nothing short of the highest. What may sound idealistic is also common sense and practical.

Educated People. What industry and business must have in their supervisory and executive groups is more educated people—not more trained seals. I realize the word "educated" may prove a stumbling block, so let me say what I mean. I am not saying that supervisors should necessarily be college or university graduates. Lord forbid! By an "educated" person I mean a person (1) who knows what he does not know; (2) who has an honest perplexity and curiosity about his personal experience; (3) who has a stop-look-and-listen attitude toward his own experience so that he is capable of reëvaluating it and learning from it; and (4) who has some skills in the direction of being able to receive communications from others.

In short, my picture of an educated person is a person with those mental attitudes which allow him to grow from his experience in the direction of learning how to live better with himself and others. We can find such people in all walks of life and with varying degrees of formal education. I find little evidence to confirm the belief that only universities turn out such people. In fact, there is some slight evidence that in such institutions one is least likely to find them.

Be that as it may, please note that my picture of an "educated person" is a far cry from a person (1) who has all the answers; (2) who knows clearly right from wrong and what the "proper attitude" of people should be; (3) who accepts the maxims of others as a substitute for reflection and reëxamination of what experience can tell him about himself and others; and (4) who is insensitive to the opinions, feelings, and attitudes of the people with whom he works. Recent studies[3] would seem to indicate, moreover, that supervisors who have the attitudes toward experience I call "educated" are also the supervisors who seem to be better able to secure the coöperation of others.

If this be so, it would seem as if the aims of "real education" are consistent with the kind of person we would like our supervisor to be. With these aims in mind, we are now in a better position to state more clearly what our role as trainer in these training sessions should be.

Facilitating Self-Learning. I shall start negatively first. We should stop giving supervisors "the word." This I imagine is going to be difficult for some of us. "Do you mean," I can hear someone ask, "that we can no longer tell supervisors anything?" Let there be no mistake about it; I mean just that. We have to stop telling supervisors how they should behave and what their attitudes should be. We have to stop trying to change their personalities. We have to stop talking down to supervisors, lecturing them, giving them pep talks and little sermonettes. We have to give up our precepts, maxims, wheezes, and even their more dignified manifestations called "principles."

Why must we stop these things? For the simple reason that once and for all we are going to take seriously the idea that supervisors learn by themselves from their own experience, and what we can do most effectively is to help them in this process. Let us remember that our

---

[3] See Whyte, *Human Relations in the Restaurant Industry,* and Daniel Katz, Nathan Maccoby, and N. C. Morse, *Productivity, Supervision and Morale in an Office Situation* (Ann Arbor, Michigan: Institute for Social Research, University of Michigan, 1950).

new objective is to assist people in learning from their own experience. We are no longer trying to change them; we are giving them the opportunity to change themselves, if they wish, by reflecting upon and reevaluating their own experience.

This last point may need to be underlined. We are not interpreting their own experience *for them;* we are not telling them *our* personal experience. Instead *we are allowing them to examine and reëvaluate their own experience.* Let us not confuse these quite different phenomena, as I fear too many people do.

So let us be clear. We are not even going to tell supervisors what they should have learned from their own experience. They are going to have to learn the hard way. No more spoon feeding, no more ten commandments. They are big boys now, and "poppa" is no longer there to provide them with the answers. Each supervisor is going to have to work out his own salvation, to find the particular answer which best fits himself and his own situation.

Under this new objective, therefore, what we do is to set the conditions which will facilitate this process of self-learning. What are these conditions? In considering this question I shall have to go back to my analyses of how and what we learn from experience. Regarding personal experience I made several assertions; let me repeat them:

1. Personal experience has a way of being very important to the person whose experience it is.

2. Not only is each person's personal experience extremely important to him, but he is an authority on the subject. Nobody else knows more about it than he.

3. Different people learn different lessons from experience, sometimes useful, sometimes not.

These facts—and I shall call them that—make our problem both difficult and intriguing. They make us realize that learning the valid and useful lessons which experience can teach us is a very complex process. It means that there is no such thing as uninterpreted experience. Experience is constantly being evaluated. And lest we forget, please remember that each one of us is doing the evaluation. Sometimes we may interpret from too limited experience. Because of certain attitudes we bring to experience, we may misevaluate it and fail to see its significance. Therefore, before we can learn some things, we have to unlearn many "things that ain't so."

But this is difficult because of the reality to each of us of his own interpretations, no matter how limited and "screwy" they may be. Try to tell the supervisor whose experience has taught him to beware of redheads that not all redheads are volatile and explosive, and you will see what I mean. How does one get out of this impasse? I shall enumerate three ways that I find helpful:

(1) One can help people to recognize the feelings and attitudes which they bring to experience. For most of us these feelings and attitudes are implicit or unconscious; often we do not realize we have them. Nevertheless, they determine in good part what we see and hear. They underlie our beliefs and conceptions. They provide the frame of reference for our interpretations. They function as ill-defined and vague questions. Until we recognize more clearly some of these feelings and attitudes, there is no way of correcting them. We do not see how they distort the meanings we assign to our experience.

(2) If experience does not speak for itself, if we have to keep asking questions of it in order to elicit its useful meaning, we can be helped to ask "better" questions of experience. By "better" I mean clear and answerable questions. There is no clear answer to a vague question, but perhaps still more important to realize is that there is no answer to an unanswerable question. It is astonishing how often we ask and persist in asking of experience questions which experience cannot answer. Scientists no longer feel frustrated because experience cannot tell them how many angels can sit on the point of a needle; they have given up asking such questions. But in human affairs we have not progressed that far; we continue to ask unanswerable questions and feel frustrated because we cannot answer them.

The most common questions we ask in matters of human affairs are: "Who is to blame?" "Who is the villain?" "What is the cause of all our woes and miseries?" That the mutually interconnected, interrelated, and interdependent character of experience makes these questions unanswerable does not bother us. This hunt for the "spherical sonofabitch"—and by that I mean a sonofabitch from every point of view—goes on. I do not need to remind you that the search for this person or entity is rampant in the world today, and that for short periods in history we think we have found him or it. In our wishful thinking there must be such an entity, and in spite of our repeated disillusionments the quest continues.

(3) Not only can we help persons to recognize the feelings they bring to experience and to ask better questions of experience; we can also help them to be better observers of experience. We can provide them with a useful way of thinking about experience, which will allow them to make their own observations. Not until they can make better observations do they have something concrete against which to check their questions and to revise their beliefs and assumptions. It is futile, for example, to ask supervisors to address themselves to the feelings of

employees when they are not yet able to recognize a feeling when it is expressed to them. If people have no capacity to observe the effect of their behavior upon others, it is little use to tell them to "listen." So many of our precepts, maxims, and principles fall by the wayside because of this limitation. The practice of a precept can be no better than the observations in the concrete territory to which the precept is applied.

THE CASE-METHOD APPROACH

The time has come to raise the $64 question which by now I feel may be lurking in the back of many readers' minds. Let me try to state it: "We accept the propositions that the process of self-learning is facilitated (1) by helping people to recognize the attitudes they bring to experience; (2) by helping people to ask better questions of experience; and (3) by providing them with a *useful way* of thinking about matters of human behavior so that they can make better observations about themselves and their relations to others. This is all very fine, but please don't leave us hanging in the air. Get out of your ivory tower and become concrete. Just how can this be done?"

At this point I shall have to become extremely personal. I cannot tell you how you should do it; I can only tell you how I try to do it. The approach I take represents my own personal understanding and adaptation of the case method of instruction as used at the Harvard Business School. For this understanding I am greatly indebted to my colleagues there, so that what I have to say is far from original. Nevertheless, I shall continue to talk in personal terms so as to avoid any possible embarrassment to my colleagues for any shortcomings in my understanding. Moreover, I am only speaking of the case method as applied to the area of human relations, since it is to this area alone that my experience has been limited.

Setting Up the Discussion. In the first place, because learning begins with concretions and not abstractions, I choose a description of a concrete case for discussion—not an "armchair case," but a description of a real situation, of something that actually happened, of what actual people said, felt, did, and thought in a particular situation. This description does not contain all the facts, but rather some of the facts that some of the people involved in the situation have or that are available to them. I have the students or trainees (it does not matter which) read and prepare this case before the discussion. This description may involve as little as two or as many as twenty pages of reading matter.[4]

[4] For examples of the kind of cases I mean, see Glover and Hower, *The Administrator.*

In discussing this case, I ask the students or trainees what they would do in such a situation if they were in a position of responsibility. I generally choose for this position of responsibility one of the minor characters in the situation, let us say a department head or foreman rather than a president of the company. I do this because it allows me very soon to ask them not only what they would do but also how they would do it. Most students are much more articulate with "what to do" than with "how to do it." This is much truer when they are assuming the role of a foreman than when they are assuming the role of the president. I am always interested in how many supervisors think the president is a free agent and can do anything. I sometimes wonder how complimented presidents would be if they realized what prodigious feats their supervisors thought they were capable of accomplishing.

By stressing not only what needs to be done but also how to go about doing it, I help the student to realize the difference, for example, between "being tactful" in general and what the particular tactful remark in a particular situation would be. By this device I hope the students will realize how often their solutions are merely verbal. Notice I am not telling them anything. After they tell me that they would be "tactful," I merely ask them to tell me what they would say in particular to this particular person in this particular situation. The sweating, fumbling, silence, exasperation, or sheepishness which generally follow this question are more meaningful to them than anything I can say.

Helping the Students to Recognize Their Attitudes. There are several different assumptions that students or trainees are likely to bring to bear on a case:

(1) While they are discussing and "solving" the case, I usually observe them "hunting for the villain." There is never complete agreement on just who in particular the villain is, but that there is one and that he should be exterminated is almost always assumed. A wants to fire Joe Blow, B wants to fire the foreman, C wants to fire the department head, and D may even want to fire the president. By the time every villain has been exterminated in some fashion or other and there is no one left in the situation to do any work, I call the group's attention to this interesting "solution" and ask for any further comments. In my best wolf-in-sheep's-clothing manner, I perhaps mutter something to the effect that it does seem odd to me that we can only correct this condition by firing everybody in it.

(2) During the discussion I observe not only the "hunt for the villain," but also the "hunt for perfection." After their energies in the direction of exterminating villains have worn a bit thin, students often like to play God. With a flip of the wrist they change the personalities

of the characters in the case. They make them objective, calm, dispassionate people who see all, know all, and hear all. I give this God-playing tendency full reign. Generally during this phase I am merely muttering such phrases as "How interesting!" "You don't say?" "Bless my soul!" "Really?" "Extraordinary!" "I wouldn't have believed it," and equally innocuous remarks.

(3) Concurrently with the hunt for the villain and the hunt for perfection there frequently occurs also the "hunt for authority." This game is a favorite pastime of people in staff positions. The reason why they cannot get certain things accomplished, these people claim, is that they do not have "authority." Without it they are impotent; with it they could issue orders and injunctions which would be immediately obeyed. Their underlying assumption is that they lack authority, never that they lack understanding or skills. The solution therefore is to put themselves in a position as close to the president as possible, so that they will have the authority to get their plans and schemes accepted by the people below them.

During this period in which they are elevating themselves to higher and higher positions in order to get things done, I merely ask them how they would get there and, assuming they did get there, in what way, if at all, their behavior would change. Do they see any difference between the "authority" which is earned and recognized by the bottom and the "authority" which is conferred from the top?

(4) By this time the group becomes restless. The teacher does not seem to be approving of their behavior, although let me assure the reader that I am deeply interested. I am neither approving nor disapproving. I am just observing and reflecting my observations; but this is not the way the stereotype of a professor should behave. So by this time the group becomes a bit "aggressive." They begin to complain, "You haven't told us all the facts. How can I tell how to do it when I don't know if Joe Blow is an introvert or an extrovert? You haven't told us." I readily confess my guilt and then ask, "Let us assume that Joe Blow is an introvert. Just what difference, if any, would it make with regard to what you would do and how you would do it?" Sometimes I ask, "O.K., you don't know, but how would you find out if Joe Blow is an introvert or an extrovert?" I wouldn't quite say that these questions have a soothing effect on the class, but, to put it crudely, it does set them "back on their heels." They have to think again for themselves, and that is disagreeable.

(5) Now the class is filled with tension. The students have exterminated villains; they have played God; they have sought for a mystical authority; they have asked for more "facts"; and still the professor or

leader does not seem to be satisfied. At this point their attitude is likely to be, "We've worked hard enough. You tell us. You give us the answer." Here is the toughest nut to crack. Being human and having also a nervous system, I would like to tell them "the solution." But so long as I am not too fatigued to hold out against them, I generally say, "The discussion has been very interesting. I'm not sure I know just what should be done or how it should be done. I can tell you what I would do and how I would go about it. But that would not be *the* answer. It would be *my* answer. Perhaps we should discuss another case next time."

Note that I am not telling the students or trainees what to do. I am merely pointing out to them the assumptions they are making and the attitudes they are bringing to the problem. I am trying to help them to recognize these attitudes so that they can question and reëxamine them. I do not force them to reëxamine their assumptions. My attitude is permissive but questioning. "So you like to exterminate villains? So you like to play God? So you like to be given the facts, the authority, and the answer? How human, how interesting, but how come? Are we engaged here in an exercise of wishful thinking, or are we realists and men of practical affairs?"

Please do not think that there is not a very difficult problem of timing the innocuous and perhaps facetious remarks I make, but then I cannot give you all my "secrets." Also please do not think that these hunts for the villain, perfection, authority, the facts, and the answer are the only assumptions students or trainees bring to these case situations. I have only mentioned some of the most common ones for purposes of illustration.

Helping the Students to Ask "Better" Questions. Before considering this step, let me emphasize the importance of helping students to recognize the feelings and attitudes they bring to experience. This phase of the case discussion is very important. It is by far the most difficult to learn for those who are beginning to teach by the case method. It is time-consuming; it requires the patience of Job; it plays real havoc upon the nervous system of the case-discussion leader. Moreover, it involves that aspect of the learning process which is most ignored—that we have to unlearn some things experience has taught us before we can learn some of its more fruitful and helpful lessons. Until this is realized by the learner—even if only in an intuitive way—knowledge in the area of human relations remains sterile.

In matters of human affairs I often find it more helpful to ask "What is going on here?" than "Why are things the way they are?" The former question often helps us to sharpen our observations about what is going on right under our noses; the latter question frequently leads to idle speculation. The clinician, for example, has to be able to diagnose a case of measles before he can help the patient to get well. Moreover, the diagnostic skill of being able to recognize that "this is a case of measles" is as important to the physician and the patient as to try to answer the question of how the patient got the measles. In fact, in medicine the recognition of a syndrome precedes any explanation of its etiology. The skill of the clinician is his capacity to identify what is before him here and now.

When we instruct in the human-relations area, this fact is often ignored. We talk as if there were no such equivalent diagnostic skill based upon an intuitive familiarity with the way people behave. We try to solve problems intellectually, abstractly, and analytically instead of trying to identify and recognize what is taking place here and now. When Joe Blow comes up to complain to us, instead of trying to listen to the feelings he is expressing to us here and now, we are wondering about how his wife treats him, whether his mother rejected him as a child, whether he has an inferiority complex. So we observe nothing and hear nothing. We do not even hear or observe ourselves responding to our speculations rather than to the feelings of Joe.

So in the discussion of cases, instead of encouraging students to speculate as to why people behave the way they do, I try to turn their attention to the way a particular person in a particular situation is behaving and the effect of this behavior upon others. "Tell me," I ask, "do you see what this particular person is doing, what he is saying, what feelings he is expressing, here and now? Can you see in this particular case that the foreman is doing all the talking; can you see how this prevents Joe Blow from talking; can you identify some of the feelings Joe Blow expressed in the few moments he was allowed to talk? Can you see whether or not the foreman responded to these feelings of Joe's or to his own preoccupation? Can you see what effect upon Joe the foreman's particular response had?"

Notice that the new questions I am raising are questions which can be answered by observation here and now. I am hoping that when the supervisors go back to the shop or office they will ask similar questions of their present situation. In this way I hope to encourage them to make better observations, which will allow them to learn from their present experience.

Helping the Students to be "Better" Observers. In discussing the previous point I have already discussed in part this one. I defined a "better" question as one that can be answered approximately by experience. Experience, if it is to be useful, requires more precise observation. Observation occurs in the present, not in the past or future. By "better" observation I therefore mean the recognition and identification of what is taking place here and now.

Before we can observe skillfully, we need a useful way of thinking about the phenomena we are observing. Because most of us do not have a very clear way of thinking about what is happening when two people are talking together, we do not observe very clearly what is occurring. As a result, we are likely to pay more attention to what is being said than to the person saying it. In human relations we are observing events which involve the relations of people. By relations I do not mean logical relations. I mean *the activities* which bring people together or separate them from one another. I mean *the sentiments and feelings* they do or do not share. I mean *the interactions* they have, how often or how few. Note that *activities, sentiments,* and *interactions* are referring to things that can be seen and heard. They are elements to be found in any human relation.

For the observer of human relations, this need for a conceptual scheme —for a way of thinking about human relations—is paramount. Without such a conceptual scheme, his observations become dissipated. Let me try to illustrate what I mean in terms of the conversations I recorded earlier between a conference leader and his trainees in a training session. What did you, the reader, observe or hear in them?

Were you preoccupied with such questions and observations as the following:

What is loyalty anyway?

Did the conference leader answer the questions of the trainee correctly?

The trainee is right when he says, "You can't be loyal when the company gives you a raw deal."

The conference leader does not seem to be too bright.

The trainees do not seem to be too bright.

The conference leader should have said this or that, etc.

Or did you see and hear the following activities, interactions, and sentiments and their interrelations, and did you consider the following questions:

The conference leader began and ended each conversation.

The one conference leader used more words than the several trainees put together and spoke more often (ten times to their nine).

The conference leader was frequently expressing how people should feel.

When they had a chance, the trainees were expressing how they felt.

The conference leader did not address himself to the trainees' feelings and thus did not seem to encourage the trainees to speak.

The feelings of the trainees acted upon the feelings of the conference leader and vice versa.

The discussion was about "words" rather than about "situations."

The conference leader assumed that words meant something—not that people meant something. As a result, the "words" discussed provoked more heat (feelings) than light (exploration).

The trainee in statement 4 might have been talking about a previous personal experience.

What is likely to be the trainee's feeling when the conference leader responds to his statement (6) with statement 7?

What is the trainee in statement 16 trying to say?

Did the conference leader help him to say it?

It is my contention that if you (the reader) made the latter kind of observations and raised the latter kind of questions, you had a more useful way of thinking about these conversations. You were thinking of man as a creature living and learning in and through a network of relations. You were thinking of what purposes are secured and what needs are satisfied in these relations. You were thinking that what man brings to his experience in terms of assumptions and feelings determines in part what he perceives (sees and hears). You were thinking that what takes place in a conversation when two or more people are talking together is more likely to be an interaction of sentiments and feelings than a strictly logical phenomenon.

Therefore you were sensitive to the feelings which the trainees were trying to express. Therefore you were sensitive to the possible effect of the conference leader's feelings upon the feelings of the trainees and vice versa. Therefore you were curious about what was going on there. In short, you had a way of thinking which allowed you to observe what could be observed instead of indulging in idle analysis and speculation.

Accordingly, in helping students to be better observers, I try to provide a useful frame in which they may observe what is occurring in a concrete situation and in which they may think and operate on the facts. Such a way of thinking not only assists the observer to make certain observations; it also helps him to see certain uniformities in the facts—certain recurring phenomena. To cite some very simple cases, he can begin to see that persons are likely to talk more freely to him about matters that are of importance to them if he tries to understand what they are saying from their point of view rather than from his own. He can begin to see how persons resist changes that do too much violence to their customary ways of behavior. These uniformities in the territory he can observe over and over again. Once they can be recognized and identified, he can begin to take them into account in his behavior and the behavior of others.

Not until the student reaches this stage of being able to recognize some of the brute and stubborn facts of human behavior does "human relations" become something more than words, good intentions, rituals, and techniques.

Helping the Students to Make "Better" Decisions and to Behave Responsibly. It is my belief that in the area of human relations making better decisions is dependent on the three points already discussed; that is, that better decisions will only follow from better observations, better questions, and more self-awareness. I assume that the conscious decision-making process in the area of human relations is only a very, very small part of the evaluational process which is constantly going on at various levels of consciousness in the minds of people in positions of responsibility. The supervisor or executive is "evaluating" every minute of the day (and night too, sometimes). These evaluations determine what he assumes, sees, hears, feels, and does in the many interactions he has each day with superiors, subordinates, and colleagues. These evaluations enter very strongly into his more conscious deliberations and decisions. To treat decision-making apart from the personal and social evaluations of persons in which it is deeply imbedded would be a grave error—a form of "misplaced concreteness."

For these reasons I allow my students to make up their own minds, to reach their own decisions. I only try to make them more aware of what they are assuming, feeling, perceiving, doing, and saying and of how these processes are interdependent. By such a process of self-awareness I assume they not only will make "better" decisions but also will act more responsibly. Responsible behavior is acting with awareness of the effect upon oneself and others of what one is doing. Without such an awareness, good intentions are not enough. Without a capacity for observation, awareness cannot be achieved.

CONCLUSION

In conclusion I should like to make four comments:

(1) I know I have treated a very serious and difficult problem in a very cavalier fashion. Articles or books, for that matter, could be written on each of the last four points I have been considering. My only excuse for my oversimplified treatment is that my purpose has been to intrigue the reader with a point of view rather than to expound it systematically.[5]

(2) What I have been trying to say is a matter of deep concern to me. My plea in this article has been for more spontaneity and humility

[5] For those readers who are interested in more scholarly presentations of useful ways of thinking about matters of human relations, I should like to recommend Homans, *The Human Group;* Rogers, *Client-Centered Therapy;* and Whyte, *Pattern for Industrial Peace.*

in the teaching of human relations. The teaching of human relations can be a great adventure, a great challenge, and a great hope. Let's not make it a farce.

(3) In the many human-relations programs in business and industry, I see an opportunity for the recovery of spontaneity, a sense of perspective, as well as a sense of humor. Too often in each of his many courses the supervisor is too much concerned with the grim, earnest, and often humorless discussion of some specialization, so that nowhere does he get a sense of perspective with regard to the nature of his job as a totality. In my opinion, the human-relations area offers an ideal opportunity to regain this lost sense of proportion about matters of supervision. It is the one place where the supervisor can be himself—without having to pretend to be an expert on all matters. Let's keep it that way.

(4) I realize that what I have been talking about is not so simple to do as my remarks may have seemed to indicate. The skills of teaching by the case method cannot be learned in three easy lessons. Nevertheless, in spite of this handicap, the case method of instruction should not remain unexplored by business. It is realistic, down-to-earth; it provides an ideal medium for helping self-learning to take place. Moreover, particularly in an institution like business which is unhampered by academic tradition, it could really grow and develop.

Executive Training by the Case Method

KENNETH R. ANDREWS

A number of companies have already adopted for first-line supervisors and for executives in higher ranks the case method of training which F. J. Roethlisberger recommends in "Training Supervisors in Human Relations." The first objective is negative: to avoid the boredom, futility, and waste of training programs that ignore the attitudes, feelings, and experience of those being trained. The more important purpose is positive: to enable the participants to learn (from reflection upon their own experience) how to approach more effectively than before the human problems of administration in their own organizations.

It is still too early to claim measurably improved executive behavior. But now, after three or four years of experimentation, it is plain that application of the case method to internal problems of company administration has succeeded in deeply interesting those exposed to it and impelling them to ask for more.

Training directors accustomed to apathetic response to their programs will be interested in training arrangements which generate enthusiasm; members of management who approve training budgets will be interested even more in signs that time and money devoted to training are well spent. This article, therefore, will describe for both training directors and company officers the intrinsic interest and the potential effectiveness of two experimental programs and will suggest the particular steps to be taken by companies inclined to follow Roethlisberger's advice.

The organizations which have recently experimented independently with training centered on the experience of their executives include J. D. Woods and Gordon, Ltd. (of Toronto, Canada); the Standard Oil Development Company; the Standard Oil Company of Indiana; the E. I. duPont de Nemours Company; the Lago Oil and Transport Company,

Ltd. (of Aruba in the Netherlands West Indies); Cargill, Inc.; the American National Red Cross; and the United States Navy. In each instance the program has been adapted to the particular needs of the organization, and in all companies the approach was experimental.

Several of my colleagues have participated in these experiments; I draw from their experience. Because my firsthand observation makes it appropriate, the two programs to be described here in detail are those undertaken by Cargill, Inc., and by the American National Red Cross. One experience involved the use of cases drawn from those made available to the public by the Harvard Business School; the other led also to the development of cases provided by the organization itself.

CARGILL'S MANAGEMENT CONFERENCES

Cargill, Inc., which buys, sells, stores, and transports grain, produces and distributes seeds, and manufactures animal and poultry feeds and vegetable oils, began its experiments in executive training by the case method in 1948. Encouraged by the reports of individual executives who had attended the Advanced Management Program at the Harvard Business School, John C. Savage, then the company's training director, visited the School, arranged for the services of an experienced case-discussion leader, and set out to develop a full-time one-week course for 16 men chosen from the level of men reporting directly to vice presidents in charge of the company's major divisions.

Setting the Objectives. The first task was to determine what subject matter to cover. The training director and the writer interviewed most of the chief executives to get their impressions of the company's executive talent. After these discussions it was clear that awareness of the problems of working with people and willingness of specialists to assume a company-wide point of view were two needs to which the conferences should be pointed.

The company's recent diversification away from sole dependence on grain merchandising made the need for new points of view acute. Accordingly, the purposes of an "intensive week of conferences" to be held in February 1949 were somewhat diffidently announced in a mimeographed statement to be *the development and exchange of at least a preliminary awareness and a practical point of view toward (1) what prompts people to work efficiently and smoothly together; (2) what is involved in building and leading an efficient team; and (3) what must be done to translate observations about human relations into action in an efficient and responsible business.*

The goals were lofty and perhaps far off. However, it was not one of the objectives of the first series of case discussions to attain them completely. A useful way of thinking about making progress toward them was enough at this early stage. To avoid promising too much and to separate the experimental course from the usual lecture and injection-type training program, the announcement concluded:

Discussion will be free and unrestricted. The success of the conference will depend, much more than on the contributions of the conference leader, upon the ideas contributed by the men at the table. The competence and experience of the members will be such that these discussions should be continuously interesting, permanently stimulating, and provocative of considerable further thinking about the crucial topics discussed. No immediate cure-alls for human problems will be available, and only a beginning attack upon persistent difficulties can be formulated during the discussion. The persons selected will have an opportunity to clarify the kind of problems that lie ahead of everyone working toward more responsible positions as he qualifies for them.

With the hope that the persons selected for the conferences would take away an "awareness of an executive's responsibility for advancing not only his own operating subdivision or line function, but the company as a whole," the course was approved by the Cargill management. Everyone recognized that the translation of this awareness into effective behavior must take place afterwards, on the job, not in the training conference.

Selection of Conferees and Cases. The training director monitored the choice of persons to attend, and the conference leader chose the cases.

Since cases and conferees were to be the flint and steel of this program, both were selected with an eye to sparks. The training director consulted every division head in the selection of at least one representative from each of the company's divisions and from a number of its branch offices. The attempt was made to choose a man at the stage of his development when a widening of his point of view to include total company objectives was more important than further development of his specialty. The group was balanced to cover the widest variety of experience. The men selected were among those who within the next ten years would, if all went well, succeed to top-management responsibilities. The group's potential capacity was thus considered to be great. They were all on the same level; no man's immediate superior attended the conferences.

It certainly cannot be said that the men selected looked forward with great enthusiasm to a full week away from their desks spent exclusively in conferences, especially when they saw that a professor was in charge of the punishing schedule. Some of the men, indeed, consented to attend only in recognition of their bosses' expressed wish to that effect. Most of the men, furthermore, came from a level at which it is conventional in American industry to assume that executive skill is as fully developed as the person's capacity will permit.

As many precautions as good sense dictated were taken to keep the initial selection from being misunderstood—for example, pointing out to the men that they were not selected because they were either expert or clumsy in human relations, that persons not included in the first series would be chosen later if the experimental conferences succeeded. But training is training, and its connotations are inglorious. Some of the conferees later reported that they were not happy about being elected.

The cases were chosen from the files which the Harvard Business School has collected and made available to the public.[1] (The "case" is a carefully written description of an actual situation in business which provokes in the reader the need to decide what is going on, what the situation really is, or what the problems are—and what can and should be done.) The conference leader's choice was guided by his own knowledge of which cases had proved interesting in past discussion and which cases were directly relevant to Cargill objectives and Cargill problems.

The cases were arranged in a folder with questions which were included to indicate the possibilities of advance preparation. The order of cases was determined not by any logical arrangement of issues or course outline but by the level at which the central figures of the case did their work. Since the week of conferences was to provide opportunity for the men attending to review their own experience, it appeared suitable to take up the cases first at the foreman and last at the presidential level. This rationale was intended not to impose a pattern upon the discussion so much as to suggest the continuity of executive experience and the familiar chronology of growth. The actual course of the discussions was to be determined by the experience and interests of those elected to attend.

Conference Place and Routine. Because it was planned to make the week of conferences a complete break in their work life, the conferees were all asked to stay at the Lowell Inn in Stillwater, Minnesota, a comfortable and attractive place 30 miles from downtown Minneapolis. Here they would be protected from office and home interruptions. The design was to provide a pleasant and different environment in which the conferees could live together, study cases, argue cases between sessions, and achieve, all told, a productive experience worth much more than the time, money, and effort devoted to it. Providing an atmosphere in which the

[1] Many of the cases used by Cargill and the Red Cross are included in Glover and Hower, *The Administrator.* Many other casebooks in other areas, of course, are in print, in use by schools, and available for use by industry.

men attending could relax away from everyday tensions was considered as important an adjunct to productive discussion as the selection of cases.

Relaxation from routine did not mean inactivity. The schedule was stiff enough to keep everyone occupied. On each day the group met around a table from 9:00 to 11:30 or thereabouts in the morning, from 2:00 to 4:00 in the afternoon, and from 7:30 to 9:00 or later in the evening. Usually one case was discussed during a session. Three cases a day, therefore, had to be studied between meetings. Once. or twice, an evening session was devoted to summary discussion instead of a more demanding "digging through the case."

The provision in the schedule for a five-day week averaging six hours of serious discussion, two or more hours of case preparation, and the same amount of time to talk in smaller groups, though it may seem in prospect intolerable, proved in fact to be burdensome but supportable. The luxury of the surroundings was thus accompanied by considerable devotion to duty. This was not a ritually alcoholic company convention, or a rest home for tired executives, but a carefully arranged new kind of hard work.

What Happened. A description of what happened in a week-long conversation among 16 men must necessarily be a personal account. I report here my own observations based on what I saw, heard, and have since deduced, and what has been reported to me by the company.

The soundness of the original arrangements was quickly confirmed. There is no doubt at all about the fact that the discussion was lively and interest high. The schedule was not too heavy; discussion often ran over the period tentatively allotted to it in advance. Fatigue accumulated visibly during the week but did not markedly interfere with attention or interest. One or two cases proved to have been inappropriately chosen; these were dropped when their uselessness for the occasion became clear, and others were considered in their place.

The discussion, particularly because at least in its early stages it was argumentative, sometimes repetitive, and consistently vigorous, is very hard to summarize. As the group came to know each other, the discussion became more systematic, searching, and pointed. The participants' comments quickly revealed their own experience and assumptions about its meaning, and they attacked and asked questions about each other's point of view. They seemed to be constantly surprised at how many views there were of a given case and at how many different analyses there were of what was going on and what needed to be done in the case situation.

Some men confessed their confusion in the face of so many points of view and were disturbed by the apparent pointlessness of uncovering so many of them. It became evident, however, that the existence of differing points of view had something to do with administration, and most of the week was taken up with the implications of this discovery.

During the course of the week, I saw developing (or perhaps thought I saw because I wished to see it) a turning away from the idea of a general "principle" for solving human problems, and a turning toward the attitudes and questions with which skillful administrators approach the problem of working with people in their own organizations. The pastime which Roethlisberger damns (the hunt for villains, for perfection, for authority) gave way to inquiry into "what the hell is going on." By the middle of the week dispassionate observations and calm questions began to appear more often and hastily contrived judgments less often. "What are we going to do for exercise," one man asked, "now that we have stopped jumping to conclusions?"

The man whose standard reaction to every instance of interpersonal friction was, "I'd put my arm around that guy's shoulder and say, 'Now look, old man, you don't want to get all steamed up about that; we can work it out,'" came eventually to distrust the universal efficacy of his prescription. He did not forsake in the process the amiability which had originally prompted the stereotyped response. His opposite number, whose instinctive response in each of the earlier cases was, "I'd pick up that guy by the scruff of the neck and fire him the hell out of the company," eventually considered more exploratory attitudes. He did not give up the stubborn insistence on high standards of performance with which he came to the conferences.

In the laughter and good nature which in the conferences highlighted the absurdity of all stereotyped response to unique situations, both men came to look upon the human aspects of administration as something more than the dissemination of either (1) brotherly love or (2) the fear of God. The group as a whole began to express a point of view toward human problems which requires one to be neither softheaded nor hardnosed but first of all alert to what is going on. Presumably at least some of this conference-born curiosity and executive detachment persisted under subsequent on-the-job pressures.

Thus, the first venture by this company into training by the case method followed in broad outline the pattern which a good case always suggests to intelligent people willing to assume responsibility for analysis of its meaning and for formulation of action appropriate to the analysis. The problems of the case, those plain or implicit, were identified; the possibilities within the organization for correction, amendment, or changed behavior were assessed; and from the point of view of the responsible executive in the case a choice of steps was outlined and specific action often decided on.

Within this form, sometimes below the surface of the discussion, the men thinking and talking applied the case to their own problems and experience. Either in the conference, in smaller groups afterwards, or by themselves they usually completed the analogy between the case and their own situations. Throughout, they looked at themselves and their colleagues in the light of the discussion. Sometimes, even after years of association, they seemed favorably surprised at what they saw.

But it is easy to claim too much. It is also undoubtedly true that some men, though unaccountably interested, profited not at all from the discussion. Some persons here as elsewhere were so loyal to what they had already "learned" from their experience that it could yield up nothing better and nothing different upon reëxamination. It is safe for me to say merely that at the last session demand was made (1) for further sessions and (2) for exactly the same sort of sessions for their own superiors. ("If I need this, my boss sure does!")

A man who had come from Omaha "over his dead body" said as much and summarized the sense of the meeting as follows: "I'm not sure exactly what I got from the conferences, but I know it's something, and something worth while." He went on to express willingness to leave Omaha once every two months for the follow-up sessions. Nothing that I may say later can better express the potential effectiveness of the case method of training than this man's remarks. No occasion on which case training within a company has been used has failed to produce interest, and none has produced any more specific guarantee of good results than the feelings reflected here.

Aftermath. Something had happened, at any rate. The president of Cargill soon reported that he had seldom observed such enthusiasm for a new venture. The members of his immediate staff were apparently interested by their juniors' recommendation that they too should undertake this experience. Even during the first week they had appeared by ones and twos to observe the evening sessions, and several months later they spent two days at the Lowell Inn wrestling with cases on their own. Because of the selection of cases (mistakenly chosen to reflect supposedly unique top-management problems and top-management attitudes) and because two days are not a week, this conference was less successful than it could have been. But it did serve to acquaint directly the officers of the company with the process involved in a discussion by the case method and to demonstrate firsthand its power—an effect which must be experienced to be believed.

Since the first experiment, two more groups of executives with roughly the same qualifications have attended the annual conferences at Stillwater. As far as I could tell, the second and third series were as pro-

ductive as the first. During the third-year conferences, the "alumni" of the
first and second years returned for two and one half days each to work
on new cases. Though the procedure now had no novelty for the participants, the sessions were again lively and interesting. Changes wrought
by time and experience were evident in some of those attending. Only
one or two men were apparently as little affected by these exposures to the
case method as they would be to any other form of influence.

Even more significant for those who hope that business will explore
further the possibilities of case training is the extension within Cargill of
the method under the auspices of the training director. Supervisory conferences with human problems of administration as their subject are discussions not only of published cases but now more often of cases drawn
directly from actual Cargill experience. I am told that these proceed,
under the rotating chairmanship of the members or under the training
director, with similar profit and gusto. Experiment here has thus led to
the incorporation of the case method as a major tool of company training,
and the program will henceforth continue without anything more than
occasional outside assistance.

Why the Conferences Prospered. After three years of watching the introduction of the case method and the discussion of human relations and
its application to administration in Cargill, I think I know why these conferences are considered to have been successful:

(1) The preparation and environmental arrangements were skillfully
managed by the training director.

(2) The objectives of the program had the active understanding, interest, and support of the company's owners and managers.

(3) The experimental method captured the interest of persons ready to
try a new departure in executive training—an interest so active that in
each of the three years the president opened the series, the chairman of
the board or the executive vice president closed it, and vice presidents
visited the sessions in between.

(4) For the men attending, this was evidence not only of management
support for training activities but of a keen interest in executive development and in the men who would eventually succeed to positions of highest
responsibility.

(5) The willingness of the top-management group to expose itself
even briefly to the same experience completely redressed the trainee
status and obliterated any lingering resentment against being sent to
learn what had long been taken for granted.

(6) The selection of place and persons was intelligently devised to
give the case method every opportunity of success.

(7) No important cleavage between the objectives set forth by the

training program and the objectives sought under daily work pressures complicated the procedings.

(8) Above all, their own interest and competence provided the men attending with whatever benefits they took from the experience.

Unless the signs were all misleading, the conferees left the case discussion more alert in various degrees than they had been to things which they could detect in their own executive activity and in their relations with others in the company.

THE RED CROSS MANAGEMENT CONFERENCES

In 1950 the National Headquarters of the American Red Cross undertook, under the leadership of Dr. Louis F. Hackemann, at that time its National Training Director, a program similar in many respects to that started a year earlier in Cargill.

The most interesting difference was the further experimentation made by the Red Cross in the second year. At that time cases drawn from the internal administrative problems of the Red Cross organization were the subject of the discussion, and the conferees were expected during the week of the training to reassess the significance of very persistent difficulties and to struggle with ways and means of dealing with them. The process of converting into recommendations the findings of the conference is still going on, but an interim report may throw further light on both the vitality and the versatility of the case method.

The Red Cross management conferences were in some ways considerably less intensive than Cargill's, and the discussion groups were larger. So far there have been two week-long sessions, a year apart. All the members of the organization's top management, more than 80 men and women, attended case discussions during the week. The general manager, the deputy general managers, and a half dozen other senior executives met in one group; their subordinates in two other groups of 30 each. The groups of 30 met for approximately six hours daily for two days each, discussing a half dozen cases. A final joint meeting of the entire staff, which included the heads of the 20-odd different services comprising the organization, was held to acquaint each group with what the others had been doing. The conferences were held in Washington hotels, away from the headquarters buildings, but unlike the Cargill conferees the Red Cross executives returned to their homes in the evening.

Objectives of the First Conferences. The cases for the first year's series were chosen following the same kind of interviews with executives as preceded the first Cargill conference. It was quickly apparent that the problems of communication, coördination, and coöperative activity were no different in the Red Cross from those facing any nationwide multiple-activity organization of formal complexity and rapidly shifting emphases. It was agreed that the objectives of the conference should be stated formally as follows:

1. To provide an opportunity for the principal executives in National Headquarters to develop and exchange ideas about administration—the process of accomplishing organization purposes through coöperative action.

2. To stimulate a renewed awareness of the human problems involved in:

(a) The formulation, dissemination, and effective execution of co-ordinated policy;

(b) The creation of effective working relations between superiors and subordinates and among groups of diverse technical interests and special qualifications;

(c) The striking of the necessary balance between demands made by an organization upon its individuals and by individuals upon their organization;

(d) The effective coördination of planning and communication aimed at mutual understanding;

(e) The practice of delegating authority and responsibility through a staff and line team;

(f) The attitudes, sense of responsibility, and administrative behavior required of an executive in high position.

What Happened—First Series. Although these objectives suggest the materials for a lifetime of reflection, the discussions drawing on a lesser amount were apparently successful. Some persons may have considered the proceedings a waste of time, but only two alluded to such views in their responses to the questionnaires which were sent to all participants after the first series. With these exceptions the entire staff welcomed enthusiastically the early experiment in case training.

Perhaps because of the promise of new patterns of relation within the organization and the suggestion that new ideas might become available to solve old puzzles, interest was high pitched. The chief problem posed by the early direction of the conferences, in fact, was to keep enthusiasm within the bounds of realism. It was not easy to prevent eagerness from obscuring the necessity for a snail's pace in changing basic organization approaches to a better coördination of diverse activities and a gentler integration of conflicting points of view.

The shorter period of the discussions and the initial inexperience with administration of some of the persons attending were probably responsible for the higher ratio of inspiration to systematic analysis of case situations.

It was to a sense of hope and an interest in the future improvement of internal procedures that the first sessions were devoted.

What the psychologist would refer to as the therapeutic element of such conferences was much more pronounced in the Red Cross series, perhaps because of differences in sophistication among the two groups. Cargill executives, in contrast to Red Cross executives, were the product of careful, systematic development within the company. The history of the Red Cross had necessarily been chaotic. Many of the present executives, for example, were catapulted into their positions without long preparation by the enormous expansion of the organization during the Second World War. It has been the purpose of recent training to round out the qualifications of the management as a whole.

Once again the use of cases from outside organizations concerned with the same type of problems as those acute within the Red Cross permitted discussions to proceed without strain or embarrassment. All told, the first session, modeled closely upon the Cargill experiment, took a different course only because of differences in organization and in persons attending.

The Use of Red Cross Cases. Persistent demands were made after the session, and also expressed in the questionnaire responses, for a repetition of the conferences, using Red Cross cases. In deference to these demands, the training director alerted the members of his training committee who had attended the previous conferences to think about the sort of issues important to the internal operation of the Red Cross and specific incidents which invoked them. Within a short time interviews with individuals who had experiences that could become cases were completed, and a casebook was prepared as the basis of the 1951 conferences.

As the work of making up the casebook proceeded, including selection from the welter of material and preparation of questions for discussion, the cases which seemed to be the most usable fell into four groups:

1. Problems of written communication and paper work.
2. Problems in individual placement and development.
3. Problems of unproductive committee effort.
4. Problems arising out of the conflicting demands of departmentalization and teamwork.

They varied in form from a single letter actually written by an executive of the Red Cross or a collection of notes about the cost of correspondence to narrative descriptions of incidents which reported without interpretation or conclusions the alleged facts.

In every instance, the origin of the case was disguised as much as possible, and in one case several incidents were put together within the framework of a disguise to comprise a single problem. Disguise, inciden-

tally, does some violence to the literal accuracy of the events being recorded and allows conferees to think that essential information has been
left out. On the other hand, it permits frank discussion of cases with
those who played an actual part in them sitting around the table, and,
at least among the Red Cross management, it was tacitly agreed that
identification of the individual cases would not be finally attempted.

There was naturally some speculation between sessions as to the
identification of the disguised situations. The fact that guesses varied
widely confirms the supposition that the basic problems implicit in the
cases were representative not only of pervasive Red Cross problems but
of perennial difficulties of all organized activity. With cases made ready,
disguised, and reproduced, a third objective was announced to supplement
those of the previous year:

3. To analyze the administrative problems currently confronting the
American National Red Cross and prepare for submission to the Executive
Vice President responsible recommendations directed toward ultimate
solution.

What Happened—Second Series. The conference leaders—one for the
small group of senior executives and another for the two groups of service
directors and department heads—approached the conference with appre-
hension. Without the previous year's pleasant experience in using cases
drawn from industry and without already tested relations to lean on,
they probably would not have approached the conferences at all.

The risk seemed great. Natural curiosity about the source of the
cases and penetration of the disguise could very well embarrass some of
the conferees, hurt others, and revive old animosities. The baldness with
which the problems were presented (the case writer, who was one of the
conference leaders, never understated the reported facts) could offend
some as being critical or provocative of disloyalty to the organization.

The very existence of organization problems as daily harassments to
many of the conferees who had helped create them promised defensive
or angry reactions. It has long been known by practitioners of the case
method that it is easier to talk about some other company's problems
than one's own; in fact, the "other-company" setting releases tension,
allows people to talk without being misunderstood, and in general serves
as the key to unlock the detached intelligence without which organization
problems are not solved. And since the conference leaders, being outsiders,
would usually not know what detailed situations the cases brought to mind
among the conferees, they felt at a distinct disadvantage.

The results could not have demonstrated more conclusively the
groundlessness of these fears. Except for a one-session letdown in each
group, caused probably by fatigue, and by General MacArthur's Washing-

ton parade, the discussions were much more searching than in the first year. Interest was even greater. Tension was often high because of the voltage of some of the material, but it was never unhealthy. None of the expected explosions or ill effects showed themselves. The application to Red Cross cases of topics discussed around business problems the year before (the conditions of effective communication, for example) astonished the conference leaders and made them glad they had consented to the experiment.

Because the ostensible objective was always the amelioration of current problems in the Red Cross, the discussions seldom wandered, and never, as occasionally in the first year, could the conferees take refuge in the "that-is-their-problem" evasion of responsibility. Yet since no one person had to propose an operating decision and since all of the participants were gathered for the only occasion which brings them together each year in one room, the atmosphere permitted sufficient detachment to permit reflection and reassessment of old experience, all without pain or discourtesy.

One or two persons who could not dissociate themselves from the thought that the organization was under attack by its own members absented themselves, but the others seemed not only constructively moved but much benefited by the discussion.

Converting Discussion into Action. Special measures were taken to make sure that the discussions would focus eventually upon what should be recommended to the executive vice president.

The training director set up, within each of the three conferring groups, four smaller groups of eight to ten members each. To each of these he assigned a specific problem area and asked that the small groups carry on in discussions of their own the explorations of the larger sessions and decide what should be done about the issues they detected. Each small group was to appoint a spokesman to represent it in a panel discussion to be held on the last day of the week.

This final meeting, to be attended by everyone, was supposed, via the panel, to identify the basic problems and to list all the recommendations seriously considered by the 12 small groups. This proved to be a device whereby everybody discovered what other members of management had made of the cases.

These arrangements, completed entirely within the organization, went well. As if six hours of discussion in the larger group were not enough, the smaller groups met at night, at dinner, and between times to complete exploration of their problems and to instruct their spokesmen. Everyone took his responsibilities very seriously.

The final panel meeting was fascinating to watch. The way in which the spokesmen informed the assembled management of the issues as viewed in their groups was to one who had attended the meetings of all three conference groups an illustration of how much practice in working together even these training conferences had provided. The small groups had been ably assembled to represent varieties of experience; the integration of what must have originally been sharply divergent ideas was marked.

The substance of the discussions cannot be reported in detail in this space. A transcript of the proceedings recorded it for the use of the training committee, which had given itself until July 31, 1951 to complete the task of further reducing the suggestions made in the panel discussion to usable form. The panel discussion (with the general discussion following) had served the purpose of pooling all suggestions and all alternatives, but it could not, of course, make the final choice among them.

Effect of the Conference. Because the promise of improved coördination and more effective administration within the Red Cross was a powerful incentive to those whose hard work made the second year's experiment with cases a success, it will be frustrating if nothing comes of the final deliberations under way. But even if no sensational result is forthcoming in terms of organization procedure, an ineradicable gain has already been recorded.

Consider the benefits. The management of an enormous organization has heard the best ideas of all its members on problems of perennial importance. The top executives have expressed their point of view about the initiative expected of the next level; the next level has expressed itself on what must be done so that initiative is not blasted in the bud by top management. Each executive has been invited by everybody else to consider what he can do in his own jurisdiction without any formal change whatever. Members of management know each other better. And the experience of working together toward common ideals of administrative skill was in itself a valuable demonstration of the power which can come to an organization when the factional views of departmental specialists disappear into the unanimity of a management looking at its organization as a whole.

No lack of drama in final formal recommendations can diminish whatever value each person took from the task of trying to understand his colleagues and merge fragmentary and divergent thinking into an organization-wide idea.

Once again, it should not be said that everyone became a better administrator because of these conferences, but at least everyone had the opportunity to reëxamine his own experience with his organization and to learn whatever this reëxamination—conducted in an atmosphere of intense activity and of complete good will—might yield. What the result is for each individual personally will manifest itself very subtly in behavior on the job. To know it in any more detail would be not only difficult but unnecessary.

EXTENSION OF THE CASE METHOD

To one interested in the growth of case training in companies, the further application of the case method is more important even than a successful series of conferences for the higher echelons of management. This has happened in both the organizations described here:

(1) In Cargill, the case method was adopted for other supervisory conferences.

(2) In the Red Cross, the case method has been similarly included in the training program in force. So far the top staffs of the Eastern, Midwestern, Southeastern and Pacific areas have undertaken the study of the business cases. It is hoped that all area headquarters will develop collectively a group of cases suitable for use by the field organizations. In the meantime "Institutes on Supervision" for the top and intermediate levels of supervision have been built around both the case method and the group-dynamics procedures also being explored by the training staff.

In both organizations it appears that the case method has survived the first test of its merits. The next discovery by these and other organizations may be that the case method can be as effective in marketing, production, and finance as in the less specialized areas of human relations and general management.

GROUND RULES FOR YOUR OWN EXPERIMENT

Now for a company interested in experimenting for itself with training in the human aspects of administration, what do the foregoing experiences suggest must be done? What appear to be the conditions essential to interesting the men who are to receive such training? What will clear the way for their thinking out for themselves the demands which their executive responsibilities lay upon them? What steps must be taken by the person in charge of establishing an initial program of case discussions?

The Cargill and Red Cross experiments may suggest a similarity of form, pattern, and schedule that could mislead. A survey of the other ventures I know of indicates that all manner of departures in environmental and nonessential features are possible:

(1) J. D. Woods and Gordon claims profit from two long weekends of conferences a year apart.

(2) The Standard Oil Development Company and duPont chose rather than a short intensive series a two-hour conference every two weeks for eight or nine months.

(3) The Navy Reserve Officers Training Program includes a year-long course entitled "Functions of the Naval Administrator," which presents a case a month in voluntary night meetings with no guaranteed continuity in attendance and often even without experienced instructors.

(4) On the other hand, the Navy Bureau of Supplies and Accounts is using 25 cases (along with some lectures by specialists) in an intensive full-time one-month course for purchasing officers.

(5) Probably because of the distance the discussion leader had to travel, the Lago Oil and Transport Company of Aruba scheduled two groups in eleven meetings within two weeks.

(6) The Industrial College of the Armed Forces, in an important departure from its traditional attack upon its courses, plans to examine cases in two two-hour sessions a week for six weeks.

(7) Johnson & Johnson scheduled six sessions three or four weeks apart.

(8) Standard Oil of Indiana provided case discussions for two groups in one four-day period.

Thus, even this early all sorts of schedules and allocations of time have been tried. They all seem to work fairly well. The courses referred to have been given under very different conditions to different persons with different objectives; they are alike only in (*a*) the use of the case method and (*b*) the enthusiasm with which they are received.

Conditions Essential. The first necessity, then, is to recognize that *in the formulation of your own training program you should pay more attention to what is possible and proper in your company than to what has been done in others.* For example, although I believe that the advantage lies in the intensive rather than the dispersed program, the decision should go to the arrangements least likely to inconvenience current operations. Nothing, in short, is essential to case training in human relations and administration except good cases, a good conference chairman, and a group of persons with executive experience.

A group of persons with executive experience you have; otherwise you would not be bothering about training or anything else. Your problem here is to interest some of them in undertaking the experiment. Good cases are no longer hard to come by. Many are published, and at least one qualified firm specializing in the development of case-training programs will consider writing cases drawn from your own company experience.[2] Good conference chairmen or discussion leaders are something else again,

[2] Harbridge House, Cambridge, Massachusetts.

but there are ways of meeting this need, and suggestions to that end will be offered shortly.

After the determination, in the interest of company conditions, to take advantage of the versatility of the case method, the second important step is to *achieve agreement on the objectives of the experimental course.* Administration, human relations, executive development, and general management embrace universes of meaning, and some narrowing is desirable in the interest of stating what you wish to accomplish by the training session. Every important top executive interested in the program should be asked to say what in his opinion most needs doing. The training director must take all the answers into account as he tries to construct a reasonable series of objectives.

The exact wording of the objectives is not especially important, so long as the phrasing is not so restrictive as to strait-jacket conference activity or dampen rather than whet interest. But it is imperative that top management concur in the goals, for its support of the attempt to achieve them—in training sessions and on the job—is essential. Topside lack of interest in training objectives is reflected downward with the speed of light, and topside behavior which is in contradiction to training objectives instantly erases new beginnings achieved by subordinates in training conferences.

For these and other reasons, the selection of personnel for the early conferences should reflect an attempt, at least, *to work from the top down.* If top-level executives are willing to give time to case discussions, their doing so will be unmistakable evidence of the weight they assign to the objectives of training. Top executives are as much interested as anybody in participating in case discussions once they know what goes on, and as little interested as any one else in run-of-the-mill lectures. Traditionally, training is for underlings. To the extent that, in the action taken to choose people for the first conference and in the talk about it, emphasis can be taken off *training* and placed on *exchange of experience,* the interest and attitudes of those selected will be more favorable than you might otherwise expect.

In the selection of persons for the first conference, do not include a man and his superior in the same session. Do not do so in subsequent conferences unless you are sure that discussion will not be hampered thereby if and when the going gets rough and the discussion becomes heated. Otherwise it is possible to have more than one level of supervision represented so long as wide discrepancies in rank are avoided. Do not expect more than a somewhat bored resignation from those selected until about ten minutes after the first conference is under way. And if you are concerned about the number of persons who should be included in the first conference, take comfort in the fact that experience to date indicates that the number is a nonessential variable. Groups of 6, 15, 30, 50, and 100 have worked well; for in-company training in general, however, a safe range is between 15 and 40.

The Training Director and Discussion Leader. The selection of persons to attend and the monitoring of objectives are properly the business of the training director. But leadership of the first series of conferences is not—and for three important reasons:

(1) Especially if the first group is chosen from the second or third echelon of management, the training director may seem to be placing himself in a position of authority and claiming more knowledge than he may wish to of the administrative process and executive responsibilities. Despite the fact that the case-discussion leader does not "tell" the conferees the solution of a problem, the word, or the answer, the conference members will still look to his chair and its occupant as authoritative until real understanding sets in.

(2) On-the-job relations including strains and tensions and imperfections in interstaff relations will affect the discussion less if the conference chairman is innocent of much knowledge of them and of having participated in any of the in-company situations which will inevitably come to mind as the cases are discussed.

(3) Experienced discussion leadership is the most important ingredient in the first experiment, and it is unlikely that a training director can be experienced in case discussion before he begins.

This then is almost a necessity: *for the first experiment an outside conference leader should be obtained.* In these early days of application of the case method to in-company training, it is the lack of skill and experience in case-conference chairmanship that is the chief handicap to the wider use of this method of training in industry. Perhaps the best source for discussion leaders is one of the graduate or undergraduate schools of business administration where at least some courses are taught by the case method; there are now a good many of these.

You are looking for a man who not only has experience in "teaching" cases but knows the subject area into which your objectives fall. At the same time, you want someone who will not substitute his own experience and knowledge for that of the conferees (unless he is lecturing and summarizing at a relatively late point); who will encourage the conferees to think for themselves; who will not inhibit a discussion by any of the thousand acts whereby a conference leader can do damage; and who still can manage to maintain direction, relevance, and intellectual curiosity. The selection of such a person may seem at first a formidable task, but it is not impossible. The vitality of the case method matches its versatility, and case discussions survive even under imperfect chairmanship.

Very early in the course of the planning of the first experiment and concurrently with the joint efforts of an outside discussion leader and a training director to formulate objectives, select cases, and run stimulating and productive conferences, the training director should *make preparation for multiplying the good effects (if any) of the first experiment within the company.* In this connection one fact in particular should be kept in mind: that just as it is wise to bring in a conference chairman temporarily from outside for the first experiment, so it is essential that ultimately this task be performed by members of the organization. The training director should therefore be looking among those attending the first experimental session for persons who in his judgment can learn, from observing the discussion leader, the mechanics of case discussion for the company's own subsequent use. (The training director himself should attend the conferences but should not actively participate to an extent which reduces his full-time observation of the process and procedure.)

Various avenues of developing skilled conference leaders are available, and the choice to be made will become clear as a company's alternatives are examined. Two considerations, however, are paramount: First, a prospective leader must experience the process as a participant, watching meanwhile the operation of the method and the interaction of the conferees and later discussing with the director the things that happened. Second, and even more important, he should make an actual trial with a group of supervisors using a case.

Rather than expecting to produce expert discussion leaders from the initial experiment, it is wise to try only to begin that process, merely giving persons confidence enough to be willing to undertake presiding over discussions. The trial may be confined to one session. Moreover, a prospective leader should be advised to proceed in the early stages on the basis that if he is to err at all, he should err by doing too little rather than too much. Under this guidance, as he develops confidence and skill, he will be able to direct the conferences more firmly in proportion as he is able to recognize what is going on.

More thorough indoctrination of persons who are to be regularly concerned with human-relations training, and indeed with questions of interdepartmental coördination and nontechnical aspects of administration, will almost immediately be in order if the first experiments are successful and a company decides to go on with the establishment of a regular case-training program. Here, too, the chief difficulty will be the acquisition of experience by the persons to be in charge of such programs.

Leadership of training in human relations, when all is said, is still a very demanding occupation. The suggestions made here for providing experienced leadership of case discussions are stopgap in nature and necessarily improvisatory in form. Meeting more systematically the long-run need in industry for persons with advanced training in human relations requires much more knowledge than is now available.

An important new experiment which may provide that knowledge has been undertaken by F. J. Roethlisberger and others with funds allocated by Harvard University from a grant made by the Ford Foundation. A facility for determining the possibilities of furnishing advanced training to postgraduate students and to persons from industry and the armed services is now under way. Representatives of companies interested in training men in observation and awareness of administrative relations, and in executive behavior appropriate to the relations observed, will now be able to explore the possibilities in detail. There is promise that to such a training institution industry will eventually be able to turn for persons to man the human-relations programs for which the need, though widely felt, is not yet satisfied.

In the days before such programs are fully operative and their research findings become available, it is far better for a company to struggle along with imperfectly experienced case-discussion leaders and to run the risk of occasional failure in case training than to wait. Certainly it is fruitless to resort to canned programs which do not succeed in interesting supervisors or in enabling them to learn how they can better handle the nontechnical portion of their responsibilities. Further experiment is in order. That it has a chance to succeed in more companies is suggested by experiments already completed.

PART THREE

RESEARCH PROBLEMS IN HUMAN RELATIONS

The Preparation of Case Material

PAUL R. LAWRENCE

A good case is the vehicle by which a chunk of reality is brought into the classroom to be worked over by the class and the instructor. A good case keeps the class discussion grounded upon some of the stubborn facts that must be faced up to in real-life situations. It is the anchor on academic flights of speculation. It is the record of complex situations that must be literally pulled apart and put together again before the situations can be understood. It is the target for the expression of attitudes and ways of thinking brought into the classroom. To be all these things, a case must essentially represent a good job of reporting. Case writing, indeed, is both as simple and as difficult as good reporting. A case writer must learn not only to report what he sees and no more, but also to see in the events he is observing things that to him are new and different.

Schools and other organizations beginning to use the case method soon become interested in preparing cases for their own particular purposes. They frequently find that preparing their own cases not only allows them to focus better on problems of concern to their own trainees, but also serves to enrich and stimulate the thinking of their instructors.

People who are starting their own program of case collection frequently ask questions about our experience. They wonder how you recognize a good case when you see one. What are the sources of the cases? What is involved in organizing a systematic case-collection program? How do you go about conducting a case study in a company? What are some of the problems of writing up your case data in finished form? What are the problems of getting a case released after it is written? This article will present some of the answers to these questions which have grown out of the experience of myself and others in preparing cases for use in the Administrative Practices and the Human Relations courses at the Harvard Business School. In collecting cases for these courses, we have drawn from the many years of experience which the school has accumulated in preparing cases for other subject areas.

WHAT ARE THE SOURCES OF CASES?

The courses in Human Relations and Administrative Practices at the Business School secure case material from a variety of readily available sources. Probably most of the cases come from the contacts which faculty and staff members make with people in business. Through these contacts Business School people hear of business incidents and situations which interest them. These case leads are followed up either by questioning the initial informant about more of the details of the situation or by arranging to have one or more trained observers get firsthand information about the situation through a more extended study of it.

Another fruitful source of case material is the personal experience of the students themselves. On occasion students have been asked, as a class assignment, to write up cases from their own experience. Some of these cases, like the Stubton Company,[1] are highly useful. In a less formal manner students often relate to their instructors incidents from their experience which can be put together as cases (Jim McFee). To a lesser extent cases have been secured from the personal work experiences of faculty personnel (Dashman Company) and from published material (Case of the Applicant's Check). Important secondary sources of cases, of course, are other schools preparing original cases and industrial concerns writing cases for on-the-job training. If faculty people are constantly on the alert to spot and follow up promising case leads, a goodly supply of cases can be procured from these several sources. However, to insure a continuing supply of new and more useful cases and to plan a developing course which is not dependent on chance encounters with new situations, *it is highly desirable to organize for case collection by training observers and case writers and by giving them adequate time for making firsthand observations in industry.*

WHAT IS INVOLVED IN A SYSTEMATIC CASE-COLLECTION PROGRAM?

Many advantages are to be gained by setting up a systematic program for the collection of case material in the human-relations area. Such a program can provide the firsthand case descriptions which are possible only when a trained observer is watching the everyday behavior of people on the job and is alert to how the different participants view their job

[1] The Stubton Company and all the other cases referred to here may be found in Glover and Hower, *The Administrator*, unless otherwise noted.

situations. Data of this kind can give to case descriptions a depth not always possible with cases secured in semidigested form from the point of view of a single informant. Such cases bring the student a little closer to the complexities of social behavior. They stretch the capacity and expand the insight of the observer and the instructor alike. They give promise of providing the data needed to expand our knowledge and understanding of human behavior in organizations. The benefits are many, but they cannot be obtained without the expenditure of time, money, and patient effort.

In the first place, the people who are to make the firsthand observations of industrial life need training to do the job well. Most of all, these observers need coaching to help them sharpen their observations and see more in the everyday events of the situation they are watching. They need help in developing both a broader perspective on the problems they are observing and a grasp of the implicit significance of the commonplace. They need to develop a way of thinking about organizations as social systems. They need coaching in developing their own skills of listening with understanding. All of this training can be accomplished while the research progresses by discussions between observer and a person with considerable experience as teacher and observer. This training requires much time and effort of the more experienced person.

In making systematic case studies in industry, we have found it wise to plan on spending several weeks, or, if possible, months, making observations in a single organization, because it takes much time to secure the particular kind of data we need. The observer in an industrial concern must develop with the people of the plant a relation of confidence and trust which enables him to learn the relevant detail of their interpersonal relations. Once people of the different levels of an organization have come in the course of time to trust the observer, it would often be uneconomical to leave that organization without staying long enough to secure the raw material for a number of cases.

There are other reasons for extending any case study. An extended exposure to the complex details of one organization puts a "sense of concrete reality" in the observer's thinking about industrial affairs. It helps to fit him for further research and teaching. Then, too, shorter case descriptions of a situation can be secured from a variety of sources, while the more complete and complex picture of a business organization can be built up only from a series of cases arising out of an extended case research study. Two examples of such a series of cases are the Marshall Company series and the Flint Electric Company [2] series. These cases have

---

[2] The Flint Electric Company series has not been published in book form.

proved very useful in the classroom. So while a systematic case-collection program can pay rich dividends in stimulating cases, such a program should allow adequate time for training and extended observation. The question still remains, however, just how such a case study in industry is carried out.

HOW DO YOU GO ABOUT CONDUCTING A CASE STUDY?

The case collector's first problem in starting a case study is the establishment of a suitable working relation with the responsible executives of the concern to be studied. We seem to get the best results in terms of cases when the company involved initiates the contact and invites people at the School to make a general study or to look at some particular problem in the business. However, many useful cases have been secured when the case collector has taken all the initiative in establishing the research contact. Regardless of who initiates the contact, it is wise to start by clarifying the basis on which the case study is to be made.

Almost all of the case studies that are undertaken by the school are done with a mutual understanding that the businessman concerned is authorizing the study for the benefit of education with no expectancy of any reciprocal services—consulting or otherwise. It is also mutually understood that the information secured will be held in the strictest confidence and that resulting cases will be submitted to the company for release before they are used in the classroom or elsewhere. It is of even more importance that the executives of the company understand and accept the fact that the observers expect to be told in confidence of the feelings and attitudes of people at all levels of the organization and that these matters must be withheld from others in the organization. Nothing can destroy the usefulness of the observer faster than to engage in any form of talebearing. Unless an understanding on these matters can be reached by frank discussion with responsible top executives of the company, it is usually best to abandon a case study. In addition to reaching an understanding with the top executives on the nature and conditions of the study, it is often advisable in a unionized concern to reach a similar understanding with the union officials.

Once the initial arrangements for carrying out the study are made, it is customary for the observers to be introduced to the people at all levels of the organization with whom they will be expected to come into contact. A brief explanation of the nature and purpose of the study is given at the time of these introductions. But this only starts the process by which the observer becomes acquainted with the people in the organization and gains their understanding and acceptance of him. Gaining the understanding and trust of the people throughout the organization is accomplished more by the observer's day-to-day behavior than through any logical explanations of the study or promises of secrecy. In time, if the observer is truly interested and listens with understanding, people will talk freely to him and accept his presence on the job without modifying their own behavior. At this point the researcher will be in pay dirt; he will thenceforth be very busy collecting and recording the data which will eventually become finished cases.

Once the final cases have been prepared, their release must be secured. If the cases are adequately disguised and if the executives and others with whom the observers worked have confidence in them, the release of the case material can usually be secured without any difficulty. Sometimes, because of the confidential nature of the material, the observer must clear his case material with the person in the company from whom it was originally obtained before showing it to the higher executives who must sign the final formal release. Occasionally some useful data must be left out of a case because the original informant is afraid to have it shown to his superiors. Such minor setbacks must be accepted. In our experience, no major case studies have been lost because of release difficulties.

Throughout the entire process of case collection—from introduction to final release—runs the problem of the observer himself. I believe that every person who has served as an observer on a case-study project has experienced the acute discomfort that comes with standing idly about, first on one foot and then on the other, while, as a stranger, he watches people in an organization busily going about their own daily tasks. Few situations are better contrived to make a person feel out of place and awkward. At such a time it is good to have a coöbserver in the same boat experiencing the same feeling. But whether the observer is working by himself or as a member of a team, if he persists in his efforts to get to know new people, he will soon find that he does come to feel at home, even as an observer, in the organization he is studying.

HOW DO YOU KNOW A "GOOD" CASE WHEN YOU SEE ONE?

Whether case data are collected from an extended firsthand case study or from the many other sources of case material, a case writer at some point must decide whether the data he has available can be written into a useful, finished case.

Nothing in any one case inherently makes it a good case. When a given instructor uses a given case with a given class at a given time, and the resulting discussion proves to be stimulating to the learning process of most of the people involved, then that case is a good case for that situation. In other words, the only test of the worth of a case is its use within a certain setting. In advance of its use an instructor can only intelligently guess from his experience whether a case will be good in a given situation. Although this statement may give the reader the feeling that success in the use of cases is determined by chance, a few criteria are useful in the prediction of success or failure for a given case.

One of the best advance tests of the usefulness of a case is the degree of interest which a case writer or instructor has in the case. If he finds a case exciting and provocative, the chances are good that the case will prove useful in class. Understanding the many purposes cases serve in class can help the case writer evaluate ahead of time the potential usefulness of the case data. The following paragraphs describe briefly and give illustrations of some of the different types of case used for different purposes in the classroom. The use of these examples does not imply that the purpose under discussion is the only purpose that these particular cases could and do serve.

One kind of case is commonly known as the "springboard" case. This is a case that proposes a problem so vital to the interests and experience of students that it stimulates a lively discussion of the more general issues suggested by the central problem of the case. Students start expressing their attitudes and feelings toward the issue, and the discussion can rapidly move to the consideration of these attitudes themselves with less attention to the particulars of the case. The discussion of the Ripton Company case often moves this way in class. The students start discussing their different abstract attitudes about the responsibility of employers to employees and problems in firing people. Such a case discussion on occasion can be very useful and case materials raising such issues can serve as a springboard to start off the general discussion. Of course, the instructor usually finds it useful at some point in the discussion to ask the students to begin to relate their various attitudes about the general issues to the specific situation which the case presents.

Some highly useful cases set up different sorts of booby traps which students get caught in and then have to work out of. For instance, some cases highlight a misleading question. Students are apt to spend considerable time trying to find answers to this question before they discover that the case evidence does not answer their original question, but will throw light on other questions. Such a case is the Universal American Corporation. In this case a top executive attempts to learn about employee grievances by having all supervisors report them by letters relayed up through the chain of command. When the students look at these letters, they usually start wondering what these letters have to say about employee grievances. They eventually discover that, while they do not throw much light on grievances, they implicitly do tell a great deal about the relations among management people. The case highlights the importance of asking the right questions—significant questions that the evidence can answer.

Along this same line is the case in which what little evidence is given is not particularly helpful in dealing with the problems facing the people in the case. Students often want to make the big decision that will solve the problem without facing up to how little they actually know. John Edwards, for example, involves the promotion of a junior man in a group of salaried office workers. The older men in the group complain about this promotion. The case gives us enough information about the backgrounds of the participants to start considerable speculation about the reasons behind the complaint. In time it is realized, however, that no amount of speculation will conclusively answer the question, and that the best course of action is probably to listen carefully to what the complainants have to say before doing anything else.

Other special types of case are highly useful. Some cases are primarily illustrative of some management procedure, type of organization, or major problem of industrial life. Arthur N. Coleman and Lincoln Electric Company as cases are primarily illustrative. Other cases, such as Jim McFee and the Lamson Company, have a dramatic flavor which stimulates discussion and gets a course off to a good start. Still others are useful because, like Letter to a Professor and the Liddick Company, they pose problems most students face as they leave school for industry.

All these cases serve certain purposes in the classroom, but still the bulk of useful cases belongs to the broad category of those which lend themselves to systematic analysis. These cases are the backbone of any course in the area. They allow the class to go beyond the clarification of attitudes and the unlearning of the wrong lessons of their experience. In the courses in Administrative Practices and Human Relations, students and instructor analyze cases which describe many different things. The primary focus of the case may be on relations among a group of management people (Porter Manufacturing Company), or among a group of workers (Joseph Longman and Livingston Company), on the introduction of change in an organization (The Calhoun Company and the Superior Slate Quarry), on the administrative methods used throughout an organization (Colebrook Box Company and Haig Chemical Company), on a single conversation between two people (Brookmay Manufacturing Company and the Corelli Case), on the relations between a staff specialist and a line supervisor (Merson Company), on relations with customers (Gibbons Finance Company), or on some problem in the relation of a boss and his subordinates (Beacon Publishing Company and Postal Retail Company). But regardless of the focus, the cases are used primarily for systematic analysis—as a basis for the class to develop a useful way of thinking about the behavior of people in organizations, and to practice the use of this way of thinking in making better observations and more suitable decisions. It is hard to name the common denominators of cases which lend themselves to systematic analysis. Most of them describe what actually happened (conversations, written memoranda, etc.) between two or more people around some specific events. These descriptions of behavior give the class some data with which to answer the recurrent question, "What is going on here?"

Cases can serve many purposes in the classroom. And it is a commonplace that cases, when put to use, serve purposes unforeseen by the case writer or instructor. If the case writer or instructor believes that a given case should serve some single purpose in class, this thinking can introduce a rigidity which will block a good discussion. So advance planning about the purpose of a given case can be overdone. The real test of a case's usefulness is in the classroom, and if the case is intriguing to the writer and the instructor the chances are high that it will prove to be a "good" case.

HOW DO YOU WRITE UP THE RAW DATA INTO A FINISHED CASE?

One of the first things to be decided in writing up a case is the degree to which the origin of the specific facts of the case is made explicit. The decision on this matter will make a real difference to the way the case works in class. This question of origin does not refer to the degree of disguise, but rather to the degree of explicitness with which facts are presented as the subjective judgments of some observer. A case might contain the sentence, "Joe was a competent foreman." Such a sentence carries an illusion of objectivity, yet we know that labeling Joe as competent is a subjective judgment that someone has made. We just do not know whether it was Joe's boss, his fellow foremen, his subordinates, his wife, or Joe himself who made the judgment. The case writer would move one step closer to a complete statement of origin if he instead wrote, "Joe's boss thought of Joe as being a competent foreman." The case writer would even be more explicit if he reported, "Joe's boss told the case writer on June 24, 1951 that he thought Joe was a competent foreman."

The above example indicates that as a case writer becomes more explicit about the origin of his facts these facts lose their illusion of objectivity and become more subjective and, some will argue, more vague.

Yet this explicitness about origin represents a more complete job of reporting the situation and forces the student to face up to the subjectivity of most facts in a way that defines true objectivity. Many useful cases have been written in the past in which most facts are stated without origin and with an aura of objectivity. Some of these cases are useful in teaching students to see through this illusion. Certainly the case writer can carry his explicitness about origin of data to a ridiculous point. (For example, "On July 2, 1951, the case writer read on the official production record that the X department had processed 5,192 crankshafts in June 1951," instead of "The X department processed 5,192 crankshafts in June 1951.") But the case writer needs always to think about how explicit he will be about the origin of his data. Most case writers err in being too vague rather than too explicit.

In writing up finished cases, another key question concerns the selection of data for the case. The primary determinant, of course, of the content of a case is the real-life situation being described. In general, the closer the case comes to describing the actual events involved, the more useful it will be for teaching purposes, but this rule by no means solves all the problems of the case writer. As any case writer knows, he is never able to learn all the relevant facts about the situation he is describing. Secondly, he can rarely include in a case all the facts he has been able to observe. He must engage in a selection process, whether this selection is done consciously or unconsciously.

Our experience indicates that there are few useful generalizations about this selection process. Nevertheless, a few rules of thumb follow. Most cases describe one or more events occurring as far as the case is concerned in the present. Most cases also present something of the background of the people, the problem, and the company. It is usually wise to include in the finished case all the available firsthand data about the key present events. These would include the available record on what people do and say and think. Background data may be used more sparingly than facts describing the current situation. The most useful background material gives a student some ideas about the thinking of the participants; there is little need for a recital of past jobs, formal education, and other inactive facts. The case writer has to decide how much background material is needed to give setting and context without giving so much as to block the students from ever coming to grips with the problems posed by present events.

Another question of concern to case writers involves the cut-off point for ending a case. In real life, events do not come to an end, as they often do in movies and fairy stories. We can never know all the future repercussions of events described in cases. The end of a case has to be arbitrary. The cases often conclude at the point where the case writer runs out of data. At other times, cases are ended before this point because such an earlier ending would, in the case writer's opinion, tend to stimulate class discussion. Frequently, endings are chosen that dramatically pose some problem requiring immediate action. Such "action" endings enliven the case discussion but they are not a prerequisite of a good case.

The above suggestions about writing up cases do not, of course, cover all the problems of the case writer. Most of the skills of a good case writer must be acquired on a trial-and-error basis. One last word of advice would be that a new case writer would profit greatly from extensive experience with cases as a student and, if possible, as an instructor. Such experience gives a familiarity with cases and their uses for which no article like this can be a substitute.

Clinical Research and Research Reports in Human Relations

GEORGE F. F. LOMBARD

THE NEED FOR CLINICAL RESEARCH IN HUMAN RELATIONS

The present state of our industrial civilization requires research in human relations which will yield results of immediate practical value to the responsible administrator. This research must also produce the data necessary to develop in the long run an understanding of the basic forces at work in our society. A program of clinical research resulting in case reports recognizes and meets both these needs.

To understand the character of such a research program, it is necessary to look first at the research methods of the natural sciences. Their brilliant achievements are best known to us as laws, principles, and theories. These results tend to conceal the careful observation of natural phenomena, laboriously accumulated over centuries, on which they are based.

Only a relatively few years ago, a careful observer noticed and recorded a spot on a culture that was free from spores where he had expected to find them. A question about the occurrence and further study of it led to the discovery of penicillin and opened new worlds to medicine. In this instance the speed from clinical observation to widely useful results was great, thanks to the centuries of successful observation of natural phenomena preceding it. We hear of the spectacular instance, but we forget the infinite amount of detailed work, the results of which, both negative and positive, now guide our scientists on the road to progress.

In the social sciences no such foundation of accurate and detailed knowledge exists, in part because the need for scientific study of human situations has not long existed. Until recently the pace of social change allowed individuals and groups to acquire the capacity to understand one another by living together without explicit attention to the process involved. In modern industrial centers, at least, these conditions no longer hold. Symptoms of misunderstanding and conflict are appearing at every level of society. Yet with all their urgency, it is important to remember in planning social research that these problems are essentially new. As a result of this newness, the unspectacular, pedestrian observation of specific situations which preceded the statement of widely useful generalizations in the natural sciences is not available as an avenue to conclusions about social problems.

Furthermore, the need for widely useful generalizations has become so urgent that planning for social research has tended to neglect the fact that the advance of scientific knowledge everywhere begins with careful observation. Wherever in the social sciences detailed study of actual phenomena has occurred, the efforts have been amply repaid. To mention only a few of those who have patiently studied concrete situations and recorded their observations before stating conclusions about their data, the work of Freud, Janet, Mayo, Leighton, and Rogers has brought significant results.

CARRYING OUT RESEARCH IN HUMAN RELATIONS
BY THE CLINICAL METHOD

A path for research in the social sciences is therefore clear. This is not to say that it is short or easy; indeed, it is sure to be long and difficult, but its general direction is known: *Careful, patient, and skillful observation and analysis of particular situations go hand in hand with statement of widely useful uniformities.*

Organizing research in human relations on this basis requires a method of study permitting detailed examination of situations as they actually unfold. In particular, the method must take account of the fact that the primary reactions of individuals and groups being studied may be less their usual responses to their own work than responses to being studied. The extent to which this may happen in human studies is, of course, unlike anything in the natural sciences. Experience has shown that the attitudes which the research worker brings to the situation and his behavior reflecting these attitudes will determine whether he will be able to study *customary* behavior.

In studying particular human situations from this point of view, the most useful techniques are interview and observation. The interview permits detailed study of individual and group attitudes by facilitating free and spontaneous expression. Observation permits the activities and behavior of individuals and groups to be studied systematically. The two tools together, used by a small team of skilled researchers, provide the familiarity about a situation from which the research group can form tentative hypotheses. These two tools are also useful in testing these hypotheses as they develop. They can be importantly supported by questionnaire and statistical techniques. With these procedures situations can be explored both extensively and intensively with the flexibility necessary to meet the widely varying phenomena of human relations.

In the clinical method successful field work depends in part on the researcher's skill in making observations and conducting interviews; it depends equally on continuous analysis of his data to suggest in what direction his skills should next be applied. Much of this analysis is best done through unhurried discussions in groups of research-minded individuals who can bring to bear on the situation being studied a variety of experiences. This permits clear determination of the activities of the people being studied, their patterns of interaction, their sentiments, and the related values of their social organization. This determination of their actual behavior establishes a base line for the assessment of any changes which the research group may wish to introduce experimentally. Statement of the criteria for an experiment without this study of the actual situation can only lead, in view of the present stage of our knowledge, to shallow interpretations at the level of verbal formulas.

THE CASE REPORT OF CLINICAL RESEARCH

Need for the Case Report. When the active field work has made sufficient progress, the major attention of the research group shifts to making a permanent record of the study and its conclusions. The verbatim transcript of the research data and the log of the research team's activities, discussions, and questions with their wealth of detail are chiefly useful to the members of the research group who have conducted the study. Once they have served their purpose in helping to isolate the uniformities of behavior being studied, another type of report is needed.

It is precisely at this point that the urgency of the need for widely useful generalizations in the social sciences has been misleading. The ensuing emphasis on results from research has led to the permanent record of many studies being confined to statements of conclusions with a minimum of attention to descriptive data. Consequently it has been impossible for those outside the group which made the study to assess the implications of its findings for other situations or to know how they should be revised in the light of other experience. This weakness is an important handicap, even for the original research group, when it desires to re-examine an earlier study in the light of subsequent discoveries after only a few years have elapsed. Yet the fact that descriptive data have not been available has played an important part in holding up the spread of the kind of clinical knowledge which would provide the close familiarity with situations from which widely useful uniformities could be derived. It is this need which the case report as a record of a research study is designed to fill.

The Two Parts of the Research Case. The research case has two parts, often but not always editorially separate. The first is descriptive of the total observed situation or some carefully specified aspects of the total situation. It is a report of a situation observed while it was occurring. The test of its quality is the accuracy with which it reflects the situation it describes. It is not written to present or defend an issue; in this sense it is to be distinguished from a case used to illustrate a principle. It is not written as history. The focus of a research case is in the present and on the forces at work in the present.

Research data prepared in this way preserve the complexity of actual human situations for analysis by others at any subsequent time. To make such a *description* of a situation a permanently useful research document, it needs an additional statement of the research team's *diagnosis* of the situation. This statement is usually recorded separately from the descriptive part of the case. The addition of this statement makes the research case distinct from the teaching case.

In some instances, the second part of the research case is simply analytical and diagnostic of the forces operating in the situation. It raises the significant questions (interim or final) posed by the study. Where the research situations raise questions regarding action and the research data warrant comment, this second part of the report states the researchers' specific suggestions for action.

The order of statement to be expected in this part of the report is not a logical theory. *It is rather that order of statement which would be useful to a person who has to administer the situation being described.* The tests of its usefulness are empirical. It should make sense to those who live in the situation; it will often enable them to take steps which they had not seen before. It should clarify for them things which they have intuitively acted upon but which they have not previously put into words.

The structure of both parts of the research-case report reflects the situation which it describes. It may be descriptive of certain elements of a situation, such as the sentiments certain persons or groups of persons in a situation express toward each other at a specified time. It may also be written around a specific point of action—the usual focus of a teaching case—to which have been added descriptions of the relations of the individuals and groups which had a bearing on it. If it is so organized, the point of action may be one at which the decisions were intuitive rather than logical, implicit rather than openly expressed. Either is equally appropriate, so long as the case reflects the actual situation.

Point of View. Unlike the writer of fiction, the writer of a research case must maintain the point of view of a responsible person in the situation he is describing; he may not be omniscient. In other words, the case writer may not enter into the minds of the persons he is describing. He may repeat their conversation, he may describe their behavior, he may draw his own inferences about what they are thinking and feeling, but he does not indulge in the fallacy that he can state what is taking place within their minds. That is, he cannot pass from inside the mind of one person to inside the mind of another. He may present what he thinks A is thinking, but what he presents remains what *he* thinks A is thinking, not A's thinking. The strict application of this simple point is of major importance in maintaining the accuracy with which a case reflects an actual situation. The case writer preserves the accuracy with which his case reflects the situation, and he maintains the point of view (with all its limitations) of a person responsible for action.

Uses of Research Case Reports. The primary objective of research case reports is to broaden the available base of clinical experience. If this objective is to be fully achieved, the reports must be publishable. It is expected that at least most of the cases resulting from this program will be suitable for articles and bulletins and, in the case of longer studies, for short books.[1] The reports will, of course, have to be disguised where it is necessary to protect the anonymity of persons and groups concerned, but this presents only a minor problem. Techniques for accomplishing it have been well worked out. Some studies may be of interest only to a limited professional group; others will command a larger audience. In general, both parts of research case reports will interest two groups, administrators and scientists.

1. *For Administrators.* For administrators, the first part of the report makes available a careful statement of previously unexpressed bases of action in the situations studied. As long as these bases for administrative action remain unstated they can be communicated only by the always difficult and time-consuming method of sharing experience. When, as in modern industrial life, situations are rapidly changing, the time is not

---

[1] The following titles are suggestive of the kind of studies described. Some of these studies, particularly those of Rogers in individual psychology, go much further toward statement of a consistent theory of behavior than is suggested here. See Zaleznik, *Foreman Training in a Growing Enterprise;* Ulrich, Booz, and Lawrence, *Management Behavior and Foreman Attitude;* Rogers, *Counseling and Psychotherapy;* Whyte, *Human Relations in the Restaurant Industry;* Leighton, *The Governing of Men;* Ronken and Lawrence, *Administering Changes.*

available for this process, and it breaks down. Explicit statements become necessary. Once stated, these intuitively determined bases of action become factors available for continued attention; unstated, they are easily overlooked.

The second part of the report, in stating the significance of the data, makes the research useful for administrators generally. It limits the kinds of situations to which the findings apply and makes possible a cautious comparison with other situations. Without such a statement, the record of the facts of a situation has often proved of little significance, even to those directly concerned in change.

2. *For Scientists.* Just as both parts of the report together are necessary to communicate the findings of the study to administrators, so are they necessary for scientists in order to provide a basis for the development of more widely useful uniformities. Since the first part of the report preserves the data of the study, uniformities stated at the time of the study may be effectively modified in the light of later research. Resulting new hypotheses may in turn be checked against the earlier data. Thus the development of sound knowledge becomes a process of continuous growth. Failure to preserve such data has too often blocked the accumulation of clinical knowledge in the social sciences and has compelled each new study to start once again from the beginning.

When the accumulation of clinical knowledge has proceeded sufficiently in some such manner as that described, widely useful statements about the uniformities in human behavior can be developed. This is a long-run objective of the case research program. Case studies will accordingly be organized with the need for the development of widely useful uniformities in constant view. Sufficient flexibility will be secured in the program to permit the talented research worker to state his hypotheses and, where the clinical research findings support them, to experiment with them. These are not objectives on which a start can be made in periods of less than three and more probably five years at the minimum. The kinds of statements described as the second part of case research reports and concerned with the diagnosis of specific situations can be obtained currently and in addition have the usefulness for the future that has already been discussed.

Self-Awareness and Scientific Method[1]

GEORGE F. F. LOMBARD

The recent successses of the natural sciences have arisen from the use of controlled experiments. In teaching and research they receive primary attention. This is entirely appropriate to the needs and opportunities of those sciences: the whole history of controlled experiments in them has been that they are fruitful of new knowledge. Their history in the social sciences, with few exceptions, is that they have not. Since one man's meat is frequently another's poison, the techniques of the controlled experiment are not what I wish students of human behavior would learn from the natural sciences. My reasons for this reside in two familiar but neglected skills without which science has nowhere progressed.

Experiments may fail for many reasons: only those based on relevant observation of nature have any chance of fruitful results. Since before Galileo's "fantastically artificial" neglect of friction in his experiments on motion, the experiments of natural scientists have, on the whole, been relevant to the nature of things; the results of the polls taken before the 1948 elections are evidence that many in the social sciences have not.

Claude Bernard said, "The experimental idea is by no means arbitrary or purely imaginative; it must always have support in observed reality, that is to say, in nature."[2] This concept of experiment is quite different from one current in the social sciences today, namely, that the

[1] Expanded from remarks made at a discussion entitled, "What the Social Scientist Would Like His Students to Know About the Natural Sciences," at the Harvard Summer School Conference on "The Place of Science in General Education," July 1949. For the ideas behind these remarks, I am indebted to F. J. Roethlisberger for clarifying for me the importance of observation in scientific method, and to C. I. Barnard for crystallizing the concept of self-awareness.

[2] Claude Bernard, *An Introduction to the Study of Experimental Medicine* (New York, 1927), p. 38.

limit of experiment is the ingenuity of the experimenter. But how are scientists to know what is relevant to nature? The difficulties here are great, especially so because research itself may distort the natural happening of events. How can that be studied which study itself distorts?

Natural scientists have long been aware of the problem posed by the relation of the researcher to his data. To be sure, in some of the natural sciences the presence of a researcher does not greatly affect the phenomena being studied. In others, the apparatus must be shielded from, for example, the heat of the investigator's body. In biology and physiology the problems are quite different and often complex, even in simple experiments. Here also, thanks to the work of such investigators as Bernard, Cannon, and others, many of the obstacles have been overcome.

In the social sciences, the sensitiveness of the phenomena being studied to the presence of an investigator is especially great. This sensitiveness of human life to interaction with other human beings is familiar to all of us, and not only in research. It is demonstrated in every relation. To clarify the point, let me take extreme examples.

Restrictive controls, short of the extinction of life itself, produce in those who are controlled diverse reactions, in all of which may be recognized attempts of the self to maintain its integrity. This seems to be true of parental, educational, administrative, military, and governmental controls. For example, this aspect of human behavior continually plagues the administrator who seeks to initiate change. In research, too, what we seek to control again and again resists the investigator and in often subtle ways upsets his plans. So, for many years, experiments in industry with rest pauses for workers were inconclusive: sometimes production increased following their introduction; sometimes it did not. Investigators cussed "human nature" until the researchers at Hawthorne began to understand the nature of their relation to the workers in the room set aside for the test.[3]

Impressive though reactions to violation of integrity are in human life, the positive effects of a relation with others can be even more startling. The capacities of human beings to respond to warmth and appreciation with adaptation and growth are tremendous, although these powers are often latent. An article by Vincent Sheean entitled "On Love," in the July 1949 *Atlantic Monthly*, gives an instance in point. Philosophy, religion, medicine, several of the social sciences, practical men of affairs, and military leaders have all documented this phenomenon. Whether human beings welcome or resist a relationship, their active response to one is apparent. My point is that in the social sciences, as in all science, an

---

[3] Roethlisberger and Dickson, *Management and the Worker*, chap. viii.

investigator's skills in handling his relation to his data are of great importance.

But, granted that an investigator needs skills in relating himself to his data, he must still make relevant observations. Although some physical scientists have had truly exceptional capacity in this direction, they have seldom made explicit the processes by which they achieved their results. Often, I suspect, they are not aware that there have been processes. Often they do not have to be conscious of them: their work has progressed far enough so that frequently they can take for granted the observations of nature on which an experiment is based. "At some time and in some way not recorded," [4] is a fairly typical description of the origin of an observation that led to fruitful experiment.

Not all records of observation are this incomplete. President Conant refers to Galileo and a pump that "was once called to his attention" [5] and to Galvani, the frog's legs, and two people who are identified only as "one of the persons who were present" and "another one who was there." The fact that such careful observers as Galileo and Galvani failed to record the particulars of the situation in which their first observations occurred is indicative of the point I wish to make. Who was the person "who was present" who noticed the movement of the frog's legs? Who was "another one" who noticed that a spark seemed to excite the action? What was the background of their thinking that made them mention these observations to Galvani as possibly significant? Particularly, what in Galvani's thinking led him to seize at once on their remarks with "incredible zeal and eagerness," even though he "at the time had something else in mind and was deep in thought"? [6] Would that all of us when deep in thought could thus turn our minds into fruitful channels.

More detailed instances of how relevant observations have occurred can readily be found in Mach, Poincaré, Bernard, and others who have documented the progress of science. Cannon's *The Way of an Investigator* supplies us with valuable material. We also know something of the observations that led to the development of penicillin and radar. In all this material three phrases are used over and over again: "an accidental observation," "a hunch," and "chance." These words make me curious. Just what do they mean?

Two possibilities occur at once. The words hardly seem adequate as

[4] J. B. Conant, *On Understanding Science* (New Haven: Yale University Press. 1947), p. 37.

[5] *Ibid.*, p. 33.

[6] *Ibid.*, p. 67. In *The Way of an Investigator*, p. 69, Cannon, without quoting sources, gives a slightly different account of these incidents, in which the same failure to record precisely the original observations is apparent.

descriptive of a *process of thought*. On the other hand, they may reflect an *attitude of mind* that glories in the obviously brilliant results of the controlled experiment, to the neglect of the skilled observation. It is as if this attitude were saying, "What could be less worthy of attention than an accident, a hunch, or chance?" The choice of these words signifies how little the process is thought to deserve attention—and how little it receives. "It happened once; it was accidental; it will not happen again." "We made the most we could of it; why pay more attention to it?" A hunch: "A small thing; random; inexplicable. Now, when we can control the variables . . ."

Webster lists fourteen meanings for the word "chance." The fourteenth is: "The fortuitous . . . element in . . . existence; that which happens . . . in connection with events to which it bears no necessary relation." The first meaning is simply, "The happening of events; the way in which things befall." I call attention to the contrast of connotations in the fortuitous, the unrelated, and the inexplicable, on the one hand, and the happening of events, nature, on the other. Priestley redefines chance as "the observation of *events arising from unknown causes.*"[7] "Chance," with causes unknown, is surely distinct from chance without cause.

Please note, my claim is not that fortune plays no role in observation. Indeed it does; but when we have said that, have we said all there is to say? To me it seems not, though what else there is, is both complex and difficult to describe.

Certainly a skill of observation is something much more than what is involved when I say, "I see you." You are visible reality—at least, I find it fruitful for many purposes to assume that you are. What I mean by the process of observation is much more complex. To observe things in this other sense involves a way of thinking about things, as well as the data that are observed. Two psychologists, Snygg and Combs, have recently stated the dual nature of the process as follows:

The progress of science . . . is in two directions. The first is toward the discovery of new facts. This unceasing search is continually turning up new facts inexplicable in the old frames of reference. In turn, the scientist is forced to develop new frames of reference. Once a more adequate frame of reference has been achieved, its effectiveness is soon demonstrated by the discovery of a great number of new facts and relations.[8]

A skill of observation is, then, a capacity to *discriminate between reality as it actually is and reality as any one of us sees it,* determined as it is for us by the frames of reference, the conceptual schemes, which

[7] J. B. Conant, *The Growth of the Experimental Sciences* (Cambridge: Harvard University Press, 1949), p. 53.
[8] Snygg and Combs, *Individual Behavior,* p. 5.

we habitually use. Some psychologists speak of this difference as the difference between "reality" and "perceived reality." To learn to step outside the conceptual schemes one habitually uses in search of new and more fruitful ones is no mean accomplishment. Science and philosophy have long pondered the problem.

President Conant's book *On Understanding Science* is helpful in giving us examples of the difficulties in the way of this learning process. Swammerdam, who experimented with frogs' legs but failed to push the work as Galvani did; Rey, whose work on calcination of tin should have exposed the phlogiston theory of combustion; the need of a new concept to "fit the times" if it is to be useful; and the "power of an old concept" to prevail against contradictory evidence are all to the point. President Conant says: "The history of science . . . fails to demonstrate any uniform way in which new experimental facts and observations generate the fruitful notions in the minds of great investigators." [9]

Bernard has this to say: "Apropos of a given observation, no rules can be given for bringing to birth in the brain a correct and fruitful idea that may be a sort of intuitive anticipation of successful research." [10]

These difficulties sound ominous for my purpose, but they give us a clue, for our question need not be the rules for getting from a *given* observation to an experimental idea. Our question can be, rather, "Are there any conditions of the mind which seem to assist the making of new observations?"

Bernard discusses at some length "a few general principles for the guidance of minds applying themselves to research (in experimental medicine)." Cannon, among others, speaks of "hard labor" and "the prepared mind." [11] Both Conant and Cannon quote Pasteur, "Chance favors the prepared mind." Henderson's statement of the "conditions [necessary] for understanding" is well known: "First, intimate, habitual, intuitive familiarity with things; secondly, systematic knowledge of things; and thirdly, an effective way of thinking about things." [12] His more precise description of "systematic knowledge" is by no means as familiar: "*Accurate observation of things and events,* selection, guided by judgment born of familiarity and experience, of the salient and recurrent phenomena, and their classification and methodical exploitation." [13]

---

[9] Conant, *On Understanding Science,* p. 17.
[10] Bernard, *Introduction to the Study of Experimental Medicine,* p. 33.
[11] Cannon, *The Way of an Investigator,* pp. 67, 79.
[12] L. J. Henderson, *Sociology 23, Introductory Lectures* (Harvard University; rev. October 1938; mimeographed), p. 6.
[13] L. J. Henderson, "The Study of Man," *Science,* XCIV (1941), p. 1. The italics are mine.

Henderson's remarks describe usefully—at least, as he was wont to say, "to a first approximation"—the *outward* organization of training necessary to prepare a mind for fruitful observation. Since it is in the mind that an idea is generated, the process of creating one has an *inner* aspect as well. These outward conditions will not be productive unless they stimulate the growth of this inner capacity. A key to the ability to observe the difference between reality and reality as our existing conceptual schemes permit us to perceive it is awareness of our own frames of reference. If we know what they are, we are in a position to distinguish between them and reality. We can "see" that the world is round, not flat; that weights and feathers fall uniformly; that not all unions are "bad" and all managements "good," or vice versa.

In many of us, awareness of this sort remains low; in others, it develops into an overriding—sometimes neurotic—conviction of sin that leads to crises of indecision and inaction. In still others, it achieves a balance that permits effective discrimination between reality and what we see as reality.

At this point I am faced with a difficult choice. The strict logic of my topic requires that I should describe as precisely as possible just what is the balance in the processes of the mind that leads to effective awareness. To do so would take me far into several theories of psychology, from which we would emerge convinced that the "gaps" in what is now known are more important than the "blocks" of what is known. Consequently, I propose to leap this hurdle by calling attention to two aspects of it: first, that the gap is there, and, second, that I am neglecting it.

Let me say only that a new idea worthy of attention seems always to spring from reflection. Consequently, balanced awareness involves an effective alternation between reflective thinking and concentrated attention. This fact is important in linking the general conditions of training of which I have been speaking with this inner process of mind; for it follows that training must supply adequate material—that is, experience— for reflection, as well as an opportunity for the two kinds of thinking to develop in effective alternation with each other. The conditions Henderson laid down meet these requirements; but it is precisely at this point that we need to know much more about what learning is, and what the conditions are that favor it.

Let me repeat, the difficulty of acquiring an awareness of one's own frames of reference is great. It is especially so in the social sciences, where the investigator's own frames of reference, from which he draws the meaningfulness of his whole life, are called into question. Difficult and even painful as this learning process may be, it is nonetheless inevitable in the accumulation of knowledge; else the researcher fails to separate what he brings to the situation from the data he is studying.

Skills in handling our relation to the data we seek to study and skills in making relevant observations are related. Both require the inner quality of awareness of self of which I have been speaking. On the one hand, awareness of self increases our capacity for handling ourselves in relation to our data by forcing on us continuous and critical inner appraisal and reappraisal of what we are doing in relation to an external reality. On the other hand, it reinforces our capacity for accurate observation by making us conscious of the difference between that which we see (perceived reality) and reality. This awareness is as necessary in the training of social scientists as it is in general education for citizenship.

In the social sciences we often proceed as though we were unaware of the existence of the need. Our attempts to meet it have until recently been in one of two directions, both relatively sterile compared with progress in other sciences. On the one hand, we study situations far removed from what is familiar to us because we hope that the gross determinants of the behavior occurring in them will persist and be obvious to the investigator in spite of his presence. Studies of primitive tribes and cultures and of other groups at the fringe of our civilization have taken this direction. These studies are eminently worth while in their own right, and much of general value has been learned from them. Yet their methods leave us with a sense of something missing when we focus them on the problems of modern life. Too often, sensing "the shadow but not the substance" of our relation to our data, we retreat into a pseudo objectivity that defeats itself. By attempting to make our questionnaires, tests, and laboratory-type experiments completely objective, we arrive at a typical norm so far removed from the uniqueness of the particular instance that the knowledge gained is all but useless in application.

Why I believe the quality of awareness is necessary in the training of a social scientist will, I hope, be clear by now. That quality in him is the seed from which new understandings of the way things happen will grow.

I believe this quality is equally needed today in general education in training for citizenship. When a boy-girl relationship becomes that of husband and wife, a couple cannot assume that communication between them over mutually created problems of children, housekeeping, and career will be eased by the understanding that arises from a common background. Indeed, most of us sooner or later have to realize that no such community of background exists. Under these conditions understanding, if it is to be achieved, must be demonstrated in face-to-face interactions in the present.

This means that each of us must be able to recognize and behave in terms of what is important in our relations here and now. Distinguishing this present reality from the way in which our past experiences have taught us to see it is vital to securing, first, understanding; then, communication and active coöperation.

Difficulties of communication between people exist not only in family relationships. They are a common symptom of our times. In industry they exist at every level of organization, between worker and worker, between foreman and worker, between staff specialist and line executive. They are particularly important and difficult between representatives of different organizations—business and government, business and labor, labor and government, government and government.

Let me take brief examples from foreign affairs; the needs are only less dramatic, hardly less acute, in the domestic economy. An administrator of the Economic Coöperation Administration interested in improving the efficiency of manufacturing in Europe, or a nutrition expert of the United Nations Food and Agricultural Organization seeking to improve the diet of southeast Asia, must each be aware of the threat to existing customs that his methods present. Without this awareness, what he is doing will inevitably seem to be destroying established ways of doing things, rather than creating new freedoms. His relation and the relation of our country to those peoples then come to be hated and feared, instead of becoming the more fortunate relations through which they can seek the help to help themselves.

Administrative skills in instances such as these go a long way toward making good intentions effective, but they are never wholly so without understanding and support in the wider community. Indeed, now that destruction for one may mean destruction for all, whole nations are called on for an awareness of self in relation to others such as has never before been required. At these levels the problems are of an entirely different order from any I have discussed up to this point. Yet, in peace and in war, citizen awareness of the effects of national policy is imperative. For example, however disastrous bombing may be to lives and property, it may also arouse to action a will to resist. The stubborn "happening of events" will then bring it about that this living resistance will replace both lives and property. If this should happen, bombing becomes a boomerang of a kind no primitive ever wished to possess. Even the *threat* of bombing may arouse such resistance.

And the threat is today a reality in the lives of all of us. Surely general education's responsibility to address the problems of communication between peoples cannot neglect these aspects of understanding: understanding of how what I myself do, of how what we as a nation do, affects and is affected by, the social realities of the divided world in which we live.

Many noted students of the social scene—Toynbee, Fromm, Rogers, Liebman, Whitehead—point to something closely akin to what I have been calling a conscious awareness of self in relation to the external world, as the chief need of civilization today. Our ignorance of what is required at these more complex levels is appalling; yet conditions today make it necessary to face the problems of research and education that are involved.

At the simpler levels, useful leads for organizing training in awareness are available, though neglected. One does not need to be a skilled observer to recognize that education does an uneven job in providing would-be researchers and citizens with foundations for the development of these skills.

In both school and college the emphasis is on systems of knowledge, a quite different thing from "systematic knowledge." Our conceptual schemes are more often "theories of explanation" [14] than fruitful ways of helping us to new observations. We leave the acquisition of "intuitive familiarity" to chance, or neglect it entirely, in spite of good examples set us in engineering, and especially in medicine.

Beyond this, experience suggests that training organized under the burden of responsibility in connection with the handling of actual situations provides a favorable climate for self-awareness to mature into active skill. Henderson makes much of this point and refers both to medical training and to what I believe was once known as "Milner's Kindergarten" as a case in point in a quite different field, that of government administration.[15] Yet, everywhere in education, especially in the training of ourselves, the teachers, neglect and chance have captured the "burden of responsibility."

I could mention "self-directive" interviewing as a promising new tool of research for some fields of the social sciences. The recent suggestion of an "internal frame of reference" as an appropriate conceptual scheme for psychology may be most fruitful. Role-playing and several forms of group discussion, such as group therapy and group dynamics, are having some success in developing effective self-awareness. Semantics and psychoanalysis also have important contributions, as may the psychodrama and sociodrama. I would be overly self-aware indeed if I did not mention, too, our rather different use of case-method instruction in human relations in General Education at Harvard College and in the Graduate School of

---

[14] *Ibid.*, pp. 8–10.
[15] See also John Buchan, *Pilgrim's Way* (Boston: Houghton Mifflin, 1940), pp. 100 ff.

Business Administration. We have plans for new, as yet untried, ways of training in social skills under the burden of responsibility.

I have now tried—I am sure, inadequately—to clarify two aspects of scientific method, the importance of which I wish students of human behavior could learn from the natural sciences. I have described them as skills of handling oneself in relation to one's data and as skills of making relevant observations of nature. An inner quality of the mind, which I have called self-awareness, seems to me a key to their acquisition. At this stage of the growth of knowledge in the social sciences, I give techniques of experimentation secondary emphasis. As social scientists learn to handle their relations with their data and to make relevant observations, I am confident that experimentation will reappear in ways that do not distort the happening of events. Our start is to learn to make accurate observations of nature.

The Need and Methods for Study

JEROME F. SCOTT AND R. P. LYNTON

Sometimes an observation essentially simple carries an importance for practical affairs far beyond anything that can be claimed for it of intellectual illumination.—Elton Mayo [1]

The utmost abstractions are the true weapons with which to control our thought of concrete fact.—A. N. Whitehead [2]

What is to be gained by the scientific study of management? If human situations vary infinitely and if the roots of management skill lie in experience of management, what can science contribute that management does not already know?

Perhaps answers to these questions may be found in, or behind, the above quotations. Both Mayo's observation and Whitehead's contain paradoxes. Mayo is saying that sometimes an outsider can see a new meaning or a new "twist" in a situation that had wholly escaped those who were involved in the situation. Perhaps the facts had become so familiar that the managers had ceased to remember the importance of them. For instance, like the husband in the films who "took his wife for granted," management had perhaps not realized that they were expecting coöperation to continue after the conditions for coöperation had been unwittingly destroyed. Something like that must account for the situation in many docks, for instance, where men who are no longer members of teams have often ceased to coöperate. Mayo is saying further that sometimes the mere articulation, the bringing to the level of conscious thought, of facts so familiar that we had forgotten them makes these facts much more useful.

Whitehead states generally what Mayo says with particular reference to industry, that the use of science to practical affairs lies in finding the true generalities that underlie behavior. The paradox is that these basic

[1] *The Social Problems of an Industrial Civilization*, p. 116.
[2] *Science and the Modern World* (New York: Macmillan, 1947), p. 48.

generalities, these "utmost abstractions," are very simple statements—often of very obvious truths. An example from industry will illustrate the point. There was a time, and not long past, when men were thought of as economic men; it was generally accepted, at the conscious level, that behavior sprang from motives of individual gain, of physical comfort. It followed that when management set out to alter behavior, for example, to increase output, they naturally turned to the carrot (of wages) or the stick (of dismissal). Now anthropological, psychological, and industrial research have made it quite clear that personal gain is only a small part of human motivation. Much of a man's behavior is conditioned by his early rearing; more is due to the influence and example of his close associates; and much depends on whether he is an accepted member of the groups in which he works, plays, lives. All this may be boiled down to the "utmost abstraction," the "essentially simple" observation, that a man's behavior is primarily and largely affected by his social relations.

Practical managers, looking at this statement and at the evidence for it, remark "Of course"; for, whatever they were wont to say, to a great extent they had *acted* as if the statement were true all along. But once conscious of the new "abstraction" that man is primarily a social, not an economic, animal, they may turn less often to the carrot or the stick.

Sometimes, indeed, the "essentially simple utmost abstraction" may wholly negate previous conceptions, both conscious and intuitive, and open entire new vistas. To draw an example from another field, such must have been the case when men were able to substitute, after much bloody controversy, the idea "the earth is round" for "the earth is flat."

In point of fact, efficient industrial organizations successfully fill two general needs of their members: the satisfaction of material requirements, and the maintenance of spontaneous coöperation. The techniques and arrangements for fulfilling these needs vary from one organization to another, and in effectiveness. The variations are due largely to the multiple processes by which members come to feel and think alike in some respects. Organizationally, the value of these processes is acknowledged by allowing free play to the forces that be, facilitating their communication throughout the organization, and formalizing the procedures that emerge. To that extent they are evolved through what Mayo calls "established routines of relationship," and Whitehead, "the pattern of habitual dumb practice and emotion."

But the conditions of modern industrial society increasingly require deliberate study of the conditions and deliberate adaptation of the processes. Technical change is rapid. Organizations are larger and more complicated, deal with a wider variety of problems and with more heterogeneous groups of people than was ever the case in the past. To a large extent, "we have passed beyond that stage of human organization in which effective communication and collaboration were secured by established routines of relationship." [3]

In many techniques, crafts, and sciences such changing circumstances have already caused the traditional method of communicating skills and attitudes—by supervised imitation and slow social conditioning—to be largely supplemented and superseded by the method of systematic observation, generalization, and explicit statement. Not so in the field of administration—in the maintenance of spontaneous coöperation. There the method has so far remained almost entirely unchanged: skills are still learned in the hard school of experience supplemented only to a very small extent by systematic methods. The interacting processes of study and deliberate adaptation have hardly got under way.

We have all seen some of the results: inadequate adjustment, crisis, finally breakdown. We need to examine the problems and possibilities of developing systematic, explicit methods of studying the processes of adjustment and of communicating the skills necessary for adaptation. Such an attempt is relevant to everyone, and not merely because we are all affected by the results of successive and ever greater failures to adapt. In a very real sense everybody is to some extent engaged in social study. All life is experiment in social science. Every home, club, factory, and office is an experiment in coöperation, varying infinitely. Most learning takes place as a result of intimate participation in such experiments.

Such a conception of "social science" may help to distinguish the special function of those whose profession is social study. The essential difference between their approach and the general approach is this: the social scientist attempts to make explicit and communicable a framework of general statements which will account for particular facts and make systematic prediction possible. Early in this process, he must, like all scientists, collect and evaluate facts.

BASIC PROBLEMS OF COLLECTING AND EVALUATING SOCIAL DATA

The collection of data for the study of current social problems raises three basic difficulties: on the one hand, observation is liable to affect the events studied; on the other hand, secondhand data are very difficult to evaluate; thirdly, the uniqueness of each social situation in all its complexity makes comparison with other situations and, consequently, generalization difficult. For the sake of clarity we will examine these three basic difficulties in turn and specially highlight them.

The observer is part of the situation he is studying. His presence affects

[3] Mayo, *Social Problems of an Industrial Civilization.*

the facts he is studying, that is, the behavior of other people. In principle this difficulty exists in all sciences: according to Heisenberg's principle of indeterminacy, it is not possible to watch even an atom without affecting its behavior. But the observer's influence is particularly great in social study. People adapt to each other in most subtle ways. In particular, they alter their behavior to suit their ideas of what any observer ought and ought not to see.[4]

The point is obvious when some crude adjustment takes place, such as occurs when a policeman intrudes on the activities of a solitary burglar. But it is of fundamental importance even when less obvious. For instance, it is unrealistic to walk up to a group of workers and expect to get a true picture of what they do and say. Immediately they adjust to the newcomer. They may shift to make room for him. More importantly, their behavior will take into account that they know him (or not); like or dislike him; that he is a fellow worker, a foreman, or the manager; why they think he has come over to join them.

The following instance, recorded in a British factory study, shows the trend of output during the attendance of an observer for purposes of study: "In February 1943 one of the consultants decided to spend a considerable proportion of his time over the next few weeks on the further study of experienced linkers at work. During the seven weeks in which he was a frequent visitor the output of the 35 girls in the department increased steadily until it exceeded their previous three months' average by 11 per cent. Within four weeks of the consultant's departure output was back at its old level. Yet the consultant's visits had not led to the ending of the impasse in the development of training. The only physical change made during the period was the installation of a new clock at the request of the linkers."

In some organizations workers delight in fooling time-study men. Occasional success has sometimes led to attempts to carry out time study unseen. To that extent a problem of collecting social data has at least been acknowledged. But this method of overcoming it is despicable, and also incompatible with coöperation—just like making use of any kind of information expected to remain confidential.

The ideas of what the observer ought and ought not to see depend largely on the nature and the quality of the group's relation with him. If the relation is satisfactory, the observer can reduce his "interference" to a minimum so that the situation remains largely natural, and can to some extent take account of his influence on it in his assessment of what he observes. We shall return to the matter of research relations in the next section.

[4] For illuminating instances of this, see Roethlisberger and Dickson, *Management and the Worker*, pp. 385–387.

Secondhand information, that is, statements made to the observer by others, raises further problems of evaluation. Even when a person is talking about himself—often particularly then—his statement usually reflects more accurately his own wishes and his relation to the listener than his actual behavior in situations he describes. The same applies when a person makes a statement about others. It applies even to what are too often regarded as virtually infallible "facts and figures," such as statistics of stocks and materials, accounts, output, which are merely statements in a certain form. Statements are not likely to be accurate in the sense of giving a wholly unbiased report of what happened in fact. They are to be considered primarily as symptomatic, referring not only to the situation under discussion but also to the reporter's own thoughts, feelings, and relations.

For instance, a worker may explain to his foreman that he was absent because of illness. In a more candid conversation with a workmate he may expand this to say that, although he was "slightly off color," he might well have been at work if he had not had something else to do; he had said "illness" to the foreman because it was the easiest explanation. In the relations between worker and foreman, "illness" was the most reassuring explanation to give. In the more candid relation, the more complete explanation was "illness" plus "personal business."

Secondhand data are difficult to evaluate also for another reason. We have noted that at best the statement consists of the reporter's views of what happened, colored by his attitudes and relations to date and in the particular situation he is describing; and that the statement is liable to be affected further by the situation in which the reporting takes place, particularly by the reporter's relation to the listener(s). Thus, mostly unnoticed by the reporter, but sometimes deliberately, his statement is distorted. It is also liable to be incomplete. This is so partly because his choice of data to report out of the numberless details that make up a social situation may not correspond to the choice the listener would have made if he were assessing the situation. A fundamental reason for incompleteness lies in the social conditioning of the reporter which leads him to take for granted, and hence not to notice or recount, what are perhaps the most important aspects of the situation. Abstraction is inevitable. But unwittingly the reporter is liable to omit from his description features of the situation which are essential to make it meaningful to a person of different background.

For instance, a case of absence may result from a complicated network of factors. The most obvious factor may be illness or business. But an equally important factor may be the failure of the absentee's desire to be at work or of his sense of responsibility to offset the inclination to absent himself. This in turn may reflect the management of the department. But only the first kind of factor is at all likely to be reported without much further thought.

The difficulties of evaluating secondhand data can be overcome to the extent that the student can get to know the views the reporter has of the situation and of the listener, and can create the conditions in which statements can be elaborated, checked, and supplemented. A wise listener will not expect a "yes" or "no" answer to a question that could not be answered without further thought and in less than a thousand words, or a balanced statement from a person afraid that what he says may do harm. He will rather attempt to create the conditions, and particularly a relation, in which the reporter can speak at length and at ease.

The following instance, taken from a British colliery study, shows, at a rather oversimplified level, how a statement becomes meaningful through elaboration:

In discussion of mining matters with a mining man, it is not uncommon for him to say something like this: "Changing 'Y' colliery over from direct current to alternating current resulted in substantial increases in output."

Such a statement does not explain a great deal. On the basis of it, one might jump to all sorts of conclusions. But one might be able to get it expanded. "How is that?" the outsider asks.

"Well, some of the machinery was changed, for one thing," is the reply.

"Oh, so better machinery accounted for the increase?"

"Not entirely. Some of the plant was reorganized at the same time."

"How did that help?" (Quite clearly the situation has a lot more to it than the outsider might have thought.)

"In the reorganization, the pit was reorganized, and some sections which had been widely dispersed were brought closer together."

"So it was easier to supervise?"

"That's part of it. But what was probably more important was that as a result of the reorganization, it was possible to work the men in smaller teams, and the spirit improved."

Thus, by going into the matter—and often only by going into the matter—the outsider discovers that a mining man's phrase may subsume whole paragraphs of relevant information. So accustomed is he to talking with his colleagues that he uses a veritable verbal shorthand.

It is important to emphasize that the difficulties of describing, measuring, and evaluating social situations are essentially inherent in the nature of social data and are not limited to the early stage of development of systematic social study. Various techniques are available to reduce the difficulties. It is technically possible, for instance, to supplement observation and memory by the use of recording instruments, and thus secure such important facts in a conversation as repeated statements, pauses, tones, overtones, and data on general behavior. It is possible also to measure certain aspects of the situation, for example, how many people are present and the length and number of observations, and to compile indices of such matters as output, absenteeism, labor turnover, and sickness. And these data can be subjected to complicated analyses. But evaluation remains and will remain most difficult. The recorders of social data remain human beings who note what they are preconditioned to note. The observations remain liable to the double effect of incompleteness and unconscious distortion. Finally, by their very nature, social data can hope to be only approximately exact.

Generalizations have to be made on the basis of accumulated observations of situations which are broadly similar but never exactly identical. In all its complexity each situation is unique. Experimentation is possible only within broad limits. There is no exact knowing what "might have been," no possibility of reëstablishing the *status quo* and trying an alternative course of action in identical circumstances. For instance, a doctor cannot compare the effects of (*a*) amputating and (*b*) not amputating a leg in one case. He can only compare the effects in similar situations. Either he can compare two patients of whom one has been operated on and the other has not, or he can compare the condition of one patient before amputation with his condition after amputation. All generalizations on social data rest on a similar procedure.[5]

Significant statistics are therefore difficult to collect and difficult to interpret. Statistics simplify complex, unique facts into standard units. To take a blatant example, we may be able to count the human inhabitants of the earth. But when we count *men* we are reducing individuals to a common denominator. For many practical purposes that would be inadequate or misleading. There are men in Britain and men in China; Britons married and unmarried; Britons with larger or smaller families or none at all, poor and rich Britons . . . and so on down to the man Smith and the man Jones. Again, in an industrial situation the "yes" and "no" responses of workers to some questions can be counted and correlated. But, should a "yes" from Jones be reckoned the same as a "yes" from Smith, or just enough to offset a "no" from Brown? Jones, maybe, is the natural group leader, Brown an unpopular member of the group. In short, classification, indispensable to measurement, eliminates detail. Now, the degree to which detail can be usefully abstracted varies with the purpose for which the data are to be evaluated. Thus, the mere number of underground workers is a good guide to the number of miner's lamps required

---

[5] In principle, the difference between the exactness of physical science and the "approximateness" of social data is, again, only a difference of degree. Much in physical science is uncertain, and physical phenomena are no more than statistically probable. But the difference is so great as to constitute for practical purposes a different order of things; by comparison with the range of behavior in social groups, the physical world is one of certainties.

to be kept at a colliery, while it is only a partial guide to, say, the number of supervisors required, and a very inadequate guide to the kind of leadership the men want. Often social statistics eliminate too much detail to be usefully judged.

The difficulty in appraising statistical data can be put in another way. The choice of phenonema to measure already implies evaluation. Statistics abstract a feature of a complicated social situation and thereby stamp it as significant, in the same way as observation and memory fasten on to facts that are regarded as noteworthy. But standards of what is and what is not significant are barely developed and may vary from situation to situation. Important features are thus liable to be omitted by the statistics and in their evaluation. At every turn the observer is thrown back on his experience of similar phenomena in their whole context, in the total situation.

We can summarize this section as follows. What are commonly called "facts" can relate to any of a variety of levels. The first level is the situation itself in its reality; this is strictly "facts." From the facts there are several stages of remove (or abstraction) thus:

	Level of remove from the facts
The situation: "the facts"	
Photographic plus phonographic record	1st
Full report by one medium	2nd
Detailed description	3rd
Generalized description	4th
Classified (statistical) description	5th
Statement of uniformities (theory)	6th

With social data there is considerable danger of falling into what A. N. Whitehead has called "the fallacy of misplaced concreteness"—to get the levels mixed up and to regard the data as more factual or more significant than they really are. The danger springs from the wider scope of social data. What physical scientists regard as "facts"—the "objective" world—is only one part of social data. The ways people see the objective situation are as important social facts as is the objective makeup of the situation. Both are parts of reality.[6] Thinking does, in a sense, sometimes "make it so."

[6] Again, the difference between physical fact and social fact in respect of objectivity is only one of degree: since the development of the concept of relativity, it has become accepted practice in physical science to describe the relation between observer and observed (physical fact). This aspect of "relativity" is far more important in the social sciences than in the natural.

For example, in one company the assistant manager of a large branch factory was thought by his subordinates and by his immediate superior to be inadequate to his job. But the organization's general manager was of the opinion that this assistant manager was quite adequate. Both these contradictory opinions were relevant "facts" about the organization and both influenced behavior, that is, the objective situation.

High levels of abstraction are as yet rarely attained in the complex and dynamic field of social science, and even then form only a small part of the total description. For instance, a doctor's observations are probably one part measurement (for example, of temperature, pulse, blood pressure, blood composition) to ninety-nine parts description. The proportions may be much the same for social data in general.

Assessing social data in terms of "factualness" is a continuous process. It guides the collection of data; and new data affect the assessment. The collection and evaluation of data are thus closely interwoven and the basic difficulties connected with them are continuously present.

Professor Homans suggests the following list of seven points as a brief guide for dealing with data:

1. Look first at the obvious in its full generality. Only then does science economize thought.
2. Do not use high-order abstractions until you have exhausted the possibilities of low-order ones.
3. Talk about one thing at a time. That is . . . in choosing your words see that they refer not to several classes of fact at the same time, but to one and one only . . . Corollary: once you have chosen your words, always use the same words when referring to the same things.
4. . . . Once you have started to talk, do not stop until you have finished. That is, describe systematically the relationships between the facts designated by your words.
5. Science consists of the "careful and complete description of the mere facts."
6. Cut down as far as you dare the number of factors considered.
7. Recognize that your description must be abstract, since it deals with only a few elements of the concrete thing. Recognize the dangers of abstraction, especially when action is required, but do not be afraid of abstraction.[7]

THE RESEARCH RELATIONSHIP

The observer affects the situation he is studying and needs to take account of this disturbance in his evaluation of the data. In assessing secondhand data, he depends on knowing the way the reporter looked at the situation he is reporting and on creating the conditions conducive

[7] G. C. Homans, "A Conceptual Scheme for the Study of Social Organization," *American Sociological Review*, XII, No. 1 (February 1947), p. 13.

to a full and accurate statement. Finally, given the uniqueness of each social situation as a whole, generalizations about the parts are difficult to draw and to apply. There is no hope of solving these basic problems of collecting and evaluating social data except within a satisfactory research relationship.

If the relationship is satisfactory, the observer's disturbance is likely to be small and capable of being assessed with fair accuracy; it is possible to secure statements from people whose points of view are known and who report as accurately and fully as they can, and to check and elaborate them; last, but by no means least, the conditions exist in which the findings can be applied. If the relationship is unsatisfactory, the observer finds it difficult or impossible to secure access to significant data; statements, when it is possible to secure them at all, are incomplete and biased—maybe deliberately so—and not capable of being evaluated accurately; and it is difficult if not impossible to apply the findings. The use and value of techniques to aid the collection and evaluation of data themselves depend on the quality of the research relationship.

Three basic features of a satisfactory research relationship may be distinguished:

Permissiveness. A satisfactory research relationship is based on the agreement of the people concerned with the study, its purposes and methods. Significant data cannot be obtained or applied against their wishes. They can sabotage the study, and, if inclined to, they will. This is known to happen sometimes in the cases of time studies prior to fixing rates, and the various devices by which organizations seek to check and control the activities of constituent units. To secure sound data it is not enough that the purposes and methods of study be essentially sound and helpful. They must be seen to be so by the people concerned.

Agreement cannot be assumed to exist even when a group or an organization itself asks for a study to be carried out. The group may not be aware of the implications of what it is asking. The suggestion may not be approved by important members. It may have arisen on the spur of the moment. The agreement needs to be real and representative, and it is necessary to learn what is "real" and "representative" in the group. A study approved, for instance, only by top management, or only by the supervisor, or by only a few of the workers, would be regarded as an extension of that section's views and activities. Where the suggestion originates elsewhere, special efforts may be required to secure adequate agreement.

This early stage cannot be skimped. Systematic study begun without agreement is likely to be inadequate and may well defeat its own purpose. Sometimes considerable time passes before agreement is secured, particularly if the observer is not well known to the group and is tested out by it to a certain extent before it agrees that systematic study might start. This stage may yield little by way of coherent data. But it allows important processes of adjustment to get to work. The group examines the suitability of the outsider to carry out the study and begins to adjust itself to him and his prospective activities. Initial relationships are strengthened. The outsider begins to learn the manners and customs of the group in which the study is to be carried out, which can differ in important respects from those of similar groups quite close by. He becomes increasingly sensitive to these local traits, widens his relationships to include other people essential to the study, notes his progress as an indication of the importance that is likely to be attached to the study and the problems it is likely to meet, and clarifies his function and the purpose and methods of the study until agreement is secured.

The outsider is, in short, permissive—he allows himself to be guided in matters of aims and procedures by the group which is the focus for study. This attitude on his part is a basic feature throughout. He does not rush, he poses problems without forcing answers, and he generally proceeds only with the substantial agreement of the group with which he is working.

The problem then agreed for study may be small and to the outsider's good knowledge inadequate in coverage. It usually is. But it performs the function of a trial run, in which the personnel, the aims, and the methods of the research are put further to the test and adjusted to requirements. Considerable insights can be gained and understanding can be significantly increased through the process and findings of a very small study. This done, it may be possible to move on to something of greater significance.

Regarding the scope of study, people may agree, for instance, to study the problem of a high labor turnover of recruits by seeking the shortcomings of the selection procedure. Before long it becomes clear that applicants have certain characteristics in common which may suggest that recruits are drawn from special sections of the community; also that there is a sharp drop in trainee performance and an increase in the rate of leaving as new workers finish training and start production alongside senior workers. Thus what started as a study of the selection of young recruits comes to include problems of contacts with the community and of change-over from training to production, and to involve new and old workers, supervisors, and other members of the organization and the environment.

The following illustrates the dependence of research procedure on developing relationships; a day or two after his introduction to the officer who was to be his main liaison with the organization, and after seeing the works and learning something about the company, a research worker asked the officer if he might spend a little time on the factory floor with no other purpose than to "get the feel" of the place. His request was instantly turned down on the grounds that "people in the shop would start all kinds of worries and rumors that the firm is to be sold or something like that." The outsider dropped the subject. Only a few days later the officer himself spontaneously suggested that the observer might "just wander about the shop and chat with whoever he liked." Clearly the relationship between them had strengthened and the same danger was no longer apprehended.

The permissive attitude of the outsider helps the process of adjustment and promotes the study. He listens to people's anxieties; enables them to raise problems they wish to raise and to raise them in their own way; helps to clarify their problems—many of them very indirectly related to the study; and reassures them, less by word than by deed, that he proceeds only by agreement. Often anxieties are greatly reduced in the process of communication. Permissive listening has further advantages over guided discussion: the sequence and ways in which issues are raised provide clues to the significance attached to them; and the reporter does not consciously or unconsciously address the outsider's preoccupations as he would if the outsider posed problems and asked specific questions.

Permissiveness is put to its ultimate test if there is a persistent failure to agree at any stage, and the outsider offers to discontinue the study. This makes it absolutely clear where the primary initiative lies, namely, with the group studied. Agreement to continue the study can result from such an extreme form of testing and reassurance. The study ends as it began, with real and representative agreement.

Collaboration. In a satisfactory research relationship, the people studied do not merely allow the study to be carried out, but participate in it. Securing their active participation is like securing a vote of confidence; they consider it worth while to collaborate. This reflects on the aims and purposes of the study, the methods for carrying it out, and the relationship between the group and the outsider.

The values of collaboration are clear. For instance, it vastly increases the resources of study. The group make up the deficiencies of the outsider in observing and assessing the total situation. Almost invariably the observer is deficient at least in his initial knowledge of the group's attitudes, habits, norms, and structure—its culture, in standing with the group, and often in appreciation of technical issues. The group, and others more or less closely involved (such as specialists in various fields), have much to contribute. They help the outsider to avoid pitfalls and to develop the study toward increasingly significant observations and analysis. The outsider is then not alone in the study; he works with the people right in the situation immediately studied and, beyond them, with others also, more or less closely according to the degree to which they are concerned.

Through combined effort, much more information can be secured than by the outsider working largely on his own. The findings can also be discussed, elaborated, and checked. The responsibility for the study is spread. Understanding increases as the study progresses. And the communication and acceptance of the eventual results are but the last, almost foregone, stage of a continuous process of joint activity.

But the closer relationship of collaboration can be secured only through overcoming several important difficulties. The study of significant problems tends to arouse anxiety in the people involved. They feel strongly about them and look forward apprehensively to the findings. Even eager welcome of outside assistance they are likely to mix with an inclination to draw the observer away to areas of slighter importance. Sometimes, indeed, it is more comfortable for a group, like an individual, to live with a deficiency—sometimes even using it as a shield or crutch— than to go through the painful process of recognizing and dealing with it. To some extent this applies to the whole group. But it often applies particularly acutely to single members or small sections of people included in the study. They may appear eager to work together, perhaps in the (conscious or unconscious) hope of guiding the study toward findings of greater comfort to themselves. They may try to monopolize the attention of the outsider. One way of doing this is to burden him with information which is expected to remain confidential. The permissive attitude of the outsider lends itself to this. The outsider may have to straighten out this confusion. He can clarify his function and his relationship. He can help individuals and sections, especially with the approval of the whole group. All can jointly agree under what conditions data are collected and evaluated.

Fundamentally, the difficulties of collaboration are overcome in the general context of the research relationship. The progress of the study is governed by it. The outsider does not disclose confidential information. His standards of ethics are as high as, and similar in kind to, those of doctors and lawyers; confidential information is, by definition, information capable of causing harm to someone if misused.

Chester I. Barnard reflected this high sense of responsibility in the course of describing a situation in which he participated:

I have not made it available in printed form sooner because it involves some criticism . . . and because I was reluctant to run any risk of appearing to make the representatives of the unemployed "guinea pigs" in a public way. The lapse of ten years now makes it unlikely that any embarrassment will follow its restricted publication. The case was not reduced to writing until after my first lecture in 1938.[8]

The same applies to insights on the part of the outsider into problems with which the group is not yet able to cope. He does not, for instance, upset a delicate situation by making relationships explicit whose balance depends on their remaining implicit. Data are jointly collected, communicated, and assessed. The decision of when and how to communicate findings to other outsiders is a joint decision. The progress of the study is joint progress of all people concerned.

Effecting and Recognizing Change. Collaboration results in change. People who participate in collecting and evaluating data themselves change. They gain understanding of their problems. And they gain understanding of the process of understanding—collecting and discussing data, seeing other people's problems, finding that problems can be resolved, working together with an outsider. Participation in a research relation thus may affect change—the attitudes, habits, norms, and structure of the group, its culture and informal organization.

Another basic aspect of the research relation relates to getting these informal changes recognized formally, for instance by corresponding changes in the formal organization of the group's activities. This may be in the complex balance of forces that make up a community, for even quite small changes are likely to have repercussions and involve many people at different levels of the organization and its social environment. It is probable, therefore, that the processes through which the study develops from its small beginnings toward significant problems gradually involve many persons to help in their solution, that the whole community becomes engaged in "working through" a problem, and that the need for formal rearrangements is generally recognized.

The features of a satisfactory research relationship which we have described in this section correspond closely to the features of any efficient organization. There is nothing surprising in this. Study and adjustment are continuous processes in healthy communities. The particular features of the satisfactory research relation reflect the general features of the community: permissiveness goes with autonomy; collaboration for study with general participation; and, as we have seen, a socially effective organization is continually concerned to have formal arrangements take account of the informal, and to be closely integrated in the community.

    [8] C. I. Barnard, "Riot of the Unemployed at Trenton, N. J., 1935," in *Organization and Management,* pp. 51–52.

"OUTSIDERS"

In discussing the basic problems of collecting and evaluating data and of their solution within a satisfactory research relationship, we have used the terms "observer" and "outsider" without specifying who this might be or when his collaboration is called for. This section is devoted to the consideration of these questions.

As suggested earlier, we are all social scientists in a more pervading sense than we are all chemists or singers. For all of us life consists of a continual process of collecting and evaluating social data and adapting ourselves to our environment. It is probably true to say that this adaptation is by far the most complex and difficult of human skills.

Often the process of checking and evaluating data and of adapting is so closely integrated that it is not noticed at all. We eat, sleep, and generally rely on habitual responses to the varied stimuli of our environment. The next stage can be seen as one in which the processes of collecting and evaluating data and making the adjustments · considered necessary are separated out. This happens whenever we are required to adapt to an "unusual" situation. With more and more difficult problems of adaptation, the process may be increasingly deliberate. But it is usually possible for us to deal ourselves with such problems as we meet, by solving them or by living with them. In the social course of events no one outside our own group is required at any stage in the process. Indeed, if an individual or a group ignores unasked-for outside assistance, this is often a sign of good health, of personal and social integration.

An outsider is, in brief, a person regarded as not closely concerned. A passer-by trying to stop the boys fighting in the street is an outsider to their conflict, though he has some interest in maintaining the King's peace. Their teacher is less an outsider, and more likely to become a significant part of the situation to which the boys are trying to adapt. Even more closely concerned are their classmates and families. The word "closely" depends for its definition on the attitudes of the boys. They are at the center of the problem, surrounded by people whom they regard as outsiders, more or less. If some "outsider" tries to interfere they are likely to feel that he ought "to mind his own business," and, if they dare, they may tell him so.

We have seen how an outsider can help in the collection and evaluation of data and in adaptation. Mostly this again is a process too usual to be specially noticed. Our habits and skills of adaptation are mostly drawn from other people—family, friends, others with special standing. We continually rely on them, as a matter of course, to help current adaptation. Thus members of a working group enlist each other's help in meeting personal or general problems. Depending on their relationships with them, the supervisor, the workers' immediate representative, and other people, are drawn in more or less frequently to assist in the solution of problems within the group, and almost always to help groups to adapt to each other. "Supervision," "coördination," "advice" are all directed primarily toward facilitating adaptation. Social processes and organization in general can be looked at in the same way.

The function of specialists is to advise on particularly difficult problems of adaptation. Thus the development engineer advises on technical problems, and the sales manager on how to dispose of the organization's products. That is, they advise on a part of the complex process of adjustment. In recent years further specialists have begun to be employed to concern themselves with the organization itself—to increase the members' capacity to adapt and to advise on organizational structure. The appointment of specialists for personnel, training, and administration is to some extent a tacit acknowledgment that adaptation is becoming more difficult.

Specialists on problems of personnel and administration are not all equally well placed to assist in the process of adaptation. Some, particularly administrative officers, tend to be concerned mainly with formal arrangements. They may often be, in consequence, too preoccupied with perfecting administrative techniques and structures, and too little concerned with formalizing arrangements that work in the particular organization. To that extent they are out of touch with the real problems of the organization. This possibility is the more likely the larger the organization, and it is usually only the large organizations which have specialist administrative officers.

A personnel officer is usually in a more advantageous position. He often sees individuals when their problems of adjustment are likely to be particularly great, for instance, when they apply for work, when they have special difficulties at work or at home, when they leave. He is usually closer to the workshop and better able to build up good relationships. He is expected to draw from his experience observations and principles to guide personnel policy.

One personnel manager puts it as follows:

One of the most important responsibilities of personnel men is to conduct constant research . . . We [personnel managers] have at our command the finest research material in the world . . . If we can but analyze this material and experience, to draw from it certain observations and principles, and to record such findings as a history of progress in our companies, we will have done a marvelous research job.[9]

[9] L. A. Appley, "Functions of the Personnel Executive," Bulletin No. 1, Industrial Relations Section, California Institute of Technology.

An officer immediately responsible for training workers for their job may be in a particularly good position to assist adaptation. (Where it is separated from general supervision at all, training is usually a part of the personnel officer's job, but sometimes there is a specialist training officer.) Like the personnel officer, he has close contact with individual workers when they are faced with special difficulties—during training and retraining—and his contact continues for a considerable period. He can often help trainees to find suitable work and to team up satisfactorily with other people. He usually has the advantage that his function is better understood by supervisors and other specialists than the personnel officer's. It is therefore less likely to be interpreted by them as a threat to their status. It is usually regarded as quite proper for him to maintain some contact with the trainees after they have joined a work group under a supervisor and to collect data for further study.

The basic advantages and disadvantages of having outsiders to help collect and evaluate social data and in adaptation are seen most clearly in the case of specialists from outside the organization. They have varied experience to contribute to solving the problems of a particular group or organization; and, having only limited status in the solution of the problems, they can ease the tension which often prevents people from facing the issues and from altering to meet new circumstances. But they know little of the intricate network of forces which make adaptation in a particular situation difficult and determine the ways by which it can be achieved; and they may disturb the situation.

Chester Barnard, again in "Riot of the Unemployed," compares the position of outsiders and insiders thus:

A mere description of the events as seen by a keen observer having no knowledge of the forces at play would be a bare recital of acts, incomplete, probably misleading, and possibly quite erroneous, because of the omission of the understanding and the intentions of the participants, although it might be dramatic and the acts even attended by important consequences. A part of the point of this observation lies in the fact that in many instances . . . the mere introduction of such an observer into the situation would itself be a sufficient change of circumstances to radically alter the cases . . . In many situations in which social forces are at work, direct objective observation is either necessarily deficient or even destructive of the data.

The alternative . . . presents the other horn of the dilemma. The statements of participants certainly are capable of describing many of the overt acts involved, and in addition much of the understanding of the participants, and of their intentions, especially those of the relator. But such statements are subjective. They are often interpretative of events much more than descriptions of events. They are notoriously unreliable, and can only be safely used, like the patient's statement of symptoms, by one skilled in interpreting such statements and possessed of a thorough knowledge and experience.[10]

[10] Barnard, *Organization and Management*, pp. 55, 56.

SPECIALIST SOCIAL SCIENTISTS

The main contribution of specialist social scientists is more general and long-term than the help they may be able to give to any group or organization. It can be separated for convenience into, first, the study of normal, healthy social conditions and processes, and second, the development of systematic knowledge and understanding.

Studying the normal. The evolution of standards and of guides in the solution of social problems depends on the study of normal behavior. Without such study it is not possible to see wherein a social problem really consists or how it might be prevented in future. The position is the same, for instance, in medicine. Illness calls for medical help. The doctor relies on his knowledge of the complex balance and activity of the healthy organism to pick out for attention and treatment, from the welter of facts to be observed, those which are relevant to the illness. The process is basically the same in all human learning. An appreciation of the nonproblematical, the normal, determines what we regard as the problematical, the abnormal, and hence select for attention.

The study of the normal is as yet little developed in the social sciences. As a result, analyses abound in which attention is concentrated, for instance, on the changes in the environment to which people find it difficult to adapt; whereas the peculiarity may lie rather in the insecurities, particularly of human association, which make adaptation so difficult.

One reason for the lack of development in this direction is that these are early days in social science, and social scientists have felt obliged to make immediate contributions to pressing problems of industrial society. Another reason is that social scientists are often not well qualified to study the normal in the society in which they live. Unless they know a culture other than their own, they do not really know their own. They are part of their culture and they are apt to take for granted the disciplines and routines which their culture takes for granted. These may include many most important features which, though "simple," "obvious," and "commonplace," are peculiar to the society in which the scientist lives. As Homans puts it, "The things we take for granted about a social system are apt to be amongst its most important features. When we say, 'People do not often commit murder,' our statement is commonplace, but it is of the first importance." [11] The study of other cultures helps us to learn what is innate and what is learned in our habits and customs. Hence anthropologists have been called "constant rediscoverers of the normal." In other cultures we find, for instance, the active practice of that "knowledge that has escaped

[11] G. C. Homans, *English Villagers of the Thirteenth Century* (Cambridge: Harvard University Press, 1941), p. 403.

us," the knowledge of the skills of maintaining spontaneous coöperation.

Developing the structure of social understanding. As Calverton writes in *The Making of Society,* "Theory without fact is worthless; but fact without theory is even more worthless." [12] Both are essential; no theory was ever formulated without facts, although the formulator may have been unaware that he was using facts, or what facts, or how selected; and no facts have any meaning without theory, however unaware he may be that his "common sense," for instance, is indeed theory. A child holds his hand under the hot water tap and concludes that doing so heats the water; he later learns other ways of observing and notices that the water gets hot whether he holds his hand under the tap or not, and changes his theory accordingly. An adult, noticing a close correlation between the human birth rate and the stork population of Canada, refuses to believe that the two are related as cause and effect. Another adult finds a correlation between the youthfulness and the rate of absenteeism of employees in factory X and assumes a causal relationship; but when he later finds that in factory Y there is no such correlation, he discards his theory and seeks another.

The social scientist's appreciation of theory, which includes his own past experience, guides his search for significant data among the limitless facts that might catch his attention in a situation in real life, and leads him to differentiate between symptoms and causes, to recognize the situation where treatment has led only to the substitution of one symptom for another, and generally to assess his data and compare them with those of other workers in his and other fields of study. The data substantiate his theory as it stands or lead him to supplement or revise it. Thus a body of knowledge is built up, differentiating between kinds of phenomena, between phenomena of varying degrees of generality, and generalities more or less well tested or hypothetical. It can happen that two apparently contradictory theories seem equally valid. In the physical sciences, for instance, current evidence suggests that light can be seen as a wave motion or as a corpuscular movement; so that, according to Sir William Bragg, physicists use the wave theory on Mondays, Wednesdays, and Fridays, and the corpuscular theory on Tuesdays, Thursdays and Saturdays—which is, Sir William observes, "after all, a very proper attitude to take," in the circumstances. As more data become available and as the structure of knowledge is tested and elaborated and advanced further, such contradictions will be found to be illusory, or be resolved in favor of the one or the other or a new theory.

The body of theory to which most social scientists would subscribe—the hypotheses which have been most widely tested—is as yet inevitably

[12] New York: Random House (Modern Library), 1937, p. 3.

small. Those of greatest generality may be summarized in six statements:

1. Man is a social animal: by which is meant that a very considerable part of his behavior is inculcated by his culture and social environment, but not that his individuality is sacrificed to the herd instinct as is the case with, say, bees and ants.

2. An individual's behavior is a composite of his reflexes, trained reflexes, socially conditioned habits, and thought—all four. The normal response in any given situation is a response of the whole being. This response is always a product of heredity, plus total experiences, plus capacity for novel thought.

3. In all his complexity each individual is unique: but though the whole defies quantitative assessment, aspects of people's makeup and activities can be usefully measured.

4. A group of individuals has a distinct character and can be considered as a unit for some purposes: which means that the group is something more than the sum of its parts, namely, a system of relationships among individuals, which modifies the behavior of members; but not that it is an organism in the proper sense, in which the parts would merely be cells of the larger unit.

5. A system of human relationships is a complex balance: a change introduced into the system will have manifold effects as the system reachieves an equilibrium integrating the new element, or seeks to regain its old equilibrium without it.

6. The relationship between cause and effect is always complex: "all (i.e. every persistent factor) is cause and all is effect," [13] and any change is likely to have ramifying effects, with causes producing symptoms and symptoms causes. (Langmuir has termed such effects "divergent phenomena.") [14]

We have noted as significant that the efficient organizations which we studied had in common these characteristics:

1. Each was made up of largely autonomous and responsible groups;

2. These groups formed a whole by collaborating with one another;

3. There was close correspondence of formal and informal procedures and structures;

4. The relations between the organization and the wider community of which it formed a part were close and complex.

These four statements could be summarized at yet a deeper level:

5. It was typical of the organizations that they provided, in col-

[13] L. J. Henderson, *Pareto's General Sociology* (Cambridge: Harvard University Press, 1937), p. 72.
[14] Irving Langmuir, "Science, Common Sense, and Decency," *Science*, XCVII (January 1943), pp. 1–7.

laboration with the wider communities, adequate, routine opportunities for intimate human association.

Now such a general characteristic is noticed and considered significant only if in assumptions about human behavior are included the six that we listed as the framework of social theory. That is, if individual behavior depends on and stems from intimate relationships with others and is complex and holistic, then the first essential of an effective industrial organization will be that individuals find in it opportunities for regular participation and collaboration, and that these experiences consolidate with their life outside working hours. Given the theory, these are the aspects that will be looked at in particular organizations.

The elaboration and refinement of the structure of social knowledge is not a "mere academic exercise," something of no practical use. The phrase itself suggests a false division of activity. It also suggests a false relationship; the social scientist is not trying to "apply science of management," as a common phrase so carelessly puts it, but trying to find the science in management, that is, the structure which leads to the understanding of social phenomena within the compass of the "oldest of the arts, newest of the professions." Structure makes the difference between knowing a fact and understanding its meaning. We have noted how theory guides the choice and evaluation of social data. It guides also the methods by which data are collected. The following, for instance, are four "tentative working principles" which a group of social scientists extracted from their experience:

1. It is essential to obtain the approval and coöperation of both management and workers before initiating research into industrial relations.

2. The study of subgroups within a firm is unlikely to be effective without a study of the over-all relationships between groups in the firm as a whole, particularly the relationships among groups at the top of the hierarchy.

3. To achieve successful changes in relationships within a firm it is likely that adaptation should go on at the top of the hierarchy as well as in groups lower down.

4. The outsiders are subject to strong influences from the social field in which they are operating, just as they affect the situation. Study of the effects upon the outsiders is, therefore, necessary in order to understand the contributions of the outsiders to social changes.[15]

The structure of social knowledge determines to what extent the observer can limit his attention to features of greater or lesser significance

[15] H. A. Hutte, "Experiences in Studying Social-Psychological Structures in Industry," *Human Relations*, II, No. 2 (1949).

and use and develop accurate diagnostic tools. Indices of productivity, earnings, labor turnover, absenteeism, sickness, accidents, and strikes are just a few of the tools we have mentioned. Others are being developed and improved. For instance, S. D. M. King has found it useful to evaluate the status and role of each member of a group according to (a) the member's own perception of his status and role, and (b) the perception of the rest of the group of the member's status and role. Somewhat similar measures have been developed by J. L. Moreno, John G. Jenkins, and others, and may eventually yield refined classifications of human qualities and relationships. Again, interview techniques are being refined and some yield quantifiable data. But such measures are useful only in relation to wider understanding.

Finally, understanding of social data governs our ability to foresee the trend of events, and can guide our actions. The better the conceptual structure, the more accurate the forecast and the guide. Thus, existing social theory allows us to assume, for instance, that each person (or a particular set of people) will have the common characteristic of wanting to associate closely with others; that requiring him to move rapidly about on his own reduces the conditions in which intimate association is possible; that the failure to meet this need will result in some sort of social sickness; and that the sickness is more likely to express itself in illness, absenteeism, or labor turnover than in, for example, a strike, which requires corporate action. We can assume again that, in intimate association with others, people develop common attitudes, habits, norms, and a structure which make them into a cohesive group; and that this group, given the opportunity to grow and to coöperate with other groups in developing the policy, procedures, and structure of an organization, is likely to be socially healthy, responsible, and coöperative. Such a sequence of events may not apply strictly to every person or every group of persons. But even at this stage of social understanding the chances are that it will.

The slightness of the structure of social knowledge to date is thus no reason for not using what there is. It provides the best available guides to the collection and evaluation of data. It makes meaningful the particular experiences of men and women in their capacities as workers, housewives, officials, administrators, educationists, and social scientists. The structure will be improved and strengthened through use, through having new experiences fed into it to be evaluated.

We cannot be certain that the progressive development of social understanding will be accompanied by equally progressive improvement in social skills. It may be, for instance, that the weight of evidence will grow to show that such aspects of modern industrial society as great geographical and social mobility are essentially ill suited to human life.

Again, we cannot be sure that consciously acquired skills will be immediately effective. The evidence suggests that the substitution of conscious for intuitive skills results at first in decreased effectiveness. But there is no other way of progress. Like the player who has reached a stage where he can improve his game no further except by changing his stroke, we may expect a period of awkwardness and decreased effectiveness while the old stroke is unlearned and the new painfully acquired. This period comes to an end only if and when the new skills are fully integrated in the dynamic pattern of everyday life.

In the matter of our own behavior we have already taken the first step. To self-consciousness we are committed: the problem now is to sift the old skills and to construct and integrate the new.

Notes on Contributors

Andrews, Kenneth R. Associate Professor of Business Administration, Harvard Business School. Doctorate in American literature from the University of Illinois. Teaches Business Policy and Administrative Practices. Five years of service in the Air Force in administrative assignments. Consultant in the application of the case method to executive training in companies. Author of *Nook Farm: Mark Twain's Hartford Circle* (an item of American social history), "Product Diversification and the Public Interest," and other articles.

Bailey, Joseph C. Professor of Human Relations, Harvard Business School. Doctorate in history from Columbia. For the last twelve years, has taught courses in Sociology, Human Relations, and Administrative Practices at Columbia, Hunter, and Harvard. Prior to teaching, fifteen years of varied work experience in sales, railroading, and ranching. For the last three summers, has taught at the summer session of the University of Western Ontario. Consultant in training. Author of *Seaman A. Knapp, Schoolmaster of American Agriculture* (biography of the founder of the county agent system).

Fox, John B. Assistant Dean, Harvard Business School. Graduated from the Harvard Business School in 1937 after seven years' experience in business. Member of the Admissions and Scholarship Boards and chairman of a research project studying the interrelation of selection, instruction, and placement procedures with subsequent development of Business School students. Liaison officer with the military services, and consultant in military education. Several years with the Human Relations research group under Elton Mayo. Author (with Jerome F. Scott) of *Absenteeism: Management's Problem* (1943).

Fuller, Stephen H. Assistant Professor of Business Administration, Harvard Business School. M.B.A. in 1947. Taught economics at Ohio University; research and teaching in Collective Bargaining and Administrative Practices. Consultant in labor relations. Four years of administrative assignments with the Quartermaster Corps during the war. Coauthor with Benjamin and Sylvia Selekman of *Problems in Labor Relations* (1950).

Fuller, Frances M. M.A. from Columbia. Research assistant at the Harvard Business School for three years; four years with the military intelligence service of the War Department. Taught Social Sciences 112 (Human Relations) after its establishment by Dean Donham in Harvard College in 1945. Case writer, researcher (particularly in hospital administration, nurses' training, and the opportunity for women in business). Taught Administration in the Management Training Program at Radcliffe College. One of the authors of *Costs of Distribution: An International Digest* (1941).

Glover, John D. Associate Professor of Business Administration, Harvard Business School. M.B.A. and Ph.D. from Harvard. Taught economics in Harvard College for three years; taught Administrative Practices at the Business School after 1946. Taught at the Army Air Forces Statistical School and served with the bombing survey during the war. A consultant to the Air Force and to business organizations. Editor (with Ralph M. Hower) of *The Administrator: Cases on Human Relations in Business* (1949; rev. ed. 1952).

Gragg, Charles I. Professor of Business Administration, Harvard Business School. M.B.A. and D.C.S. from Harvard. Faculty service includes participation in many courses—Marketing, Public Relationships and Responsibilities, Business and American Society, Administrative Practices, Report Writing, and others. War service with the War Production Board, chairman of the Committee for the New England Economy (established by the President's Council of Economic Advisors), and advisor to the Salary Stabilization Board. A consultant to business and author of numerous articles and case books.

Hower, Ralph M. Professor of Business Administration, Harvard Business School. Degrees from the University of Kansas and Oxford; doctorate from Harvard. After twelve years of research, authorship, and teaching in Business History, served with the Quartermaster Corps in the European Theater of Operations from 1942 to 1945. After the war, taught Administrative Practices in the Advanced Management and M.B.A. Programs. Currently heads the course in the M.B.A. Program. Consultant in training. Author of *History of an Advertising Agency* (1939; rev. ed. 1949), and *History of Macy's of New York* (1943), editor (with John D. Glover) of *The Administrator: Cases on Human Relations in Business.*

Lawrence, Paul R. Assistant Professor of Business Administration, Harvard Business School. M.B.A. and D.C.S. from Harvard. Has written cases in Production and Human Relations and teaches Administrative Practices. Currently associated with the second-year course in Human Relations and with the Human Relations Training Clinic. Coauthor (with D. N. Ulrich and D. R. Booz) of *Management Behavior and Foreman Attitude* (1950), and (with Harriet O. Ronken) of *Administering Changes: A Case Study of Human Relations in a Factory* (1952).

Learned, Edmund P. Professor of Business Administration, Harvard Business School. M.A. in economics from Kansas University, M.B.A. and D.C.S. from Harvard. Twenty-five years of faculty service at the Harvard Business School include teaching and directing courses in Marketing, Statistics, and other subjects. In charge of and taught Administrative Practices from 1946 to 1950. Currently teaching Administrative Practices in the Advanced Management Program. Research in cotton textiles, gasoline pricing, and bigness in business. During the war served as head of the Air Forces Statistical Officers School and consultant to the Commanding General of the Air Forces for program control. From January 1951 to June 1952, Assistant for Program Coördination, Deputy Chief of Staff for Materiel, United States Air Force. Holder of the Distinguished Service Medal and a medal for exceptional civilian service. Author of many case books and articles and (with D. N. Ulrich and D. R. Booz) of *Executive Action* (1951).

Lee, Irving J. Professor of Public Speaking in the School of Speech, Northwestern University. Formerly president of the Society of General Semantics;

now trustee of the Institute of General Semantics and director of the International Society for General Semantics. Member of the executive council of the National Society for the Study of Communication. Author of *Language Habits and Human Affairs* and *How to Talk with People,* and editor of *The Language of Wisdom and Folly.* Dr. Lee visited the Harvard Business School for a few weeks in 1950–1951; his article draws on the observations made at that time, and his conversations with students and faculty.

Lombard, George F. F. Professor of Human Relations, Harvard Business School. M.B.A. and D.C.S. from Harvard. Participation in the Human Relations Research Program, in the Harvard College course in Human Relations, and in the course in Administrative Practices from its earliest days, and in the new second-year course in Human Relations. Responsible for the training of research workers. Author (with Elton Mayo) of *Teamwork and Labor Turnover in the Aircraft Industry of Southern California,* of an unpublished clinical study of human relations in a department store, and of widely used, annotated reading lists. Interest in research includes association with the National Research Council and the Office of Naval Research.

Lynton, Rolf P. A machine operator in an engineering factory during the war while taking a degree in economics. Has also worked as industrial consultant, as research worker for an industrial publication, and since 1948, as Field Research Officer of the British Institute of Management, in the coal, docks, and other industries. Author of *Incentives and Management in British Industry* (Routledge & Kegan Paul, 1949) and with Jerome F. Scott of *Community and Technology* (Unesco, 1952).

The British Institute of Management is a nonprofit making body with a council made up of industrialists, Trades Union executives, and industrial consultants, set up for the general purpose of raising standards of management. One of its activities is conducting field research into management problems and practices.

Ronken, Harriet O. A member of the Human Relations group at the Harvard Business School. Graduate of Radcliffe. Assisted in the development of the undergraduate course in Human Relations; taught that course and its equivalent in Radcliffe's Management Training Program. In the Human Relations Research Program, has taken part in most of the major postwar field studies. Presently working with the Human Relations Clinic. Author of the article on "Communication in the Work Group" listed in the bibliography, and (with P. R. Lawrence) of *Administering Changes: A Case Study of Human Relations in a Factory* (1952).

Roethlisberger, Fritz J. Wallace Brett Donham Professor of Human Relations, Harvard Business School. Degrees from Columbia and Massachusetts Institute of Technology. Member of the Harvard Business School Faculty since 1927. Has participated in all the research and teaching activities of the Human Relations group, beginning with the Western Electric experiment. Presently teaches the second-year course in Human Relations and heads the experimental clinic (designed to provide advanced training in human relations for men who wish to conduct training within industry). Coauthor of *Management and the Worker* and author of *Management and Morale,* as well as many articles in business and professional journals. He is successor to Elton Mayo as the professional director of the Human Relations Program.

Scott, Jerome F. M.B.A. from the Harvard Business School and a degree in economics and accounting (combined with work in a life insurance office) at the University of Minnesota. Until 1947, did research work for Professors Mayo and Roethlisberger and taught undergraduates. British Legion Lecturer in Industrial Sociology, Roffey Park, 1947–1948; Field Research Officer, British Institute of Management, since 1948. Author, with John B. Fox, of *Absenteeism: Management's Problem* (1943) and, with R. P. Lynton, of *Community and Technology* (Unesco, 1952).

Towl, Andrew R. Assistant Director of Research at the Harvard Business School. With other duties of research administration, oversees the case-collection and research activities of the junior faculty. Taught Administrative Practices for several years. Eight years' experience in investment analysis for the Provident Trust Company of Philadelphia. Consultant to private business and advisor to the Salary Stabilization Board. Author of a recent study of executive compensation and, with Dr. Melvin T. Copeland, of *The Board of Directors and Business Management* (1947).

Ulrich, David N. A graduate of the Harvard Business School and a doctoral candidate in clinical psychology in the Graduate School of Arts and Sciences in Harvard University. Wartime service in the Navy. Member of the research staff in the Human Relations Program from 1946 to 1950. Author of many cases and participant in the field studies which resulted in the Marshall and the Flint Company cases. Coauthor (with P. R. Lawrence and D. R. Booz) of *Management Behavior and Foreman Attitude* and (with E. P. Learned and D. R. Booz) of *Executive Action*.

References to Relevant Books and Articles

I. *Teaching: Aspects of the Case Method*

Albrecht, Milton, and Llewellyn Gross, "Nondirective Teaching," *Sociology and Social Research*, XXXII (May–June 1948), pp. 874–881.

Berrien, F. K., *Comments and Cases on Human Relations* (New York: Harper, 1951).

Bradford, L. P., and J. R. P. French, Jr. (ed.), "The Dynamics of the Discussion Group," *Journal of Social Issues*, IV (Spring 1948).

Cabot, Hugh, and J. A. Kahl, "Teaching Human Relations," *The Journal of General Education*, V (July 1951), pp. 303–312.

—— *Human Relations: Cases and Concepts in Concrete Social Science* (Cambridge: Harvard University Press, 1953).

Cantor, Nathaniel, *Dynamics of Learning* (Buffalo: Foster & Stewart, 1946).

Culliton, J. W., "The Question That Has Not Been Asked Cannot Be Answered," in *Education for Professional Responsibility* (Pittsburgh: Carnegie Press, 1948), pp. 85–93.

Donham, W. B., *Education for Responsible Living* (Cambridge: Harvard University Press, 1944).

—— "An Experimental Course in Human Relations in Harvard College," *The Journal of General Education*, II (October 1947), pp. 8–16.

—— "The Unfolding of Collegiate Business Training," *The Harvard Graduates' Magazine* (March 1921), pp. 333–347.

—— "Why Experiment? The Case System in College Teaching of Social Science," *The Journal of General Education*, III (January 1949), pp. 145–156.

Elliott, H. J., *The Process of Group Thinking* (New York: Association Press, 1928).

Fraser, C. E. (ed.), *The Case Method of Instruction* (New York: McGraw-Hill, 1931).

Glover, J. D., and R. M. Hower, *The Administrator: Cases on Human Relations in Business* (Chicago: Richard D. Irwin, 1949, Rev. ed. 1952).

—— *Some Notes on the Use of* The Administrator (Chicago: Richard D. Irwin, 1949).

Hunt, Pearson, "The Case Method of Instruction," *Harvard Educational Review*, XXI (Summer 1951), pp. 175–192.

Kelley, E. C., *Education for What Is Real* (New York: Harper, 1947).

National Industrial Conference Board, Studies in Personnel Policy, *Techniques of Conference Leadership* (New York, 1946).

Perry, W. G., Jr., "Conflicts in the Learning Process: The Student's Response to Teaching," in B. B. Cronkhite (ed.), *A Handbook for College Teachers* (Cambridge: Harvard University Press, 1950).

Sheffield, A. D., *Creative Discussion: Methods for Leaders and Members of Discussion Groups* (New York: Association Press, 1933).

Smith, G. A., *Policy Formulation and Administration* (Chicago: Richard D. Irwin, 1952).

U. S. Department of Agriculture, Bureau of Agricultural Economics, *Group Discussion and Its Techniques* (Washington: Superintendent of Documents, 1942).

Whitehead, A. N., *The Aims of Education* (New York: Macmillan, 1929).

II. *Research: Problems of Observation and Interpretation, and Application of Findings to the Administrative Process*

Barnard, C. I., *The Functions of the Executive* (Cambridge: Harvard University Press, 1938).

——— *Organization and Management* (Cambridge: Harvard University Press, 1948).

Cannon, W. B., *The Way of an Investigator* (New York: Norton, 1945).

Copeland, M. T., *The Executive at Work* (Cambridge: Harvard University Press, 1951).

——— and A. R. Towl, *The Board of Directors and Business Management* (Boston: Division of Research, Harvard Business School, 1947).

Donham, W. B., *Administration and Blind Spots* (Boston: Division of Research, Harvard Business School, 1952).

Gardner, Burleigh, and D. J. Moore, *Human Relations in Industry* (Chicago: Richard D. Irwin, 1950).

Gillespie, J. J., *Free Expression in Industry* (London: Pilot Press, 1948).

Golden, C. S., and H. J. Ruttenberg, *The Dynamics of Industrial Democracy* (New York: Harper, 1942).

Hayakawa, S. I., *Language in Thought and Action* (New York: Harcourt, Brace, 1949).

Homans, G. C., *The Human Group* (New York: Harcourt, Brace, 1950).

Jennings, Elizabeth, and Francis Jennings, "Making Human Relations Work," *Harvard Business Review*, XXIX (January 1951), pp. 29–55.

Johnson, Wendell, *People in Quandaries* (New York: Harper, 1946).

Learned, E. P., D. N. Ulrich, and D. R. Booz, *Executive Action* (Boston: Division of Research, Harvard Business School, 1951).

Lee, I. J., *Language Habits in Human Affairs* (New York: Harper, 1941).

——— (ed.), *The Language of Wisdom and Folly* (New York: Harper, 1949).

——— *How to Talk with People* (New York: Harper, 1952).

Leighton, A. H., *The Governing of Men* (Princeton: Princeton University Press, 1945).

Mace, M. L., *The Growth and Development of Executives* (Boston: Division of Research, Harvard Business School, 1950).

Marquis, D. G., "Research Planning at the Frontiers of Society," *The American Psychologist*, III (October 1948), pp. 430–438.

Mayo, Elton, *The Human Problems of an Industrial Civilization* (Boston: Division of Research, Harvard Business School, 1946).

——— *The Social Problems of an Industrial Civilization* (Boston: Division of Research, Harvard Business School, 1945).

—— *Some Notes on the Psychology of Pierre Janet* (Cambridge: Harvard University Press, 1948).

McGregor, Douglas, "Getting Effective Leadership in the Industrial Organization," *Journal of Consulting Psychology*, VIII (1944), pp. 55–63.

—— "The Staff Function in Human Relations," *The Journal of Social Issues*, IV (Summer 1948), pp. 5–22.

Metcalf, H. C., and L. Urwick (ed.), *Dynamic Administration: The Collected Papers of Mary Parker Follett* (New York: Harper, 1942).

National Research Council, *Fatigue of Workers* (New York: Reinhold, 1941).

Redfield, Robert, "The Art of Social Science," *The American Journal of Sociology*, LIV (November 1948), pp. 181–190.

Roethlisberger, F. J., "Efficiency and Coöperative Behavior," *Journal of Engineering Education*, XL (December 1949), pp. 233–241.

—— "The Foreman: Master and Victim of Double Talk," *Harvard Business Review*, XXIII (Spring 1945), pp. 283–298.

—— "Human Relations: Rare, Medium, or Well-Done?" *Harvard Business Review*, XXVI (January 1948), pp. 89–107.

—— *Management and Morale* (Cambridge: Harvard University Press, 1941).

—— "A New Look for Management," in *Worker Morale and Productivity* (General Management Series Number 141, American Management Association, New York, 1948), pp. 11–22.

—— and W. J. Dickson, *Management and the Worker* (Cambridge: Harvard University Press, 1939).

Rogers, C. R., *Client-Centered Therapy: Its Current Practice, Implications, and Theory* (Boston: Houghton Mifflin, 1951).

—— *Counselling and Psycho-Therapy* (Boston: Houghton Mifflin, 1942).

Ronken, H. O., "Communication in the Work Group," *Harvard Business Review*, XXIX (July 1951), pp. 108–114.

Ronken, H. O., and P. R. Lawrence, *Administering Changes: A Case Study of Human Relations in a Factory* (Boston: Division of Research, Harvard Business School, 1952).

Selekman, Benjamin, *Labor Relations and Human Relations* (New York: McGraw-Hill, 1947).

Snygg, Donald, and A. W. Combs, *Individual Psychology* (New York: Harper, 1949).

Ulrich, D. N., "A Clinical Method in Applied Social Science," *Philosophy of Science*, XVI (July 1949), pp. 243–249.

—— D. R. Booz, and P. R. Lawrence, *Management Behavior and Foreman Attitude* (Boston: Division of Research, Harvard Business School, 1950).

Whyte, W. F., *Human Relations in the Restaurant Industry* (New York: McGraw-Hill, 1948).

—— *Pattern for Industrial Peace* (New York: Harper, 1951).

—— *Street Corner Society* (Chicago: University of Chicago Press, 1943).

Zaleznik, A., *Foreman Training in a Growing Enterprise* (Boston: Division of Research, Harvard Business School, 1951).